Entertaining *with* Booze

Entertaining *with* Booze

DESIGNER DRINKS, FABULOUS FOOD & INSPIRED IDEAS FOR YOUR NEXT PARTY

RYAN JENNINGS
& DAVID STEELE

whitecap

Whitecap Books is known for its expertise in the cookbook market, and has produced some of the most innovative and familiar titles found in kitchens across North America. Visit our website at www.whitecap.ca.

Edited by Lesley Cameron
Proofread by Joan Tetrault
Design by Five Seventeen / picapica.ca
Food photography by Geoffrey Ross
Photographic digital artist Jeff Mayhew

Printed in China

LIBRARY AND ARCHIVES CANADA CATALOGUING IN PUBLICATION

Jennings, Ryan
Entertaining with booze : designer drinks, fabulous food & inspired ideas for your next party / Ryan Jennings, David Steele.

Includes index.
ISBN 978-1-55285-930-8

1. Cookery. 2. Alcoholic beverages. 3. Menus. 4. Parties.

I. Steele, David, 1973– II. Title.

TX731.J46 2008 641.5'68 C2008-900652-6

The publisher acknowledges the financial support of the Government of Canada through the Book Publishing Industry Development Program (BPIDP) and the Province of British Columbia through the Book Publishing Tax Credit.

08 09 10 11 12 5 4 3 2 1

To Yaman and Jack

Thanks for making every day feel like Saturday night.

—Ryan

To my family and friends—Helen, Paul, Jen, Michael, John and Paula

You inspire me and (on occasion) drive me to the bottle.

—Dave

Contents

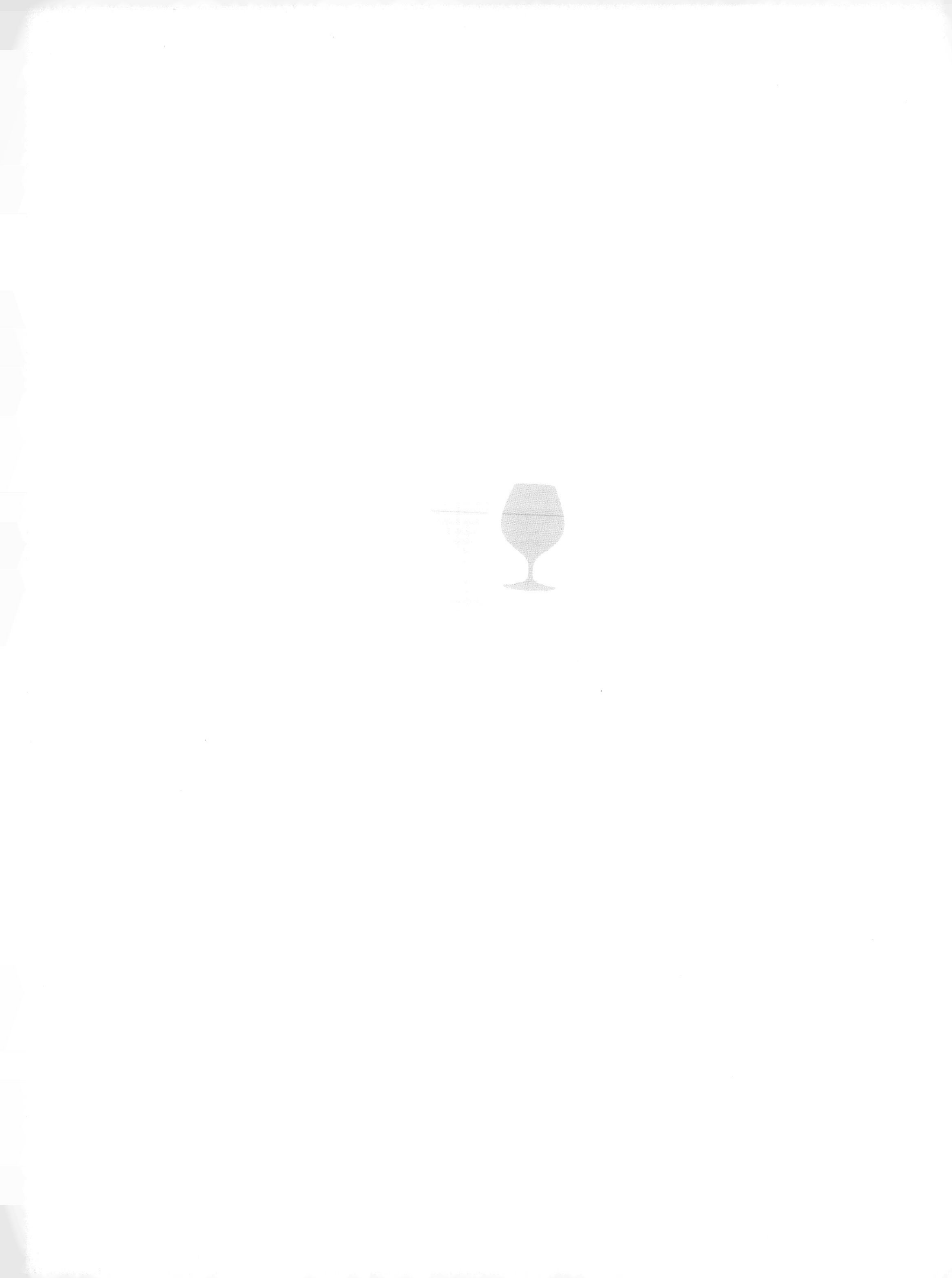

FOREWORD
BY DAVID ADJEY

How many times have we heard that the party *always* starts in the kitchen? No one knows this better than Ryan Jennings and David Steele. I've spent my whole career cooking on the fly, but to watch these guys magically create the most stunning cocktails, which they've specifically designed to go with individual morsels of food, is a real treat.

Armed with an array of dazzling recipes for cocktails, their charm almost dangles off the side of every glass. As they fearlessly combine the world of food and drink, they remind us that great presentation, both visually and tastefully, always stands out.

The first time I had dinner with Ryan, he came to my home to cook for me. For a chef, this is an invitation I receive far less than none, and it compelled me to engage in the night's events. As the evening went on, I watched him bring his famous Spicy Rum Punch Wings and Jack Daniel's Sticky Ribs to life, both of which you'll find in the Tailgate Blowout menu (page 219). His technique flowed so precisely, and I recall being fascinated by the complex plane between the two realms of dish and drink; they are the same ones that I, in fact, exist in on a daily basis. My only question by the end of the night: "How many Cream Sodas did I have?" (See page 161 for the recipe.) I will be keeping a permanent bookmark in page 11, where they've so perfectly placed the info on hangover remedies!

Entertaining with Booze delves into the soul of each dish, and reinvents the combination between the two major components of any great party—food and drink—and it is (of course) an indispensable guide for ideas when combining these two elements. The art, as a whole, seems like a balancing act these guys not only love, but have also perfected.

ONE REASON I DON'T DRINK IS THAT I WANT TO KNOW WHEN I AM HAVING A GOOD TIME.

Nancy Astor

Introduction

BY RYAN & DAVE

We're back and we're boozier than ever. Did you miss us? We sure missed you. With that eager need to douse your breakfast with brandy or dip your nose into a big glass of Cabernet, we know how much you like cooking with booze. So we sat ourselves down with a glass (or three) of wine to mull over what we could do to keep that spirit going strong. How about an entertainment bible, filled with more than 100 booze-based dishes all beautifully organized into complete party menus? Party-planning made simple. But you might also notice that there's not booze in every recipe. This time we're exercising some restraint and adding it only when absolutely necessary—approximately 95.6463% of the time.

But because moderation has never come easy to us we didn't stop there. Each gorgeously delicious party comes with serving suggestions, décor and music ideas, and drink recipes, wine matches and tips on pulling the whole thing together. Whether you're throwing a casual fondue party or an elegant wine-tasting event, you'll find everything you need for setting the appropriate mood.

Before you get started, check out our invaluable sections on stocking your bar and pantry, then kick-start your snob ascent with our quick and dirty guide to the world of wine, beer and spirits—a great reference for buying, pairing, cooking and, of course, drinking. We've also included a separate glossary for common bar terms and one for cooking. Yes, we know, we really do think of everything. We've even included a few of our favorite flavor combos from *Cooking with Booze*, just in case you haven't had a chance to buy our first book, *yet* (and yes, that was intended to sound threatening).

Booze has long inspired us and we want to pass that inspiration on to you. Take what we've done and make it your own. Expand, alter and experiment. Unleash your inner socialite and become a stress-free host by pulling off big family get-togethers with ease. Or dim the lights, spin some Sade and let our intimate dinners add a seductive edge to your dining room.

Whatever your next event, make sure you use the freshest ingredients you can find and never, ever settle for second best. Entertaining doesn't have to be complicated, and using the best ingredients you can afford goes a long way to creating the best results. We wish you and your next party great success—and with the addition of a little booze, that's nearly guaranteed.

Getting Started

Safety First

It's no secret that from time to time we enjoy a cocktail or two. And, come to think of it, you're probably a lot like us—always ready for good friends, good food and good times. However, remember the old playground adage, "it's all fun and games until somebody loses an eye." An inebriated chef is not only annoying but also dangerous in the kitchen. And be mindful of your guests. As host it's your responsibility to manage how much they're drinking and to plan how they'll get home. Keep a list of cab numbers handy, encourage people to designate a driver and be prepared (and sober yourself) so you can step in and take the keys away from an out-of-hand guest if necessary. Be an "asshole" tonight. He'll thank you in the morning.

Always have plenty of nonalcoholic options available for your guests (see page 9) and encourage everyone to drink in moderation. Trips to the hospital and phone calls from the cops can have more than just sobering effects on your party's atmosphere, they can ruin people's lives. Don't let that be the thing your guests remember about your last bash.

Remember, a drink is a drink, is a drink. One 5 oz (150 mL) glass of wine is equal to 1 oz (30 mL) of spirit or a 12 oz (341 mL) bottle of beer. Be in charge of your bar so you can monitor how much your guests are consuming, and always serve alcohol with food.

Being responsible feels good, too.

Stocking the Bar

Just about everyone has his or her favorite booze and every bar has a bottle that lingers untouched at the back of the cupboard, like the awkward kid at the school dance. What are the essentials for a good bar? We've pulled together a list that will give you a broad range of options. And, if your budget is as big as your liver, we've also included some premium suggestions.

MUST-HAVES

Most cocktails start from the five basic boozes below and any bartender worth his blender should have these on hand at all times.

- Gin
- Rum
- Tequila
- Vodka
- Whisky (Rye/Bourbon/Scotch)

1ST TIER

A couple of good liqueurs and mixers can turn a novice bartender into a great bartender. Choose your own favorites from the list below.

- Amaretto
- Brandy
- Coconut rum
- Coffee liqueur
- Crème de banane
- Crème de cacao
- Crème de cassis
- Crème de menthe
- Irish cream liqueur
- Kirsch
- Limoncello
- Lychee liqueur
- Melon liqueur
- Ouzo
- Peach schnapps
- Peppermint schnapps
- Pernod
- Port
- Sambuca
- Sherry
- Triple Sec
- Vermouth (dry/sweet)

2ND TIER

Stock a couple of these bottles for special occasions, like Tuesday night suppers and days the dog needs a walk. They make even the most routine jobs worth doing.

- Absinthe
- Armagnac
- Calvados
- Campari
- Chambord
- Cognac

Drambuie
Grand Marnier
Jägermeister
Premium Gin
Premium Rum
Premium Vodka
Single Malt Scotch

MIXERS

Apple juice
Bitters
Clamato and tomato juice
Club soda
Cola
Cranberry juice
Freshly squeezed grapefruit juice
Freshly squeezed lemon juice
Freshly squeezed lime juice
Freshly squeezed orange juice
Ginger ale
Iced tea
Lemonade
Lime cordial
Pineapple juice
Simple syrup
Tonic

FINISHES AND GARNISHES

Celery salt
Celery stalks
Cinnamon
Coarse salt
Fresh fruit (lemon, limes, oranges)
Grenadine
Ground black pepper
Mint leaves
Nutmeg
Pearl onions
Preserved fruit (pineapple chunks, maraschino cherries)
Stuffed green olives
Superfine sugar
Tabasco sauce
Worcestershire sauce

EQUIPMENT ESSENTIALS

Bar cloth
Bar glass
Bar knife
Bar spoon
Blender
Cocktail skewers
Ice bucket
Ice tongs
Muddler
Openers (bottle, corkscrew, can)
Pitcher
Reamer
Shaker
Shot glass
Strainer
Straws

TRICKS OF THE TRADE

Move your game from amateur to expert with these simple tips.

RELAX

Take your time, you can't rush perfection. If you're not a professional bartender, mix slowly. That way your drinks will end up in the glass and not on the floor—or on your guests.

GLASS CHILLING

Chilling your glassware first is an important step in keeping your drink cold, especially for martinis and other cocktails enjoyed straight-up. Place glasses in the freezer for 10 minutes or simply fill the glass with ice and top up with water. Meanwhile, mix your drink in a cocktail shaker then discard the ice water. Voilà—chilled glass.

SIMPLE SYRUP

Use in daiquiris, mojitos and any other cocktail that calls for simple syrup or sugar. (Sugar dissolves faster in water than in alcohol.)

Combine equal parts water and granulated sugar in a saucepan and heat until the sugar dissolves. Cool before using and store in an attractive bottle in your liquor cabinet, ready to sweeten any cocktail. The mixture keeps indefinitely, but may need reheating if it crystallizes.

RIMMING

To rim a glass for a margarita or Bloody Caesar, slice into a wedge of citrus and run it around the edge of the glass. Dip the rim in coarse salt or celery salt—or a homemade mixture of four parts Montreal Steak Spice to one part ground cardamom for a more exotic Caesar—then add ice and the other ingredients to the glass.

For specialty coffees, dip the rim of the cup in a saucer of water then into granulated sugar. Run a flame around the rim to melt the sugar—and blow your guests' minds.

JUICE

Freshly squeezed juices make all the difference in your cocktails as they don't contain added sugar or preservatives that dampen their flavor. When freshly squeezed isn't an option, use the premium, not-from-concentrate types of juice. Frozen juice is best reserved for propping up the ice tray in your freezer.

BRING ON THE BUBBLES

Ensure your mixes are fully carbonated. There's absolutely no point in using a premium gin if your tonic's flat. Buying small cans of soda instead of big bottles helps keep the bubbles going.

GOT THE SHAKES?

When shaking a cocktail with ice, start with a generous amount before you add the liquid ingredients. This helps prevent unnecessary dilution. The worst thing a bartender can be accused of is watering down the drinks.

FINISHING TOUCHES

Proper garnishes can make or break a drink and are used not only for decoration but for final balance. A wedge of citrus adds a touch of sour to something sweet, while a maraschino cherry bumps up the sugar content. It's about matching flavors and choosing a garnish that complements the drink. You wouldn't want a lemon wheel adorning your White Russian.

PIOUS ALTERNATIVES

Always have lots of nonalcoholic alternatives on hand like ice water, sparkling water, juice and soda. Remember that some people either don't drink booze at all, or simply opt to be responsible. (We don't know any of those, but we'd like to.)

Glassware

1. RED WINE

Each red variety can have its own glass, but it's generally large and more bulbous than a white wine glass.

2. COLLINS

Tall and slender, and used for ice-packed drinks. Also called a "highball."

3. SHOT

For serving shooters and measuring alcohol. Before trying the drinks recipes in this book, find out the size of your shot glass. A standard shot glass measures 1½ oz (fluid ounces), or 45 mL, but they come in 1, 2 or 3 oz (30, 60, or 90 mL) sizes as well.

4. WHITE WINE

Usually more slender and narrow than red wine glasses, but these also vary greatly.

5. MARGARITA

Use to serve daiquiris, frozen libations and, of course, its namesake.

6. ROCKS

For serving booze straight-up or on the rocks. Also called a low ball.

7. CHAMPAGNE FLUTE

Use to serve bubbly and bubbly-based cocktails.

8. PILSNER

For serving lagers and light ales. (The darker beer the shorter and wider the glass.)

9. SPECIALTY COFFEE

Use for hot toddies, hot chocolates, hot times.

10. MARTINI

Use for serving shaken cocktails straight-up.

Stocking the Pantry

The pantry is less of a physical place than a state of mind. Thoughtful as ever, we've decided to keep you from losing your mind and have created a list of ingredients that are used frequently in this book. If you keep the essentials on hand, you can always throw something together, say, for your mother-in-law who just happened to drop by. Our advice: make it a little too spicy and she might not come back.

FRESH

Bacon
Basil
Carrots
Cilantro
Garlic
Lemons
Limes
Onions (green, red, yellow)
Oranges
Potatoes (red, russet, Yukon Gold)
Prosciutto or pancetta
Rosemary
Thyme
Tomatoes

BREADS, PASTA AND RICE

Bagels, pitas or other breads
Pasta (assorted shapes and sizes)
Rice (basmati, arborio, jasmine)
Tortillas (flour or corn)

DAIRY

Butter
Cheese (assorted)
Cream (light 5–18%, heavy 35%)
Eggs
Mayonnaise
Milk
Sour cream
Yogurt

REFRIGERATED

Capers
Chili sauce
Chutney (mango, tomato, etc.)
Hot pepper sauce
Mustard (Dijon, Russian)
Olives (green, kalamata, ripe)
Pesto
Salsa
Sun-dried tomatoes
Tahini
Tapenade
Worcestershire sauce

CANS, BOTTLES, TUBES AND TETRAS

Chipotle peppers
Oils (olive, sesame, vegetable)
Soy sauce
Stock (chicken, beef, vegetable)
Tomatoes, whole canned
Tomato paste
Tuna, canned
Vinegar (red/white wine, balsamic, cider, rice, etc.)

BAKING INGREDIENTS

Baking powder
Baking soda
Breadcrumbs (dry)
Chocolate (white, dark 65%+)
Cocoa, unsweetened
Coffee (instant crystals, espresso)
Corn syrup
Cornmeal
Cornstarch
Cream of tartar
Custard
Dried fruit (apricots, cherries, cranberries, figs)
Flour (all-purpose, cake and pastry)
Graham crackers
Honey
Maple syrup
Molasses
Nonstick cooking spray
Nuts (almonds, cashews, peanuts, etc.)
Peanut butter
Preserves (strawberry, raspberry, apricot)
Sugar (granulated, brown, confectioner's)
Yeast

HERBS AND SPICES

Basil
Bay leaves
Cardamom
Cayenne pepper
Chili powder
Cinnamon
Cloves
Coriander seed
Cumin, ground
Curry powder
Garlic powder
Ginger, ground
Mustard seeds
Nutmeg, whole
Oregano
Paprika
Pepper (black, white, pink, etc.)
Rosemary
Sage
Salt (sea, kosher, etc.)
Sesame seeds
Tarragon
Thyme
Vanilla extract

FROZEN

Chicken breast (bone-in skin on, boneless skinless)
Phyllo pastry
Pork tenderloin or ribs
Puff pastry
Shrimp
Smoked salmon
Tart shells
Various types of sausage

SUNDRIES

- Aluminum foil
- Butcher's twine
- Parchment paper
- Plastic wrap
- Skewers (bamboo or metal)
- Toothpicks
- Waxed paper

Meat Doneness Guide

A digital thermometer is an essential tool in the kitchen. You can buy a basic model if you're on a tight budget, or you can indulge your inner gadget geek with a high-end version. In our experience, it's helpful to have two types: a magnetic one with a remote probe for oven- and barbecue-roasting and an instant-read, handheld type for pan-frying and grilling.

PROBING QUESTIONS

When probing for temperature, ensure the thermometer penetrates at least 2 inches (5 cm) into the thickest area of the cut. For grilled steaks or hamburgers, use tongs to hold the meat and slide the probe in parallel to the grilling surface. When probing a whole bird, penetrate the probe between the leg and the rest of the body.

REST FOR THE WICKED

Letting meat rest is critical to keep it juicy and moist. While cooking times vary depending on the size of the cut and type of meat, a good rule is to cover individual portions (such as steak or roast chicken breast) in aluminum foil and let them rest at room temperature for 5–7 minutes before serving. Larger carving roasts or roast chickens should get about 10–12 minutes. Full-sized roasts, turkeys and other very large cuts can rest for 30–60 minutes.

During the resting period the internal temperature of the meat will continue to climb, usually about an additional 10°F (8°C) for an average cut, or up to 25°F (15°C) for a whole turkey. Take this into consideration when reading the internal temperature and remove the meat before it's at the desired temperature. Once you've taken your meat out of the oven, keep an eye on the thermometer. The resting process allows the water vapor in the meat to recondense and be reabsorbed into the food. This happens just as the core temperature begins to cool, making it the ideal time to serve.

MEAT DONENESS CHART

BEEF	
Rare	125°F (50°C)
Medium-rare	130°F (55°C)
Medium	140°F (60°C)
Medium-well	150°F (65°C)
Well done	160°F (70°C)

LAMB	
Rare	125°F (50°C)
Medium-rare	130°F (55°C)
Medium	140°F (60°C)
Medium-well	150°F (65°C)
Well done	160°F (70°C)

CHICKEN	
Rare	not recommended
Medium-rare	not recommended
Medium	not recommended
Medium-well	165°F (75°C)
Well done	175°F (80°C)

VEAL	
Rare	125°F (50°C)
Medium-rare	135°F (57°C)
Medium	140°F (60°C)
Medium-well	150°F (65°C)
Well done	160°F (70°C)

PORK	
Rare	not recommended
Medium-rare	not recommended
Medium	145°F (62°C)
Medium-well	150°F (65°C)
Well done	160°F (70°C)

TURKEY	
Rare	not recommended
Medium-rare	not recommended
Medium	not recommended
Medium-well	165°F (75°C)
Well done	175°F (80°C)

Setting the Mood

Getting the right feel for a party is key to its success. There's no point in pretending that this doesn't require some planning. The trick is to not let yourself feel overwhelmed by it all. Just take it in stages. Understanding what type of party you're having and what mood you're hoping to achieve is the first step. Use as many of your senses as possible to help create atmosphere.

THEMES AND DÉCOR

The best way to create a theme is to add subtle cues for your guests to pick up on and one or two elements to focus their attention. If your event is fall-inspired, for example, you may want to decorate the table with attractive twigs and berries or make a centerpiece out of mini-gourds and fall leaves—very classy. Cardboard cutouts of scarecrows and pumpkins, plastic turkeys and fake flowers—um, perhaps not. (Unless you're entertaining a party of kindergartners, in which case you're reading the wrong book.) Always choose real and fresh over fake or plastic.

Centerpieces are good focal points as long as they don't interfere with dinner conversation. If you can't see the person across from you then the centerpiece is too big. Buffets have more flexibility for décor options but they also invite the temptation to drape everything in thematic table coverings. *Non.* Instead, choose a simple color theme for your linens and tableware and build from there.

LIGHTING

This is perhaps the most overlooked element of any party. Some people believe their existing light fixtures blazing with 100-watt bulbs are the perfect mood enhancer. Not us.

Proper lighting adds drama and creates illusion. Aiming small halogen spotlights up a wall creates a dramatic frame around a table, door or fireplace. Color can evoke playfulness and energy, while two strings of small lights hung from a center point gives the illusion of being under a tent. Make sure your lights can dim and avoid fluorescents at all costs.

The main purpose of lighting is to provide focus for your eye, which means you decide what people will look at by lighting it properly. Decide what you want to showcase and put the focus on it. Perhaps it's the buffet table, or the bar, or maybe you just received a PhD and want your guests to coo at it on the wall. You can also use the same technique to hide things you don't want people looking at, like the crack in the wall or your roommate's collection of vintage pizza boxes.

INDIRECT LIGHTING

Indirect lighting is a fancy term that describes lighting something without revealing the fixture or the bulb. This is a key trick to creating mood, especially with small halogen lights. Even masking the fixture by creating a small, sturdy three-sided shell will do the trick.

FLOODS AND SPOTS

Halogen lights come in two types, floods and spots. Floodlights create a wide soft beam which can be good for washing a whole wall in light, while spotlights create a narrow focused beam of light that can create drama with frames and pillars of light.

CANDLES

Candles create great accents but don't rely on them to provide your main lighting. Place them in small pots on shelves or a mantel to create wells of light on the wall. Make sure they can't be accidentally knocked over and don't leave them unattended.

OUTDOOR LIGHTING

Lighting outdoor spaces can be tricky: the space is usually large and finding the right contrast between light and dark is difficult. Strings of white lights can provide a good ambient source while spotlights aimed up into a tree can add drama and focus to the space. The motion light that saves you from the monster in the backyard should either be switched off or fitted with a low-wattage bulb. Bring some of the indoor feel outdoors by lighting tables with lamps or lanterns.

DINNER PARTIES

Most of the parties we've included in this book are casual and informal. That means you can ask your guest(s) to help bring out food or utensils and plates. We recommend serving most meals family-style, which means the dishes are served in bowls or platters so guests can help themselves. Make sure you have enough serving dishes and utensils to accommodate what you're preparing. Cloth napkins are sophisticated *and* environmentally friendly but paper napkins with bold and attractive patterns also have their place, adding a punch of color or whimsy to your party.

The simplest way to make your get-together feel more formal is to set an elaborate table. Start with chargers under your dinner plates, multiple forks or spoons for multiple courses and several type of glassware for water, white wine and red wine. Plate the meal in the kitchen and serve your guests individually. Presentation is key, so decide beforehand how you'll plate the meal most attractively. All the plates should look uniform. Remember to wipe off any drips or drops with a clean, damp cloth before serving. And keep your fingers and thumbs out of the food.

COCKTAIL RECEPTIONS

What makes a cocktail reception a cocktail reception is the ability to mingle. Make sure you've worked out your traffic patterns in advance to prevent any bottlenecks. It's a good idea to serve food and drink from two different stations. This gives people the opportunity to politely escape tedious conversation while keeping the mingling flowing. If you have the space, create seating areas for intimate conversation. This can be done by rearranging your furniture and focusing the lighting strategically.

MUSIC

Nothing creates atmosphere quite like music, from the high-energy beats of hip-hop to the dreamy, romantic sounds of jazz. Music is a powerful tool and in the wrong hands it can flatline the best parties in seconds. Aim for ambient. Guests should be able to converse easily. The fidgety fingers of tech-savvy pseudo-DJs should be kept well away from the equipment or be co-opted into managing the right ambience.

FRAGRANCES

The sense of smell is the one most closely associated with our memories. It has a powerful effect on setting the mood, but it can be very personal. For some the smell of cinnamon can evoke warm memories of pies baking, for others it can conjure a night spent drinking too much Goldschläger. Keep it subtle and you'll be fine.

HERBS AND SPICES

Mint, chamomile, rosemary, sage, thyme, cinnamon, allspice, black pepper, ginger, basil, coriander, clove and cardamom. Herbal notes relax and calm by adding an element of comfort and familiarity or romance.

FLORAL

Rose, jasmine, lilac and lavender. Floral notes evoke elegance and sophistication.

CITRUS

Lemon, lime, grapefruit and orange. Citrus notes awaken and invigorate.

FRUITY

Apple, berry, apricot, banana, melon, coconut and grape are informal, and can evoke a wide range of memories like coconut suntan lotion or grape punch sold from a child's drink stand. Fruity notes are generally playful and fun.

WOODY

Pine, cedar, birch eucalyptus, juniper berries and burnt leaves. These scents tend to refresh and conjure up holiday yuletide, fall harvest and winter sports.

SWEET

Vanilla, bubble gum, cotton candy, chocolate, caramel and other bakery fragrances like yeast-based breads. These scents relax and bring about a familiar, casual sensation.

PERSONAL APPEARANCE

Having said all that, the best way to set the sophistication level of your party isn't through the silver napkin rings, it's through what you wear as host. This is your production and your guests will look at you to set the bar. If you're serving a six-course meal and you're wearing track pants and a ripped T-shirt, it's difficult for your guests to trust that you know what you're doing.

HOUSE RULES

More guidelines than hard-and-fast rules, these tips will have you looking like a pro at your next function, a relaxed and confident host.

---

1 **PREPARE FOR THE TEETOTALERS.** Some people don't drink booze (can you believe it?!) while others may have to drive home. That doesn't mean you shouldn't make them feel special. Prepare a virgin cocktail (see Mocktails on facing page) or serve them sparkling water in wine glasses and garnish it with a few frozen berries. Pretty, delicious and road-safe.

2 **ROTATE THE HAND TOWELS HALFWAY THROUGH THE EVENING.** While you're visiting the washroom, check the saturation level on the hand towels. You may only need to switch them back to front but if they're soaked through you should replace them with fresh towels. It's a small thing that your guests will notice.

3 **SPLIT THE FOOD IN HALF.** Cut wedges of cheese in two, keep a bag of shrimp on reserve and save a box of crackers, for example. This way you can replenish and refresh—it keeps the buffet table looking good and ensures food isn't sitting out for several hours at a time.

4 **DON'T ASK YOUR GUESTS TO REMOVE THEIR SHOES.** Unless there's a snowfall coinciding with your party there's really no excuse. Shoes are part of the ensemble, for both men and women, and sock feet clash with almost every décor. Hardwood, laminate and tile floors can be cleaned with a quick mop. If you're still hanging on to your carpeted floors, well, invest in a heavy-duty vacuum or consider resurfacing.

5 **ROLL UP AREA RUGS,** stash the fragile objets d'art and clear space for chat circles and a possible dance floor. It helps keep things open and gets the party moving.

6 **RENT GLASSWARE, DISHES AND LINENS.** Party rentals are relatively inexpensive and they show up clean and go away dirty. No dishes and no worries about breakage—worth every penny the next day, and so much more sophisticated than plastic, not to mention environmentally friendlier.

7 **HIRE HELP.** Dinner parties for more than 12 and cocktail parties for more than 30 should be catered. Even if you insist on preparing all the food yourself, hire a bartender and one or two servers to staff the ovens, clear the mess and mix the drinks. It's your party and you should be mingling with your guests, not stuck in the kitchen.

8 **CREATE A PLAYLIST.** Music should never be overlooked and yet it's often put off until the end of the party-planning stage. Having five hours (8 pm to 1 am) of music preprogrammed means you'll have time to focus on your guests instead of frantically tossing CDs into the stereo. Start with mellow lounge music and progress into more upbeat and danceable tunes later on.

9 **LIGHTING, LIGHTING, LIGHTING.** Invest in dimmer switches and accent with candlelight. Everyone looks (and feels) wonderful in subdued lighting. If you can't switch all your lighting to dimmers (say in the kitchen or bathroom) change the bulbs to 25 or 40 watts for the night and add candles to brighten the space if necessary.

10 **BREW SOME COFFEE WHEN YOU WANT YOUR GUESTS TO LEAVE.** It's a surefire way to hammer the point home that the party's over. If your guests don't get the hint, start washing dishes. That'll do it.

Mocktails

Every good bartender should also have a repertoire of nonalcoholic drinks ready to go at any function. Guests who choose not to drink booze shouldn't be patronized with a warm can of diet soda. They should be respected and cared for, especially if they're the designated drivers. Mocktails are not only great thirst-quenchers, but also a special way to make those who choose not to drink feel welcome. As a host you might want to stir one of these up between alcoholic drinks for yourself; you'll last all night and you'll thank us in the morning.

GINGER MINT MOJITO

Make this virgin mojito when you're mixing up the real things—you can tell the nonalcoholic version by the slices of ginger.

2 slices fresh ginger

½ fresh lime, quartered

1 sprig fresh mint

1 tsp (5 mL) granulated sugar

Soda

Muddle the ginger, lime, mint and sugar together in a rocks glass until fragrant. Fill with ice, top with soda and garnish with a lime wheel, if desired.

STRAWBERRY BELLINI

Pick up a bottle of sparkling cider on those occasions when you're drinking champagne to mix up this pink-hued gem.

2 oz strawberry juice or purée

4 oz sparkling cider

Add the strawberry juice to a champagne flute and top with cider. Garnish with a fresh strawberry.

LEMON BOMB

Perfect on a hot summer day.

1 oz freshly squeezed lemon juice

1 tsp (5 mL) confectioner's sugar

2 oz apple juice

Soda

Stir the lemon juice and sugar together in a collins glass until dissolved. Add ice and the apple juice and top with soda. Garnish with a couple of lemon wheels.

POM POMME

Full of vitamins, antioxidants and sweet-tart flavor, this drink should come with a stamp of approval from Health Canada.

3 oz pomegranate juice

3 oz apple juice

Soda

Combine the pomegranate juice and apple juice in a collins glass filled with ice and top with soda. Serve with a couple of straws.

JA-MAKIN' ME TEA?

Refreshing, with just a hint of spice from the ginger beer, this is the perfect afternoon barbecue drink.

4 oz iced tea

2 oz ginger beer

Pour the iced tea and ginger beer into a rocks glass filled with ice and garnish with a lemon wheel, if desired.

RED SUNSET

Like that trip to the Dominican—except you'll actually remember the party this time.

3 oz pineapple juice

3 oz cranberry juice

Dash grenadine

Shake the pineapple juice, cranberry juice and grenadine together over ice and strain into a rocks glass filled with ice. Garnish with an orange slice and freshly grated nutmeg, if desired.

Classic Cocktails

Having these in your repertoire will make you practically invincible as a bartender. You'll never be stumped again for a delicious drink when a party guest asks to be "surprised."

COSMOPOLITAN

2 oz vodka

1 oz cranberry juice

Dash triple sec

Dash freshly squeezed lime juice

Shake the ingredients with ice and strain into a chilled martini glass. Garnish with an orange twist.

BLOODY CAESAR

1½ oz vodka

6 oz Clamato juice

2 dashes Worcestershire sauce

Dash Tabasco sauce

Pour the ingredients into a celery salt–rimmed collins glass filled with ice. Garnish with a stick of celery and a lemon wedge.

GIBSON

Dash dry vermouth

2½ oz gin

2 pearl onions

Rinse a martini glass with the vermouth then discard the vermouth. Shake the gin gently with ice and strain into the martini glass. Garnish with the onions.

OLD-FASHIONED

1½ oz rye

2 dashes Angostura bitters

Dash simple syrup

Combine the ingredients in a rocks glass filled with ice. Garnish with a lemon twist.

NEGRONI

¾ oz gin

¾ oz Campari

¾ oz sweet vermouth

Combine the ingredients in a rocks glass filled with ice. Garnish with an orange twist.

CUBA LIBRE

1½ oz white rum

4 oz Coca-Cola

Splash freshly squeezed lime juice

Combine the ingredients in a rocks glass filled with ice. Garnish with a lime wedge.

MANHATTAN

2 oz rye

½ oz sweet vermouth

Dash Angostura bitters

Shake the ingredients with ice and strain into a chilled martini glass. Garnish with a maraschino cherry.

VODKA GIMLET

2 oz vodka

½ oz lime cordial

Combine the ingredients in a rocks glass filled with ice. Garnish with a lime wedge.

MARGARITA

1½ oz tequila

3 oz freshly squeezed lime juice

¼ oz triple sec

Shake the ingredients with ice and strain into a salt-rimmed margarita glass. Garnish with a lime wheel.

NOTE: Blend the ingredients with 1 cup (250 mL) of ice for a frozen margarita.

TEQUILA SUNRISE

¼ oz grenadine

4 oz freshly squeezed orange juice

1½ oz tequila

Pour the grenadine into a collins glass then pack it with ice. Slowly pour in the orange juice and tequila. Garnish with an orange wheel and maraschino cherry.

BRONX

2 oz gin

1 oz freshly squeezed orange juice

½ oz dry vermouth

½ oz sweet vermouth

Shake the ingredients with ice, strain into a chilled martini glass and garnish with an orange twist.

DAIQUIRI

1½ oz white rum

3 oz freshly squeezed lime juice

Splash simple syrup

Shake the ingredients with ice and strain into a chilled martini glass. Garnish with a lime wheel.

Hangover Remedies

We've done extensive clinical research on this topic and found that hangover remedies are about as subjective as choosing a favorite booze. The next time you stumble home after an evening of too many libations, try one of these suggestions the morning after—it might just be the cure for what ails you.

TECHNICAL MUMBO JUMBO

A hangover is caused by a combination of factors, mostly the result of your liver and kidneys trying to process the alcohol as a toxin. This results in a build-up of free radicals (a byproduct of the liver's attempts to process the alcohol), dehydration and the loss of salt (alcohol is a diuretic) and sugars.

PREVENTION IS THE BEST MEDICINE

Obviously the best prevention is abstinence (isn't it always?) but let's assume that's not an option. Drink plenty of water throughout the evening to help minimize the effects of dehydration. This also dilutes the alcohol, making it easier for your liver and kidneys to process. Eating before or during drinking also helps to cushion the effects of booze.

Greasy and fried foods coat the lining of the stomach and help slow down the absorption of alcohol. Apparently, a tablespoon of olive oil before a night of boozing is used as prevention in some Mediterranean countries. We'll stick to pizza and poutine, thank you.

GET CRACKIN'

There is some pseudo-science to support the claim that eggs are a hangover cure. The whites are packed full of protein and the yolks contain fats, both of which provide energy and are easily metabolized. Eggs also contain the nonessential amino acid cysteine, which has antioxidant properties and breaks down the hangover-causing toxin acetaldehyde.

THE EURO TOAD

1 slice bread

1 tsp (5 mL) extra virgin olive oil

1 egg

1 slice spicy salami

1 wedge brie

1 tsp (5 mL) Dijon mustard

Preheat broiler. Line a baking sheet with parchment paper.

Brush 1 side of the bread with olive oil. Cut a round 2-inch (5 cm) hole in the center of the bread with a pastry cutter. Place the bread and cut-out hole, oil side up, on the prepared baking sheet. Crack the egg into the hole. Place on the middle rack of the oven under the broiler until the egg white becomes opaque (about 5 minutes). Remove from the broiler and layer the salami and brie on top. Return to the broiler until the brie is melted and creamy. Spread Dijon mustard over the cut-out hole and place on top of the brie.

HAIR OF THE DOG

This method involves facing your enemy head-on and taking a drink to cure your hangover. There is some short-term gain, as a tipple takes the edge off the hangover (mostly by numbing it) but as your liver catches up to process it, the hangover just intensifies.

MOUTHWASH

While it might not cure a queasy stomach, it'll sure make your cotton mouth feel minty-fresh.

1 oz vodka

1 oz green crème de menthe

Pour the vodka and crème de menthe into a rocks glass filled with ice. Swish accordingly.

FRESH AIR APPROACH

There are those (and they tend to be of the athletic persuasion) who believe that nothing cures a hangover better than a brisk walk in the cold morning air. This is all well and good, but in our testing we couldn't seem to get past the front door. Somehow we were always pulled back to the sofa for another marathon session of *Sell This House* on A&E.

HEALTH NUT APPROACH

For this test, we slipped on our Birkenstocks, skipped our morning showers and headed to the local juice bar. We had to fight our way through the kelp-lined yoga wear to get our fix of an antioxidant smoothie. To our surprise we felt better—great, even. Then we got the bill. Next time we'll make it at home.

ANTIOXIDANT SMOOTHIE

A good smoothie has all the qualities required to help counteract the damage inflicted by a night of drinking. It should have a good balance of sugars, liquid and a stomach-soother like dairy. Blueberries have the highest concentration of antioxidants of any fruit, while bananas replenish the potassium your body lost due to frequent bathroom breaks.

½ cup (125 mL) frozen blueberries

1 banana

½ cup (125 mL) pomegranate juice

¼ cup (50 mL) plain yogurt

Combine the blueberries, banana, pomegranate juice and yogurt in a blender, blending until smooth. Garnish with an ibuprofen and a sprinkling of self-pity.

SPORT AND ENERGY DRINKS

In theory, isotonic sport drinks (isotonic means salts that are in the same concentration as found in your body) should be a great way to replenish your body's depleted salts, electrolytes and sugars and offer you a good hit of caffeine to boot. The problem is that most energy drinks contain so much sugar that they can cause further dehydration, and that energy boost from the caffeine can mask inebriation. Be careful when using an energy drink as a mix and be sure to balance it out with a good portion of unsweetened fruit juice.

RED DAWN

4 oz Red Bull

4 oz freshly squeezed orange juice

Shake over ice and serve in a collins glass. Garnish with some dark sunglasses.

4-STEP PROGRAM

While we've given a fair shake to most hangover remedies, some are beyond the realm of possibility—including any cocktail that calls for a raw egg. Instead, our 1-2-3-4 approach seems to work.

1 cup of coffee

2 extra-strength ibuprofen tablets

3 eggs with bacon

No appointments before 4

DRINKING MAKES SUCH FOOLS OF PEOPLE, AND PEOPLE ARE SUCH FOOLS TO BEGIN WITH, THAT IT'S COMPOUNDING A FELONY.

Robert Benchley

CHAPTER 1

Occasions for Booze

EVERYTHING IN MODERATION,
INCLUDING MODERATION.

Julia Child

Boozy Birthday Party

SERVES 6

Menu

Roasted Sweet Potato and Cumin Soup

Green Apple and Fennel Slaw with Honey Citrus Vinaigrette

Exotic Braised Short Ribs

Devil's Food Cake with Whipped Dark Chocolate Ganache

Remember when you were a kid and couldn't wait for your birthday to come around every year? Well, time has a certain way of turning what was once the most anticipated event of the year into one that many of us would rather let slip past unnoticed. Hmmm, it's a good thing we've got booze—it almost makes the passage of another year bearable. Our delicious, fall-off-the-bone short ribs and velvety smooth Cointreau-spiked chocolate cake also help soften the blow.

Wine Pairing

Serve this meal with the same wine you use in the sauce—a big and bold New World variety suits it well (think Aussie Shiraz or Californian Cab).

Setting the Mood

Birthdays should be casually elegant—your table and décor should look thought-out but effortlessly put together. Think of the guest of honor and choose color schemes, music and lighting that best suit him or her. Upbeat jazz or lounge-y cocktail grooves are appropriate but if your guest is more rock 'n' roll than Verve Remixed, spin some Van Halen and suck it up.

Serving Suggestion

Serve the soup first in attractive cups or small bowls, keeping the portion lean to save room for coming courses. Bring the salad and ribs to the table in large serving dishes and have your guests serve themselves—it makes things easy for you and allows them to control their portion size.

Of course, dim the lights even lower when it's time to sing "Happy Birthday" and have the guest of honor cut and serve the cake at the table.

NOTE: If you have little faith in the culinary skills of the birthday girl or boy, offer to cut and serve the cake yourself. Nothing's worse than having someone butcher your culinary efforts—it'll be a relief to the guest of honor, too.

RUBY TUESDAY

Greet your guests with one of these celebratory cocktails. The addition of port adds incredible depth and just a touch of sweetness—enough to soften even the most bitter of birthday girls. Try it with champagne for those who really need to forget the wrath of Father Time.

½ oz ruby port

Sparkling wine or champagne

Pour the port into chilled champagne flutes and top with sparkling wine.

A PORT FOR ALL OCCASIONS

Ruby port, which has a wonderful rich claret color, is the youngest, cheapest and most widely produced of all the ports available. It's also easy-drinking. It's aged in concrete or stainless steel tanks—as opposed to oak barrels which dull the color but impart additional character to the wine—for between three and five years whereas tawny, white or vintage port can spend upward of 40 years aging in oak.

SERVES 6

Roasted Sweet Potato and Cumin Soup

- 2 large sweet potatoes, peeled and cut into large cubes
- 3 Tbsp (45 mL) extra virgin olive oil
- Salt
- Freshly ground black pepper
- 1 Tbsp (15 mL) ground cumin
- 1 small onion, diced
- 1 stick celery, diced
- 1 medium carrot, diced
- 1 clove garlic, minced
- 2 tsp (10 mL) minced ginger
- 1 cup (250 mL) white wine (an oaked Chardonnay works well)
- 4 cups (1 L) chicken stock
- 2 Tbsp (30 mL) heavy (35%) cream (optional)
- Sour cream, for garnish (optional)
- Chili powder, for garnish (optional)

Fragrant and smoky, but not too heavy, this soup will warm you up without weighing you down. We suggest a bit of cream for added richness but feel free to omit it if your metabolism—like Dave's wit—is a bit slower than it used to be.

Preheat oven to 425°F (220°C).

Toss the sweet potatoes with 1 Tbsp (15 mL) of the oil and sprinkle with salt and pepper. Place on a rimmed baking sheet and roast for 20–30 minutes, or until tender. Remove from the oven and set aside.

Meanwhile, heat the remaining 2 Tbsp (30 mL) of the oil in a large frying pan or soup pot over medium heat. Add the cumin and cook for 1–2 minutes, or until very fragrant. Add the onion, celery, carrot, garlic and ginger and continue cooking until the vegetables are soft, about 15 minutes. Add the wine and sweet potatoes and cook for another minute, then add the chicken stock. Bring the soup to a boil, reduce the heat, cover and simmer for 15 minutes.

Purée the soup with a handheld immersion blender or in small batches in a regular blender. Add the cream (if using) and season to taste with salt and pepper. Garnish each cup of soup with a swirl of sour cream and sprinkle with chili powder, if desired.

SERVES 6

Green Apple and Fennel Slaw with Honey Citrus Vinaigrette

Slaw

2 Granny Smith apples, peeled, cored and grated

1 medium fennel bulb, very thinly sliced

2 medium carrots, peeled and grated

3 green onions, finely chopped

Vinaigrette

2 Tbsp (30 mL) extra virgin olive oil

1 Tbsp (15 mL) honey

1 Tbsp (15 mL) freshly squeezed lemon juice

1 tsp (5 mL) Dijon mustard

½ tsp (2 mL) salt

½ tsp (2 mL) freshly ground black pepper

Sweet and tangy, crunchy and tender, this salad has it all—and it's a snap to throw together, which is ideal if you still need to run out and pick up a last-minute birthday gift.

For the slaw, toss the grated apple, fennel, carrots and green onions together in a bowl.

For the vinaigrette, whisk together the olive oil, honey, lemon juice, Dijon, salt and pepper in a separate bowl. Pour over the apple and fennel mixture and serve in individual ramekins.

NOTE: To make ahead, sprinkle the apple mixture with the lemon juice, cover with plastic wrap and refrigerate. Right before serving combine the dressing ingredients (omitting the lemon juice), toss lightly and serve.

SERVES 6

Exotic Braised Short Ribs

- 2 Tbsp (30 mL) canola oil
- 4–5 lb (2–2½ kg) beef short ribs, cut into chunks
- 1 Tbsp (15 mL) Chinese five-spice powder
- 1 tsp (5 mL) salt
- 1 tsp (5 mL) freshly ground black pepper
- 1 large onion, diced
- 1 medium carrot, peeled and diced
- 1 celery stalk, diced
- 4 cloves garlic
- 2-inch piece (5 cm) fresh ginger, peeled and sliced
- 2 cups (500 mL) red wine (Shiraz or Cabernet Sauvignon)
- 2 cups (500 mL) beef stock
- one 28 oz (796 mL) can diced tomatoes

This recipe is wonderful with short ribs but you can also use boneless stewing beef or lamb shanks, if you prefer. We prefer a world without televised celebrity dance competitions, but, alas, you can't always get what you want.

Preheat oven to 350°F (180°C).

Heat the oil in a large Dutch oven until smoking.

Season the ribs with the Chinese five-spice powder, salt and pepper. Add the ribs to the pot in batches and brown on all sides, about 4–5 minutes, transferring them to a large bowl once browned.

Pour off all but 2 Tbsp (30 mL) of any excess fat that has accumulated in the pot. Add the onion, carrot, celery, garlic and ginger to the fat in the pot and cook over medium heat until the vegetables have softened, about 10 minutes. Add the wine, stock and tomatoes, making sure to scrape up any brown bits from the bottom of the pot. Return the beef to the pot and bring to a simmer.

Cover and transfer to the oven. Braise until the ribs are fork-tender and most of the fat has rendered, about 2–3 hours. Start checking the meat at the 2-hour point (possibly later if your ribs are exceptionally fatty). Remove the ribs to a serving dish and cover with a lid or tent with aluminum foil. Strain the vegetables out of the sauce and discard, reserving the sauce and skimming off as much fat as possible. Return the sauce to the pot, bring to a boil, reduce the heat and simmer for about 10–15 minutes, or until the sauce coats the back of a spoon. Season to taste with salt and pepper then pour over the ribs. Sprinkle with sesame seeds and chopped green onions, if desired.

NOTE: If you can't find Chinese five-spice powder at your local supermarket you can make your own at home by combining 1¼ tsp (6 mL) ground fennel seed, 1 tsp (5 mL) cayenne pepper, 1 tsp (5 mL) ground star anise, ½ tsp (2 mL) ground cinnamon and ½ tsp (2 mL) ground cloves.

SERVES 6

Devil's Food Cake with Whipped Dark Chocolate Ganache

Cake

¼ cup (50 mL) milk

1 tsp (5 mL) white vinegar

½ cup (125 mL) salted butter

3 oz (75 g) bittersweet chocolate, chopped

1½ cups (375 mL) granulated sugar

2 eggs

1 cup (250 mL) strong black coffee

2¼ cups (550 mL) all-purpose flour

1½ tsp (7 mL) baking soda

2 tsp (10 mL) pure vanilla

Whipped Dark Chocolate Ganache

12 oz (350 g) bittersweet chocolate, finely chopped

1¾ cups (425 mL) heavy (35%) cream

½ cup (125 mL) sour cream

2 Tbsp (30 mL) Cointreau or triple sec

NOTE: Place strips of waxed or parchment paper under your cake while frosting it to prevent messing up your serving plate. Remove them carefully after decorating and delight in your wicked-ass skills.

Cointreau, a delicious orange-flavored liqueur, is our booze of choice for this cake but before you run screaming because you loathe the combo of chocolate and orange, take a breath, have a sip of your Ruby Tuesday and allow us to expand your mind. The taste of Cointreau in the frosting is so subtle that you or your guests might not even be able to detect its citrus origin, but we're absolutely convinced that you'll agree it's utterly delicious.

Preheat oven to 350°F (180°C). Grease and flour two 9-inch (23 cm) round cake pans and line the bottoms with parchment paper.

For the cake, combine the milk and vinegar in a small bowl and set aside.

Melt the butter and bittersweet chocolate together in a small saucepan over low heat. Set aside to cool slightly.

Cream together the sugar and eggs until light and fluffy. Add half the chocolate mixture to the eggs and beat well before adding the remaining chocolate. Add the coffee and blend until incorporated. The mixture will be very wet.

Add the flour, baking soda and vanilla all at once and beat until completely incorporated, then add the milk mixture and blend well. Pour into the prepared pans and bake for 30–35 minutes, or until a toothpick inserted in the center comes out clean. Remove from the oven, cool in the pans for 10 minutes then invert onto racks and cool completely before frosting.

For the ganache, combine the chocolate and heavy cream in a glass or stainless steel bowl over a pot of gently simmering water. Stir until the chocolate melts then whisk over the heat until well blended. Remove the bowl from the heat and cool for 10 minutes. Stir in the sour cream and liqueur then set aside to cool to room temperature, stirring occasionally. (The frosting will be very runny and you'll question our sanity—but trust us, it will whip up and set beautifully.) Beat the ganache with an electric beater until it becomes lighter in color and thick enough to spread.

To assemble, place 1 cake round top side down on a serving plate and cover with about one-third of the whipped ganache. Place the second cake layer top side down onto the first layer and cover with a thin layer of ganache to seal in any crumbs before thickly covering the entire cake with the remaining ganache. Decorate with a few thin orange slices if desired.

Menu

Salmon Bites with Sticky Glayva Bacon

Chappit Tatties

Roasted Cock with Leekie-Banger Stuffing

Butterscotch Bread Pudding

SERVES 12

Robbie Burns-Inspired Scotch Sampling

HOT ROBBIE

We named this cocktail after Rob Roy MacGregor, considered by some to be the Robin Hood of Scotland and by others a rogue, depending on which end of the sword you were on.

1-inch piece (2.5 cm) fresh ginger, peeled and sliced

1-inch piece (2.5 cm) orange zest

2 Tbsp (30 mL) honey

2 oz Scotch

Simmer the ginger, orange zest and honey with 1½ cups (375 mL) of water for 15 minutes. Strain into a specialty coffee mug with Scotch. Garnish with an orange twist, if desired.

January 25 is the traditional high-holy day for any Scot: it's the B-day of national poet Robert Burns, author of such New Year's greats as "Auld Lang Syne." This celebration is an opportunity to reacquaint yourself with some Scottish traditions and sample Scotland's signature malt export, whisky.

A traditional Burns supper requires a variety of foods that are near impossible to find outside the old country and are frankly not appealing to the modern North American palate. So, for this get-together we've opted to take inspiration from the ingredients of Scotland's cuisine to create a sophisticated cocktail-style evening of food and drink.

Wine Pairing

Scotch is the natural choice here, but if your fancy leans a little more toward the grape than the grain, you could try a lean, refreshing white, like a Pinot Gris or Pinot Grigio.

Setting the Mood

Scotland has one of the most recognizable cultural identities on the planet and getting carried away with the décor can be easy—and disastrous. Try to focus your décor on two tables: one to serve appetizers from (unless you choose to have them passed) and one to act as the Scotch bar. For freshness, purple heather, a small, hearty Scottish shrub, is readily available from florists and adds wonderful color to any room, especially in January. Use hints of tartan in your napkins or for a table runner, but don't overdo it.

Hang a map of Scotland as a backdrop to the bar, and mark a spot for the distillery of each different whisky being offered. It gives your guests an understanding of the terrain and region from which each comes. Little notebooks make excellent mementos of the evening and allow your guests to record sampling notes. Get crafty and wrap the notebooks in tartan paper to personalize them. Borrow books from the public library on whisky, Robert Burns and Scotland to provide your guests with good reference material. Pretty picture books work especially well.

FLIGHT SCHOOL

FLIGHT TYPES

HORIZONTAL FLIGHT

In the world of wine, a horizontal flight means sampling the same type and style of wine from different producers. Do the same thing with whisky by selecting three scotches from the same region. A horizontal tasting allows you to distinguish the nuances and character of each whisky and it's great for snooty conversation.

FOR EXAMPLE:

- The Balvenie, 12 year old
- Highland Park, 12 year old
- The Glenmorangie

VERTICAL FLIGHT

This is a tasting that uses several vintages from the same producer. With whisky this is easy to do: just select a Scotch with multiple cask vintages. A vertical tasting allows you to distinguish how a Scotch matures as it ages. Should you have an extra $30,000 lying around you could even try The Balvenie Cask 50 year old.

FOR EXAMPLE:

- The Balvenie, 10 year old
- The Balvenie, 12 year old
- The Balvenie, 15 year old

Setting the Mood, *cont.*

Now you have to be realistic. Single malts can be expensive. So, to make it easier on the pocketbook, ask your guests to each contribute a bottle. (Hey, we never claimed to be etiquette experts.) If they're experienced whisky drinkers, ask them to bring their favorite; if they're still a little novice, explain your plans and ask them to pick up a bottle that fits the tasting program. Have guests introduce their Scotch and provide some basic tasting notes—these can easily be found online.

Set an appropriate high-spirited atmosphere with a mix of traditional bagpipe and Celtic music: *Songs of Robert Burns: Celtic Collections* and *Heat the House* are both good choices. Loosen this up with a smattering of songs by contemporary artists like Franz Ferdinand, Belle and Sebastian or The Proclaimers.

Serving Suggestion

WHISKY FLIGHTS

To create a Scotch sampling flight, pour ½ oz of three different types of Scotch into three separate glasses; sip, compare and take notes. (See sidebar.)

SCOTCH 101

There are two types of scotches: single malt and blended. The latter consists of the various blends of the former, which allows the distillery to tune flavors. Single malt scotches are generally considered to be better quality but don't dismiss the blends just yet. Johnny Walker Blue, a famed blend, is perhaps one of the most buttery, smooth and delicate scotches widely available. It's also priced to keep it in the "ultra premiums" category rather than something you'd buy on a whim for a Thursday evening drinkfest. (See "Scotch 101," on the following page.)

TASTING SCOTCH

This requires using your eyes, nose and mouth. By looking at the Scotch you can determine the intensity of its flavor. Richer scotches will appear deep gold, while pale gold scotches tend to be lighter and milder in flavor. Smoky Scotch or Scotch with a lot of peat flavor will look dark caramel and display a smoky hue. Next, use your nose. Run the Scotch under your nose, swirl it gently in the glass, then pass it under your nose a second time. Do you smell anything different? Apple? Burnt wood? Caramel? Finally, take a sip, inhaling slightly at the same time and slightly swirl the Scotch in your mouth. What's the first flavor you detect? Does the flavor change? How long does it last? These are all things to keep a note of.

SCOTCH SAMPLING

SCOTCH 101

SCOTCH TYPES

SINGLE MALTS

Scotland is divided into two Scotch-producing regions, Highland and Lowland, and each has characteristically different flavors. Highland scotches are generally peaty in flavor, a characteristic brought about by the burning of peat moss to dry the malted barley. Lowland scotches, on the other hand, are lighter in color and, to the unsophisticated palate, smoother and more enjoyable. The lighter the Scotch, the less peaty the flavor.

LOWLAND MALT SCOTCHES

Lowland scotches are a good place to start for the novice whisky drinker. They're delicately flavored with honey notes and fruits, including apple. Lowland malts can be served neat as an aperitif.

HIGHLAND MALT SCOTCHES

The Highland region is Scotland's largest Scotch-producing region and consists of two subregions: Speyside and Island. Generally, the Highland malts are best served after dinner, although a light Highland malt—comparable to a Lowland malt—can be served as an aperitif.

SPEYSIDE—Speyside is the Highland subregion located around the River Spey. It produces whiskies that tend to be clean with subtle honey-like notes. Speyside malts are perfect for after dinner and blended-whisky drinkers will find them the most familiar.

ISLAND—Island is the Highland subregion comprising the islands that surround Scotland's northern tip and east coast. Highland and Island malts are typically full-bodied and heavily peated. Approach these with caution since it takes a practiced palate to appreciate their subtleties. Island scotches cover a collection of islands so each region can again be sub-categorized: the Orkneys, Isle of Skye, Mull, Jura and Islay—yours to discover.

SERVES 12

Salmon Bites with Sticky Glayva Bacon

Six 1-inch (2.5 cm) thick salmon fillets

12 slices bacon

¼ cup (50 mL) Glayva or Drambuie

Freshly ground black pepper

Freshly squeezed lemon juice

Glayva is a rich and sweet Scotch-based liqueur similar to Drambuie. It's filled with spice and herb notes and pairs wonderfully with the saltiness of bacon and the tender salmon. Salmon would stop swimming upstream if they knew they tasted this good.

Preheat oven to 450°F (230°C). Line a baking sheet with parchment paper.

Remove the skin from the salmon fillets by sliding a sharp knife between the skin and flesh. Cut each salmon fillet into 4 bite-sized pieces.

Cut each slice of bacon in half. Using a large frying pan over medium-high heat, cook the bacon until the fat has rendered but the bacon is still tender. Drain the renderings and add the Glayva. Cook until liquid bubbles up and thickens, about 30 seconds. Remove the bacon from the frying pan and set on a plate to cool.

Wrap each salmon fillet in a piece of bacon, using a toothpick to secure. Place on the prepared baking sheet and bake for about 10 minutes, or until the outside of the salmon is flaky but the inside is still pink. Top with freshly ground black pepper and a squeeze of lemon juice and serve immediately.

SERVES 12

Chappit Tatties

2½ lb (1.1 kg) Yukon Gold potatoes, cut into 1-inch (2.5 cm) chunks

¼ cup (50 mL) milk

¼ cup (50 mL) mayonnaise

1 tsp (5 mL) salt, or to taste

½ tsp (2 mL) freshly ground black pepper

Translation: mashed potatoes. We racked our brains for a way to sneak some booze into mashed potatoes, but instead we decided to give you a really great mashed potato recipe. The mayonnaise gives the potatoes a rich flavor and smooth texture. Mash away, potato fans, mash away.

In a large stockpot or Dutch oven, boil enough water to cover the potatoes. Add the potatoes, cover and reduce the heat to medium-low. Cook for 20 minutes, or until the potatoes are fork-tender. Thoroughly drain the potatoes and mash using a potato masher, or for better results use a food mill or ricer. Stir in the milk, mayonnaise, salt and pepper and adjust the consistency to your personal preference with additional milk. To make the potatoes light and fluffy, beat with an electric mixer.

I'D HATE TO BE A TEETOTALER. IMAGINE GETTING UP IN THE MORNING AND KNOWING THAT'S AS GOOD AS YOU'RE GOING TO FEEL ALL DAY.

Dean Martin

SERVES 12

Roasted Cock with Leekie-Banger Stuffing

Chicken

2 large chickens, each weighing 3½–5 lb (1.75–2.2 kg)

¼ cup (50 mL) extra virgin olive oil

1 Tbsp (15 mL) salt

Stuffing

1 lb (500 g) British bangers (sausages), casing removed

1 cup (250 mL) leeks, sliced (white part only)

1 cup (250 mL) dark ale (such as McEwans Scotch Ale)

2 Golden Delicious apples, peeled, cored and chopped

4 cups (1 L) cubed bread

1 tsp (5 mL) thyme

1 tsp (5 mL) freshly ground black pepper

Our inspiration for this dish came from a deconstruction of the classic Cock-a-Leekie soup. Of course, we stuff our chicken with sausage and beer, which is pretty hard to do with a soup, but if you like a challenge, give it a go. This dish is not only a great way to feed a hungry pack of Scotch drinkers, it's also a great excuse to use some inappropriate words at the dinner table. Of course, you could make this recipe using turkey, but then you'd have to call it Bubbly-Jock with Leekie-Banger Stuffing, wouldn't you?

Preheat oven to 450°F (230°C).

Remove the giblets or other icky parts from the cavity of the chickens, brush the skin with olive oil and sprinkle with the salt.

For the stuffing, combine the sausage meat and leeks in a large frying pan over medium-high heat. Cook the sausage, breaking up large pieces with a fork as required, until it's lightly browned. Drain off any excess renderings, add the beer and apples and continue to cook for about 10 minutes, or until the apples are soft and the liquid has reduced by about one-third. Transfer to a large mixing bowl and fold in the bread, thyme and pepper.

Divide the stuffing into 2 equal portions and stuff the chickens. Tie the body cavities closed with butcher's twine. Place the chickens in a deep ovenproof dish or roasting pan and roast in the middle of the oven for about 40 minutes, or until the juices run clear and the internal temperature has reached 165°F (75°C). Remove from the oven and tent with aluminum foil for 10 minutes before serving.

SERVES 12

BUTTERSCOTCH BREAD PUDDING

Butterscotch Sauce

1 cup (250 mL) heavy (35%) cream

1 cup (250 mL) granulated sugar

½ cup (125 mL) butter, cubed

½ cup (125 mL) Scotch

Bread Pudding

6 day-old croissants, torn into 1-inch (2.5 cm) pieces

1½ cups (375 mL) milk

1 cup (250 mL) heavy (35%) cream

5 eggs, lightly beaten

1 cup (250 mL) brown sugar, loosely packed

1 tsp (5 mL) vanilla extract

½ tsp (2 mL) cinnamon

Pinch salt

This rich and creamy dessert is sure to warm the cockles of your heart, whatever those might be. A perfect accompaniment to a Scottish-inspired dinner, this peasant dish gets a gourmet makeover by using buttery croissants. You can substitute French or Italian bread, but why?

To make the butterscotch sauce, heat the cream and 1 cup (250 mL) of water in a small saucepan over medium-low heat, until just below simmering point.

Meanwhile, in a second medium-sized saucepan, heat the sugar over medium-high heat until melted and slightly golden, about 8–10 minutes. Slowly add the butter and Scotch into the sugar mixture, stirring constantly to keep smooth. Be careful adding the Scotch as it will react with the hot pan and splatter; add only small amounts at a time. Slowly stir in the hot cream into the sugar mixture. Remove from heat and set aside.

To make the bread pudding, lightly grease a 9- × 13-inch (3.5 L) casserole dish. Evenly distribute the croissant pieces over the bottom of the dish. In a large mixing bowl, combine the milk, 1 cup (250 mL) of cream, eggs, brown sugar and vanilla. Slowly whisk in the butterscotch sauce, working with small amounts at a time to prevent curdling. Pour the sauce over the croissants and sprinkle with cinnamon and a pinch of salt. Allow to sit for about 30 minutes, or until the bread has absorbed most of the liquid.

Preheat oven to 350°F (180°C).

Bake for about 50–60 minutes, or until the center is set but still a wee bit jiggly. Remove from the heat and allow to cool for 15 minutes before serving.

Serve with a drizzle of cream, whipped cream, ice cream or your favorite cream liqueur, if desired.

Menu

Forest Mushroom and Irish Ale Soup

Salmon Arugula Wraps

Leprechaun Roast Rack of Lamb

Black and Tan Brownies

SERVES 8–10

St. Paddy's Day Beer Fest

BLACK RASPBERRY

Serve this drink in tall pilsner glasses when your guests arrive, or in smaller stemware such as champagne flutes for dessert. Its tangy sweetness is an amazing complement to the Black and Tan Brownies.

Raspberry lambic, such as Mort Subite Framboise

Guinness

Half-fill a pilsner glass with the raspberry lambic then top with Guinness.

Out of the cold dark days of winter comes a holiday so anticipated and revered it needs no introduction. St. Patrick's Day heralds in spring with spurts of green shamrocks, flashes of gold bouillon (in the form of pint glasses) and an excuse to shed winter's nesting habits and join in a parade. Afterwards, gather the gang for a beer tour through Ireland with frequent stops for mushroom soup and roast rack of lamb. Rubbing of the Blarney Stone is optional.

Wine Pairing

For St. Paddy's Day it's got to be beer—see the notes at the bottom of the following pages as well as page 230 for our quick and dirty guide to some of the most popular brews, their tasting notes and what dishes they're best suited to.

Setting the Mood

St. Paddy's Day is relaxed and casual so instead of a fussy sit-down meal, go for a cocktail party buffet. It means less work for you and allows your guests to mingle—and once the food is on the table you're free to join in the beer-tasting.

Bunches of fresh herbs make wonderfully fragrant centerpieces. Simply arrange them in small, gold-colored pots or pewter beer steins filled with water for an effective display. Encourage your guests to tear off small pieces to add to their soup bowls. Gold coins (the chocolate sort) also make easy décor options. Fill an attractive glass bowl or make stacks and tie them with emerald ribbon.

Look to the country of honor or Canada's east coast for your musical inspiration: U2, The Thrills, Mary Jane Lamond, The Barra MacNeils and, of course, The Pogues.

Serving Suggestion

Serve your guests their soup in attractive latte cups or small bowls—you can offer this course from the kitchen or place on the table in a soup tureen with your serving vessels arranged around it.

SERVES 8–10

Forest Mushroom and Irish Ale Soup

2 Tbsp (30 mL) extra virgin olive oil
1 large onion, chopped
1 clove garlic, minced
2 cups (500 mL) sliced cremini or portobello mushrooms
2 cups (500 mL) sliced shiitake or porcini mushrooms
2 Tbsp (30 mL) brandy
1 Tbsp (15 mL) fresh thyme leaves
½ tsp (2 mL) salt
½ tsp (2 mL) freshly ground black pepper
4 cups (1 L) vegetable stock
2 cups (500 mL) Irish ale, such as Kilkenny

Perfect for warming the belly and the soul, this soup can nourish a family of four right through the cold, wet winter—or on a lovely spring day in March.

Heat the oil in a large stockpot. Add the onion and garlic and cook until soft, about 10 minutes. Add the mushrooms and cook for 3 minutes, gently tossing with the onion mixture to combine. Add the brandy, thyme, salt and pepper and cook for 1 minute. Add the stock and beer. Bring to a boil, cover, then reduce the heat and simmer for 20 minutes.

Serve with a garnish of fresh thyme leaves and soda bread, if desired.

NOTE: Dried porcini mushrooms may be substituted if fresh are unavailable. Add them directly to the soup, heating until softened.

THE BEERS OF IRELAND IN A FEW WORDS

KILKENNY (CREAM ALE)

This bright amber-colored ale features soft grain and malt aromas that translate to a rich malty taste and bitter, hoppy finish.

Enjoy a pint of Kilkenny with the Forest Mushroom and Irish Ale Soup.

SMITHWICK'S (ALE)

A lovely reddish-copper color features tones of sweet and smoky malt and rich chocolate malt flavor. Finishes bitter.

Also an excellent match with the Forest Mushroom and Irish Ale Soup or Leprechaun Roast Rack of Lamb.

WINE COMES IN AT THE MOUTH
AND LOVE COMES IN AT THE EYE
THAT'S ALL WE SHALL KNOW FOR TRUTH
BEFORE WE GROW OLD AND DIE.

William Butler Yeats, "A Drinking Song"

SERVES 8–10

Salmon Arugula Wraps

4 small salmon fillets (1 inch/2.5 cm thick)

1 Tbsp (15 mL) extra virgin olive oil

1 tsp (5 mL) salt

½ tsp (2 mL) freshly ground black pepper

½ cup (125 mL) mayonnaise

¼ cup (50 mL) finely chopped chives

2 Tbsp (30 mL) Cointreau or triple sec

8 small flour tortillas (plain, whole wheat or flavored)

1½ cups (375 mL) baby arugula

1½ cups (375 mL) shredded red cabbage

Perfect for the buffet table, these sandwiches not only take little time to prepare, they can be made a few hours in advance, freeing up precious parade-watching time. Begorra!

Preheat oven to broil.

Brush the salmon with the olive oil and season with the salt and pepper. Broil skin side down until flaky, about 6 minutes, or until desired doneness. Set aside.

Meanwhile, combine the mayonnaise, chives and Cointreau and season to taste with more salt and pepper. Break the fillets into bite-sized pieces, discarding the skin. Divide the dressing among the tortillas, top with salmon, arugula and cabbage and roll tightly. Cut in half on the bias and secure each roll with a toothpick. Arrange on a serving plate, cover and refrigerate until ready to serve.

NOTE: Baby arugula has a wonderfully peppery flavor so season the dressing conservatively. You can also substitute baby spinach or smoked salmon, if you prefer.

MORE BEERS OF IRELAND IN A FEW WORDS

HARP (LAGER)

Rich and smooth with a medium gold color. Aromas of grain lead to a crisp and slightly bitter finish.

A wonderful choice for a Black and Tan (see page 219), and a winning combo with the Salmon Arugula Wraps.

SERVES 8–10

Leprechaun Roast Rack of Lamb

1 cup (250 mL) chopped chives
4 cloves garlic
¼ cup (50 mL) Irish whiskey
¼ cup (50 mL) extra virgin olive oil
¼ cup (50 mL) brown sugar, packed
2 Tbsp (30 mL) freshly squeezed lemon juice
1 tsp (5 mL) salt
1 tsp (5 mL) freshly ground black pepper
3 racks of lamb (1½ lb/750 g each), frenched*

This recipe is equally delicious when made with fresh mint or rosemary instead of the chives, or a combination of herbs—and it scales easily too if you're serving a table of four or a party of twelve.

Preheat oven to 375°F (190°C).

Blend the chives, garlic, whiskey, olive oil, brown sugar, lemon juice, salt and pepper in a food processor or blender until smooth. Rub the mixture over the lamb and place it bone side up in a roasting pan. Cover the bone tips loosely with aluminum foil and roast for about 25 minutes, or until the internal temperature reaches 125°F (50°C) on a meat thermometer for medium-rare, or for 30–35 minutes for medium. Remove the meat from the oven, tent in aluminum foil and let rest for at least 10 minutes before slicing. Slice the lamb between each bone and arrange on large platter, garnished with a good bunch of fresh herbs.

NOTE: If time permits, marinate the racks of lamb in the chive mixture overnight or a few hours in the refrigerator before roasting.

* For more on "Frenching," see page 128.

STILL MORE BEERS OF IRELAND IN A FEW WORDS

GUINNESS (STOUT)

Inky color with cascades of brown waves falling under a thick and creamy tanned head. Aromas of roasted barley; slightly sweet and a little bitter. A perfect brew. Some bar staff pride themselves on being able to carve a shamrock into the head of the Guinness as they pour it from the tap.

Serve Guinness with the Leprechaun Roast Rack of Lamb and mix up a Black Raspberry (page 33) for a wonderful complement to the Black and Tan Brownies (page 39).

SERVES 8–10

Black and Tan Brownies

- 1 cup (250 mL) all-purpose flour
- ¾ cup (175 mL) cocoa powder
- ¼ tsp (1 mL) salt
- ⅓ cup + 1 Tbsp (90 mL) unsalted butter, cubed
- 8 oz (250 g) bittersweet chocolate, chopped
- 3 oz (75 g) white chocolate, chopped
- 4 eggs, at room temperature
- 1 cup (250 mL) granulated sugar
- ½ cup (125 mL) chopped pecans (optional)
- 1¼ cups (300 mL) stout, such as Guinness
- 1½ cups (375 mL) peanut butter chips
- ¼ cup (50 mL) ale

Adding Guinness to the batter brings out the full flavor of the chocolate and adds a malty richness to this dessert. Adding ale to the fudge-like frosting is just fun, to be honest. Don't tell anyone what the secret ingredient is. Make them guess. The kids will probably get it right away.

Preheat oven to 375°F (190°C). Grease and flour a 9- × 13-inch (3.5 L) baking pan or line it with parchment paper.

Whisk together the flour, cocoa and salt in a medium bowl; set aside. Melt the butter, bittersweet chocolate and white chocolate in a glass or metal bowl over a pot of gently simmering water, stirring constantly. Remove from the heat. In a separate bowl, beat the eggs and sugar on high speed for 3 minutes. Slowly add the melted chocolate mixture and beat until combined. Stir in the flour mixture and chopped pecans (if using) until just combined. Do not overmix. Stir in the stout (batter will be very runny). Pour the batter into the prepared pan and bake for 20–25 minutes, or until a toothpick inserted near the edge comes out clean. Do not overbake. The center should be soft. Let the brownies cool completely before frosting.

Melt the peanut butter chips and ale together in a glass or metal bowl placed over a pot of gently simmering water, stirring until smooth. Spoon dollops of the frosting onto the cooled brownies and spread evenly overtop, working quickly before the frosting hardens. Cut the cooled brownies into squares.

NOTE: Dip your knife into a glass of hot water to keep it clean between slices.

NOTE: Brownies can be made up to 2 days in advance and they stay moist for up to 5 days.

YEP, EVEN MORE BEERS OF IRELAND IN A FEW WORDS

MURPHY'S IRISH STOUT (STOUT)

Less bitter than Guinness with notes of coffee and roasted nuts, this smooth and creamy beer features a thick head that remains after the pint has been drained. Has a thinner mouthfeel than Guinness.

Enjoy a cold Murphy's with the Leprechaun Roast Rack of Lamb (page 37) or mix with Raspberry lambic (page 33) and enjoy with the Black and Tan Brownies.

SERVES 6

Mother's Day Brunch

Menu

Mushroom and Bacon Frittata with Balsamic and Pomegranate Mixed Greens

Orange and Raspberry Parfaits

Blueberry Poppy Seed Loaf

PRETTY LADY

½ oz pomegranate liqueur

Champagne

Pour pomegranate liqueur into chilled glasses and top with champagne. Garnish with an orange twist, if desired.

POMEGRANATE CLUB

Made from fresh juice and alcohol, pomegranate liqueur is a wonderful addition to martinis, margaritas and mojitos (oh my!), but its exotic sweet-tart flavor is also a great match with chicken and pork dishes, as well as vinaigrettes and dipping sauces.

Eighteen hours of labor, sleepless nights and endless laundry have taken up too much of Mom's time already. Show her how much you love her and appreciate all she does for the family by making her the guest of honor at a simple yet impressive brunch. A little bit of effort now will pay dividends later. You might even get her into a romantic mood—just remind Dad to use protection this time.

Wine Pairing

Serve the frittata and salad with an unoaked Chardonnay or Chablis or try it with a light and fruity red such as Beaujolais.

Setting the Mood

The corporate machine didn't stick Mother's Day in May out of pure whimsy. Smack-dab in the middle of spring it's the perfect time to hand your credit card over to your local florist and have her create bouquets, centerpieces and a corsage for the guest of honor. Heck, get yourself a boutonniere while you're at it. Soft, pastel colors are always a safe bet.

Pull out all the stops for Mom and use those fancy plates and shiny silverware that hide behind cherrywood doors for most of the year. Set the table with freshly pressed linens, low votive candles and, of course, those fresh flowers you blew the budget on.

Make a playlist featuring Mom's favorite artists or create your own with some lively jazz, soul or classic R&B.

Serving Suggestion

Start Mom off with a Pretty Lady cocktail and a cup of freshly brewed coffee. Next, serve the frittata with the mixed-green salad and finish off with the Blueberry Poppy Seed Loaf and another cup of coffee. Follow with a relaxing foot rub, if the moment strikes. And don't ask Mom to do the dishes.

SERVES 6

Mushroom and Bacon Frittata with Balsamic and Pomegranate Mixed Greens

Frittata

6 slices bacon

½ onion, finely chopped

1½ cups (375 mL) sliced mixed mushrooms (cremini, shiitake, oyster, etc.)

½ tsp (2 mL) freshly ground black pepper

¼ tsp (1 mL) salt

6 eggs

½ cup (125 mL) milk

1 Tbsp (15 mL) Dijon mustard

1 cup (250 mL) shredded Gruyère cheese

Mixed Greens

2 Tbsp (30 mL) extra virgin olive oil

2 Tbsp (30 mL) balsamic vinegar

2 Tbsp (30 mL) pomegranate liqueur

Pinch salt

Pinch freshly ground black pepper

½ lb (250 g) mixed greens, rinsed and dried

Frittatas make wonderful brunch fare because they serve a crowd from one pan and can be made ahead of time and served at room temperature—and they're a helluva lot easier than flipping out omelets.

Preheat oven to 350°F (180°C).

Cook the bacon in a large nonstick, ovenproof frying pan over medium-high heat until crisp, about 5 minutes. Remove from the pan and drain on paper towel, then crumble into bite-sized pieces.

Drain all but 1 Tbsp (15 mL) of the bacon renderings from the pan. Add the onion and cook for 2–3 minutes or until softened. Add the mushrooms, pepper and salt and cook for an additional 2–3 minutes.

Meanwhile, lightly whisk the eggs, milk and Dijon together in a medium bowl and add to the frying pan. Cook until the frittata is set at the edges and the underside is golden, about 5 minutes. Sprinkle the egg mixture with cooked bacon and shredded cheese and bake in preheated oven for an additional 5 minutes, or until the cheese is melted and the egg mixture is set. Serve either hot or at room temperature.

For the mixed greens, whisk together the olive oil, vinegar, liqueur, salt and pepper. Drizzle over the greens in a large bowl and toss to coat the leaves evenly. Plate and serve.

SERVES 6

Orange and Raspberry Parfaits

3 large or 4 medium navel oranges
2 cups (500 mL) fresh raspberries
¼ cup (50 mL) Grand Marnier or Cointreau
1 cup (250 mL) vanilla-flavored yogurt

Simple flavors and striking presentation. 'Nuf said.

Slice the ends off the oranges then cut away the rest of the rind; cut the orange flesh into slices, then cube. Place a few orange pieces in the bottom of 6 small parfait or martini glasses, cover with a few raspberries and another layer of oranges, and finish with the rest of the raspberries. Drizzle each parfait with 2 tsp (10 mL) of Grand Marnier and a dollop of yogurt.

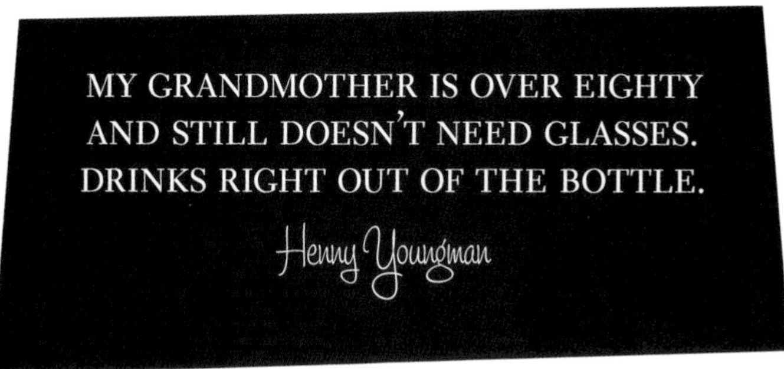

SERVES 6

BLUEBERRY POPPY SEED LOAF

Loaf

- ½ cup (125 mL) butter, softened
- 1 cup (250 mL) granulated sugar
- 2 eggs
- 1 Tbsp (15 mL) limoncello (see page 216 for a recipe)
- 1½ cups (375 mL) all-purpose flour
- 1 tsp (5 mL) baking powder
- 1 tsp (5 mL) salt
- ½ cup (125 mL) milk
- 1 cup (250 mL) fresh or frozen blueberries
- 2 Tbsp (30 mL) poppy seeds

Glaze

- ⅓ cup (75 mL) confectioner's sugar
- 1 Tbsp + 1 tsp (20 mL) limoncello

You can make this cake up to one day in advance to save precious time on the morning of the big event. Just cover it with plastic wrap and a layer of aluminum foil to seal in the freshness—then lock it in the family safe to keep temptation out of sight.

Preheat oven to 350°F (180°C). Grease and flour a 9- × 5-inch (2 L) loaf pan and line the bottom with parchment paper.

Cream together the butter and sugar until light and fluffy. Add the eggs 1 at a time, beating well after each addition. Stir in the limoncello. In a separate bowl whisk together the flour, baking powder and salt. Add half the flour mixture to the egg mixture with ¼ cup (50 mL) of the milk and beat until just combined. Add the remaining flour and milk and beat well. Fold in the blueberries and poppy seeds. Pour the batter into the prepared pan and bake for 45–60 minutes, or until a toothpick inserted in the center comes out clean. Remove to a wire rack and cool for 10 minutes before removing from the pan.

Meanwhile, make the glaze by stirring together the confectioner's sugar and limoncello until smooth. Drizzle over the loaf and serve warm or cool completely before serving.

NOTE: Place a piece of waxed paper under the wire rack to catch any excess glaze. Wrap any leftover cake in plastic wrap or aluminum foil and store for up to 3 days.

NOTE: Decrease oven temperature to 325°F (160°C) and increase baking time to 55–65 minutes if using a glass loaf pan.

SERVES 6

Father's Day Surf 'n' Turf Barbecue

Menu

BLT Tavern Salad

Wine-Soaked Potato Salad

Grilled Sirloin with Coffee Cognac Barbecue Sauce

Whole Blackened Snapper

Strawberry Margarita Shortcake

GINGER ALE

This, we think, is what the folks at Canada Dry were aiming for . . .

½ oz ginger cordial

1 bottle crisp, sparkling ale

Add the cordial to a beer glass and top with ale. Garnish with a wedge of lime if desired.

NOTE: Ginger cordial can be found at most major grocery stores and specialty food shops.

Designing a Father's Day menu for Dad is really a no-brainer: BBQ. What's even better is that we've put together a menu he'll not only enjoy eating but also enjoy preparing. Send him outside with the meat and let him do what he loves—cook stuff over an open flame. Mom could use the peace and quiet.

Wine Pairing

Serve this menu with a medium-bodied red such as Chianti or Merlot or with a full-bodied white like an oaked Chardonnay. Otherwise stick with beer—a crisp pale ale or dry porter should keep the Old Man happy.

Setting the Mood

Go out to the garage for inspiration if you must but really just aim to keep things casual and unfussy. Opt for patio lanterns over candlelight and placemats rather than Grandma's lace tablecloth. And feel free to program the iPod to play all of Dad's favorites whether it's Elvis, AC/DC or Finger Eleven.

Serving Suggestion

No need to plate this meal for your guests. Instead, serve it buffet style and have everyone help themselves. Prepare roll-ups (fork and steak knife rolled into a napkin) and present them in galvanized tins or together with S&P and extra napkins in Dad's brand-new-Happy-Father's-Day-Pop toolbox. Ah, isn't it great seeing him this happy?

SERVES 6

BLT Tavern Salad

8–10 strips bacon (double-smoked if you can find it)

½ cup (125 mL) mayonnaise

1 Tbsp (15 mL) white wine vinegar

1 Tbsp (15 mL) lemon vodka

¼ cup (50 mL) buttermilk

⅓ cup (75 mL) crumbled blue cheese

1 tsp (5 mL) freshly ground black pepper

1 large (or 2 small) head iceberg lettuce, cut into 6 wedges

2 large ripe tomatoes, roughly chopped

This is the best accessory a barbecued steak could ask for—crisp, cold lettuce, juicy, ripe tomatoes, crunchy bacon and a boozy blue cheese dressing. Beautifully simple, it's like a trophy wife for beef.

Cook the bacon until crisp then drain on paper towel and crumble into manly pieces.

Stir together the mayonnaise, vinegar, vodka and buttermilk. Add the blue cheese and pepper. Cover and refrigerate until ready to serve.

Place a wedge of lettuce on a salad plate and spoon over a couple of tablespoons of dressing. Sprinkle with chopped tomato and some crisp bacon.

NOTE: You can substitute 2 tsp (10 mL) vodka + 1 tsp (5 mL) freshly squeezed lemon juice if you don't have any lemon vodka.

SOUR PUSS

A mix of milk and white vinegar is a suitable substitute for buttermilk in baking but it doesn't have the same camouflaging powers when consumed raw. For this dressing you'll need the real thing, but don't fret, it keeps for a very long time in the refrigerator after opening and it's surprisingly low in fat—only 1%.

SERVES 6

Wine-Soaked Potato Salad

1 cup (250 mL) chopped asparagus (1-inch/2.5 cm pieces)

1½ lb (750 g) baby potatoes (red, white or a mixture)

2 Tbsp (30 mL) white wine

2 Tbsp (30 mL) chicken stock

⅓ cup (75 mL) extra virgin olive oil

3 Tbsp (45 mL) freshly squeezed lemon juice or white wine vinegar

1 Tbsp (15 mL) grainy mustard

2 tsp (10 mL) salt

1 tsp (5 mL) freshly ground black pepper

¼ cup (50 mL) chopped fresh dill

¼ cup (50 mL) chopped fresh Italian parsley

Warm potatoes soak up liquid—in this case wine and chicken stock—and pack them with flavor. Be sure to slice the potatoes as soon as you can handle them, as cold spuds will repel the wine. It's like potato foreplay.

Blanch the asparagus in a large pot of boiling water for 1 minute. Remove from the pot and rinse with cold water to set the color and stop the cooking.

Carefully add the potatoes to the same pot and boil for 15–20 minutes, or until tender but still firm. Pour into a colander and set aside until cool enough to handle. Cut the potatoes in half, or into quarters if large, and toss with the wine and chicken stock. Mix in the asparagus and set aside.

Whisk together the olive oil, lemon juice, mustard, salt and pepper. Pour this vinaigrette over the potato mixture and toss with the dill and parsley. Serve warm or at room temperature.

THE TROUBLE WITH JOGGING IS THAT THE ICE FALLS OUT OF YOUR GLASS.

Martin Mull

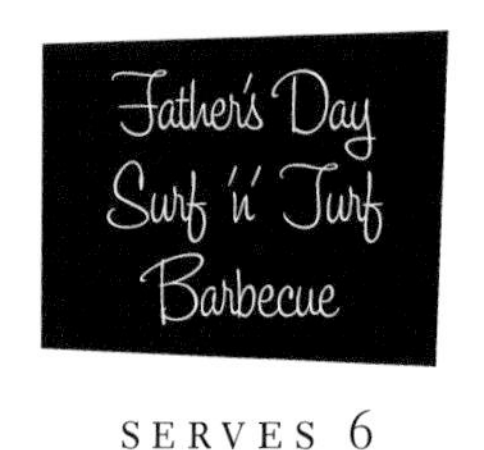

SERVES 6

Grilled Sirloin with Coffee Cognac Barbecue Sauce

Steak

2–3 lb (1–1.5 kg) sirloin steak

½ cup (125 mL) beer (crisp ale works well)

2 cloves garlic, crushed

1 tsp (5 mL) salt

1 tsp (5 mL) freshly ground black pepper

Coffee Cognac Barbecue Sauce

½ cup (125 mL) crushed tomatoes

¼ cup (50 mL) espresso or strong coffee

2 Tbsp (30 mL) cognac or brandy

1 Tbsp (15 mL) molasses

1 tsp (5 mL) chili powder

½ tsp (2 mL) salt

Dash hot pepper sauce

If this doesn't put a smile on Dad's face, there may be no hope. The full-flavored sauce is also great with burgers and ribs.

Marinate the steak in the beer and garlic for at least 1 hour, or overnight if possible. Remove from the marinade and season with the salt and pepper before grilling.

For the sauce, combine the tomatoes, espresso, cognac, molasses, chili powder, salt and hot pepper sauce in a small saucepan. Simmer until reduced by half, then remove from the heat and set aside.

Preheat the barbecue until very hot. Rub the grill with oil and cook the steak for 4–5 minutes per side, or until cooked to the desired doneness.

Wrap in aluminum foil and let rest for 5 minutes before slicing against the grain into thin strips. Arrange on a platter and spoon over the sauce or serve it on the side.

VEGETABLES ARE INTERESTING BUT LACK A SENSE OF PURPOSE WHEN UNACCOMPANIED BY A GOOD CUT OF MEAT.

Fran Lebowitz

ALSO PICTURED: WHOLE BLACKENED SNAPPER (PAGE 52)
WINE-SOAKED POTATO SALAD (PAGE 49)

SERVES 6

WHOLE BLACKENED SNAPPER

- Two 2 lb (1 kg) whole red snappers, cleaned and scaled
- 1 Tbsp (15 mL) paprika
- 2 tsp (10 mL) onion salt
- 2 tsp (10 mL) ground cumin
- 1 tsp (5 mL) freshly ground black pepper
- ¼ tsp (1 mL) cayenne pepper
- 2 cloves garlic, thinly sliced
- 1 small lemon, sliced
- 4 sprigs fresh thyme
- 4 sprigs fresh oregano

Few boozes can stand up to the intense blackening spice and charring nature of the BBQ so we've shown restraint in this recipe. That's right, no booze. We like to call it being frugal.

Rinse the fish inside and out with cold water and pat dry with paper towels. Cut 2 diagonal slashes into the thickest part of the fish on both sides.

Combine the paprika, onion salt, cumin, black pepper and cayenne and rub onto the outside of the fish. Sprinkle any remaining seasoning into the cavities. Stuff the garlic, lemon and fresh herbs into the cavities. Cover and refrigerate for 30 minutes.

Heat the barbecue until very hot then brush it lightly with oil. Cook the fish for 8 minutes on each side, or until the flesh flakes easily when tested.

NOTE: To fillet the cooked fish first remove the dorsal fin on the back (if still attached) with a sharp knife, then the tail and head. Now that that's over, have a drink. When you're ready, slide a wide knife or cake server under the fillet and lift it gently from the bones onto your serving platter. Pull away the bones from the bottom fillet and add it to your platter. You can peel away the skin if you prefer—though it's all wonderfully charred and tasty.

SERVES 6

Strawberry Margarita Shortcake

- 2 cups (500 mL) cake-and-pastry flour, sifted
- 1 cup + 2 Tbsp (280 mL) granulated sugar
- 1½ tsp (7 mL) baking soda
- 1 tsp (5 mL) baking powder
- 1 tsp (5 mL) lime zest
- ⅓ cup (75 mL) limoncello
- ⅔ cup (150 mL) water
- 1 cup (250 mL) mayonnaise (full-fat is best)
- 8 cups (2 L) fresh strawberries, sliced
- ¼ cup (50 mL) tequila
- 2 cups (500 mL) heavy (35%) cream
- ½ cup (125 mL) confectioner's sugar

This adult version of the classic summer dessert requires macerating the berries in tequila to make them deliciously potent.

Preheat oven to 350°F (180°C).

Whisk together the flour, 1 cup (250 mL) of the sugar, baking soda, baking powder and lime zest in a medium bowl. Stir in the mayonnaise water, and limoncello, and beat until smooth. Pour the batter into an ungreased 9-inch (23 cm) round cake pan and bake for 40–45 minutes, or until a toothpick inserted in the center comes out clean. Cool for 5 minutes then invert onto a wire rack, remove the pan and let the cake cool completely.

Meanwhile, combine 4 cups (1 L) of the strawberries with the tequila and the remaining sugar in a medium bowl. Cover with plastic wrap and let sit at room temperature until you're ready to serve the cake.

Beat together the cream and confectioner's sugar with a handheld mixer until very stiff. Slice the cake in half. Layer 2 cups (500 mL) of the remaining strawberries over the bottom half of the cake, spread half the whipped cream over the berries and top with the second half of the cake. Repeat, layering with the remaining 2 cups (500 mL) of strawberries and whipped cream then refrigerate until ready to serve. Slice the cake and serve with a spoonful of tequila-soaked strawberries.

SERVES 8

Urban Orphan Thanksgiving

Menu

Roasted Garlic, Potato and Ale Soup

Roasted Carrots and Beets

Apple and Walnut–Stuffed Pork with Cognac Sauce

Pumpkin and Coconut Mousse with Candied Ginger

APPLE MARTINI

1 oz apple schnapps

1 oz vodka

1 oz apple juice

Combine the apple schnapps, vodka and apple juice in a cocktail shaker with ice. Shake and strain out into a martini glass. Garnish with a slice of Granny Smith apple, if desired.

Every family has its own particular traditions. For Dave's family, it's pulling together the perfect broken-home holiday. Whether the dysfunction can be traced back to divorce, death, separation or recently committed parents, everyone is welcome. Dave's mom's technique is to never host the festivity on the actual holiday—it's always a week or two before or after the actual date. This allows children with multiple familial obligations to spend some time with "the other family" as well.

Wine Pairing

For this meal we recommend a dry Riesling or Gewürztraminer.

Setting the Mood

No matter how dysfunctional your guests are, you can't remove the harvest theme from Thanksgiving. That would be like trying to separate Christmas from endless shopping trips to the mall. But if we catch you laying down bouquets of Indian corn, not only will we revoke your right to use this book, but we may also give you a stern finger wagging. A basket of apples or pears by the door is a great way to greet your guests and introduce the fall theme. The fruit also makes a really great parting gift. Fall leaves are a splendid touch, but stick to one or two colors and don't feel you have to represent the entire fall spectrum. A mini gourd or pumpkin holding a name card or acting as a centerpiece makes the event a little more formal.

With winter just around the corner, it seems appropriate to showcase singers like Macy Gray and Amy Winehouse with their smoky-and-gravelly voices. Mix that up with the twang of Patsy Cline and you should have the perfect balance between heartbreak and healing.

Serving Suggestion

There's something soul-filling about sharing a meal around a table. Serve the food family-style, on platters and in bowls so guests can serve themselves. The soup and the mousse can be made the day before and the veggies can be part-roasted in advance and finished while the pork is resting.

SERVES 8

Roasted Garlic, Potato and Ale Soup

- 1 head garlic
- 3 Tbsp (45 mL) extra virgin olive oil
- 6 baking potatoes, peeled and cut into 1-inch (2.5 cm) cubes
- 1 onion, quartered
- 4 cups (1 L) chicken stock
- one 12 oz (341 mL) bottle dark ale
- ½ tsp (2 mL) dried rosemary
- ½ tsp (2 mL) dried thyme
- ½ tsp (2 mL) ground black pepper
- 1 tsp (5 mL) salt
- 2 cups (500 mL) milk
- Gorgonzola, crumbled (optional)
- Rosemary, to garnish (optional)

Finally, beer soup with a potato content! And that isn't a typo in the ingredients list. We really do mean an entire head of garlic. When it's roasted, garlic's intensity mellows significantly and the result is a deep and slightly sweet flavor, which goes great with the maltiness of the dark ale. Pretty much the same thing happens to Ryan after he's been left in the sun too long.

Preheat oven to 425°F (220°C). Line a baking sheet with parchment paper.

Slice the top off the garlic head and drizzle with ½ Tbsp (7 mL) of the olive oil. Wrap the head in aluminum foil and roast for 25–30 minutes, or until the garlic cloves are soft and golden. Set aside to cool.

In a large bowl, toss the potatoes and onion with 2 Tbsp (30 mL) of the olive oil. Transfer to the prepared baking sheet and roast for 25–30 minutes, or until the potatoes are golden on the underside.

Heat the remaining oil in a large stockpot or Dutch oven over medium-high heat. Add the roast potato mixture and squeeze in the garlic cloves from the roasted garlic head. Cook for 3–4 minutes. Add the stock, ale, rosemary, thyme, pepper and salt and bring to a boil. Reduce the heat and simmer with the lid on for 25–30 minutes. Using a handheld immersion blender or working in batches with a regular blender, process the mixture until smooth. Return to the pot and add the milk gradually to reach your desired consistency. Keep at a simmer until ready to serve, then garnish with crumbled Gorgonzola and a sprig of rosemary, if desired.

SERVES 8

ROASTED CARROTS AND BEETS

1½ lb (750 g) assorted beets
1½ lb (750 g) assorted carrots
1 lb (500 g) shallots, peeled
¼ cup (50 mL) olive oil
Salt
Freshly ground black pepper

Check your local veggie stand at this time of year and you're bound to find a variety of beets you've never seen before—golden, albino, baby varieties and some that feature rings of purple or white inside. Similarly, carrots can be found in yellow or purple varieties. Use these to add interest and drama to an otherwise ordinary dish.

Preheat oven to 425°F (220°C).

Peel the beets and cut them into quarters. Peel the carrots, trim the ends and cut them into large chunks or leave them whole if they're small. Toss the beets, carrots and shallots in olive oil and season with salt and pepper to taste. Transfer the vegetables to a roasting pan or large baking sheet and roast for 25–35 minutes, or until tender but not mushy, turning the vegetables halfway through cooking time so they caramelize evenly. Transfer them to a platter and serve with Apple and Walnut–Stuffed Pork with Cognac Sauce (next page).

I ENVY PEOPLE WHO DRINK. AT LEAST THEY HAVE SOMETHING TO BLAME EVERYTHING ON.

Oscar Levant

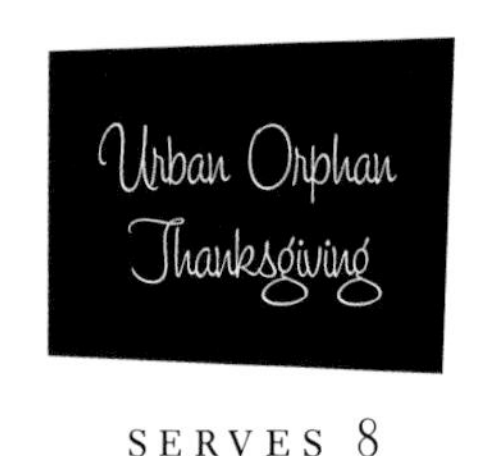

SERVES 8

Apple and Walnut–Stuffed Pork with Cognac Sauce

Stuffing

2 Tbsp (30 mL) butter

1 onion, minced

2 cloves garlic, minced

¼ cup (50 mL) chopped celery

1 Golden Delicious apple, cored, peeled and chopped

1 tsp (5 mL) grated fresh ginger

1 Tbsp (15 mL) chopped fresh sage

¼ cup (50 mL) Riesling

¼ cup (50 mL) chopped walnuts

Salt

Freshly ground black pepper

Pork

2 pork tenderloins (1¼ lb/625 g each)

2 Tbsp (30 mL) extra virgin olive oil

Fresh rosemary

Cognac Sauce

3 Tbsp (45 mL) butter, softened

3 Tbsp (45 mL) all-purpose flour, sifted

3 Tbsp (45 mL) cognac or brandy

½ cup (125 mL) apple purée

2½ cups (625 mL) chicken stock

The-other-white-meat just screams for apple, so we've given it what it wants with a double hit in the stuffing and the dipping sauce. We also doubled up on the booze. You can prepare this recipe the day before and store it in the refrigerator until ready to cook.

For the stuffing, melt the butter in a medium saucepan over medium-high heat. Add the onion and garlic and sauté until the onion becomes translucent, about 4–5 minutes. Add the celery, apple, ginger, sage and Riesling and continue to cook for 8–10 minutes, or until the liquid has slightly reduced. Stir in the walnuts and season with salt and pepper. Set aside to cool.

For the pork, butterfly the tenderloins by slicing 1 lengthwise along the center, but not all the way through, leaving about ½-inch (1 cm) thickness. Flip the tenderloin over and slice lengthwise again on either side of the center cut, making a W pattern. Cover with plastic wrap and pound with a meat mallet until the meat is about ½–¾ inch (1–2 cm) thick. Repeat with the second tenderloin. Overlay the edges of the 2 tenderloins, then use the mallet to flatten them together.

Spread the apple mixture across the tenderloins. Roll up lengthwise, and tie with butcher's twine. Season to taste with freshly ground black pepper.

Preheat oven to 325°F (160°C).

Heat the oil over medium-high heat in a large ovenproof frying pan. Sear the tenderloin for about 2–3 minutes per side. Transfer the frying pan to the oven and cook for 20–30 minutes, or until the internal temperature reaches 145°F (62°C). Remove from the oven and tent with aluminum foil for 10 minutes.

Slice the roast on an angle and transfer to a serving platter. Garnish with sprigs of fresh sage.

For the sauce, mix the butter and flour together in a small bowl until well blended. Melt the butter and flour mixture in a small saucepan over medium heat, stirring constantly until smooth. Stir in the cognac and apple purée until bubbly. Gradually add the chicken stock and any pan drippings, continually stirring until it's completely incorporated and the sauce is smooth. Bring to a boil, reduce the heat and simmer until slightly thickened. Pour into a gravy boat and serve.

ALSO PICTURED: ROASTED CARROTS AND BEETS (PAGE 57)

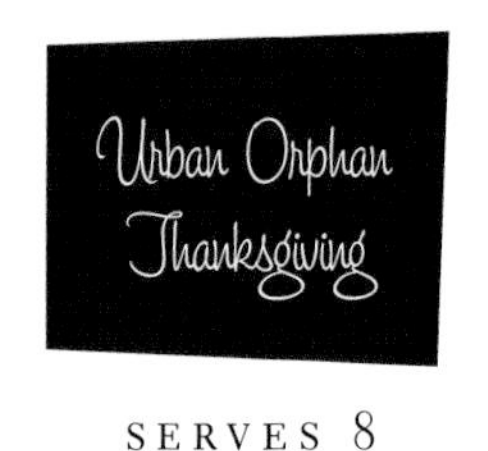

SERVES 8

Pumpkin and Coconut Mousse with Candied Ginger

- 2 tsp (10 mL) unflavored gelatin
- ¼ cup (50 mL) coconut rum
- 3 eggs, separated
- ¾ cup (175 mL) honey
- 1 cup (250 mL) light (18%) cream
- 1½ cups (375 mL) pumpkin purée
- 1 tsp (5 mL) ground cinnamon
- 2 tsp (10 mL) orange zest
- ½ tsp (2 mL) ground nutmeg
- 2 Tbsp (30 mL) minced candied ginger
- 1 tsp (5 mL) vanilla extract
- 3 Tbsp (45 mL) granulated sugar
- 1 cup (250 mL) heavy (35%) cream, whipped

Pumpkin and coconut are flavor buddies, complementing each other really well. Instead of using a real coconut, though, we've opted to get the flavor from its boozy, screw-cap cousin, which is much easier to get into.

Dissolve the gelatin in the coconut rum and set aside. In a double-boiler or a metal bowl placed over a pot of simmering water, whisk together the 3 egg yolks with the honey. Whisk in the coconut rum mixture and slowly add the light cream until smooth. Continue to whisk until the mixture thickens. Stir in the pumpkin purée, cinnamon, orange zest, nutmeg, ginger and vanilla. Remove from the heat and set aside to cool.

Using a handheld electric mixer whip the egg whites and sugar in a medium bowl until glossy, stiff peaks form. Once the pumpkin mixture has cooled, gradually fold the egg whites into the pumpkin mixture to ensure consistency. Spoon into dessert glasses, cover with plastic wrap and refrigerate for a few hours or overnight. Garnish with a dollop of whipped cream and additional candied ginger, if desired, just before serving.

NOTE: This recipe contains raw eggs, which should not be consumed by pregnant women, children or the elderly.

New Year's Eve

SERVES 6

Menu

Endive Spears with Orange-Scented Goat Cheese and Pomegranate

Oysters Rockefeller

London Broil–Stuffed Yorkshires

Blood Orange and Champagne Sabayon

Baked Brie with Lobster, Mushrooms and Madeira

Here's a menu as classic as the night that inspired it with recipes as elegant as the great cities that inspired them. As the New Year is heralded in from ports of call like Rome, London and New York, you and your guests will feel transported. Global cuisine never felt so appropriate.

Wine Pairing

We could write an entire book on how to choose a great sparkling wine and whether or not to splurge on champagne but frankly, we have neither the time nor the space. Buy the most expensive champagne you can afford—you'll never go wrong. Serve the London Broil with a full-bodied red with a hint of sweetness, such as Amarone, Merlot or Malbec.

Setting the Mood

Here's the night to break out the polished silver, crystal stemware and fine linens. You'll be dressed in your finest and your table should be, too. Opt for a palette of black and hot pink, or white and turquoise. Add flashes of silver or gold for even more drama. Glass or silver bowls make a great presentation for a selection of hats and noisemakers, streamers and confetti (if you dare).

Compile a playlist of your favorite music from the past year mixed with perennial favorites and keep everything on an up-tempo plane—it facilitates aerobic activity, making one last night of indulgence a little easier to swallow.

Serving Suggestion

This menu can easily be doubled to accommodate a larger soiree but it's important to gauge what you can realistically accomplish. Any party larger than 12 guests should be catered (see page 8). If you insist on cooking all the food yourself (you're an entertainer after our own hearts!) you should at least wrangle in some servers and a bartender to ensure the plates are cleared and no one is left perpetually parched. Also consider renting stemware, plates and linens. This makes clean-up a breeze as the rental company may even come and pick up all the dirty dishes.

CAIPIRINHA

As a tribute to Rio de Janeiro, which we're quite sure has one of the largest New Year's bashes south of the equator, we give you Brazil's national cocktail, the caipirinha (pronounced *kay-pi-ri-nya*). It's very similar to a mojito, with muddled lime and sugar, but instead of rum the booze of choice is cachaça, a sugarcane, distilled alcohol with a flavor somewhere between rum and tequila. A perfect thirst-quencher year round. *Feliz ano novo!*

½ lime, quartered

2 tsp (10 mL) unrefined brown sugar (if available)

1½ oz cachaça

Muddle together the lime quarters and sugar in the bottom of a rocks glass with a wooden spoon. Cover with crushed ice and pour in the cachaça.

NOTE: You can use equal parts white rum and tequila if you don't have cachaça.

SERVES 6

Endive Spears with Orange-Scented Goat Cheese and Pomegranate

½ lb (250 g) goat cheese, room temperature

¼ cup (50 mL) light (10%) cream

3 Tbsp (45 mL) orange marmalade

1 Tbsp (15 mL) Grand Marnier

2–3 heads Belgian endive, washed and separated (approximately 24 leaves)

⅓ cup (75 mL) pomegranate seeds

Not yet a classic but sure to become one, this brightly colored hors d'oeuvre achieves its wow factor from simple ingredients and quick work. Entertaining need not be complicated—save that for tax returns and cell phone bills.

Beat together the goat cheese and cream until smooth. In a separate bowl combine the marmalade and Grand Marnier; stir this into the cheese mixture. Spoon dollops of goat cheese into the endive spears and arrange in a circular pattern on a serving plate. Sprinkle with pomegranate seeds. Cover and refrigerate for up to 5 hours before serving.

ALSO PICTURED: OYSTERS ROCKEFELLER (PAGE 66)
LONDON BROIL–STUFFED YORKSHIRES (PAGE 67)

SERVES 6

Oysters Rockefeller

- 4 green onions (including green part), chopped
- ¾ cup (175 mL) unsalted butter, softened
- ½ cup (125 mL) dry breadcrumbs
- ¼ cup (50 mL) fresh grated Parmesan cheese
- ¼ cup (50 mL) chopped Italian parsley
- ¼ cup (50 mL) fresh celery leaves
- 1 Tbsp (15 mL) fresh tarragon leaves
- 1 Tbsp (15 mL) fresh chervil leaves
- 2 Tbsp (30 mL) Pernod
- Dash hot pepper sauce
- Salt
- Freshly ground black pepper
- 4 lb (2 kg) rock or kosher salt
- 24 fresh oysters, shucked

Created in New Orleans by Chef Antoine Alciatore and so named because of their exquisite "richness," these oysters are meant for popping into your mouth as the crystal ball drops in New York City.

Preheat broiler.

Blend together the green onions, butter, breadcrumbs, Parmesan, parsley, celery leaves, tarragon, chervil, Pernod and hot pepper sauce in a food processor or blender until well combined but still with some texture. Season this herbed butter to taste with salt and pepper.

Spread the rock salt over a large baking sheet and place the oysters shell side down in the salt to keep them stable while cooking. Top each oyster with a dollop of the herbed butter and broil on the middle rack of your oven for about 5 minutes, or until the edges have curled and the butter mixture is bubbling. Do not overcook. Serve immediately.

NOTE: Oysters can be prepared ahead of time, covered and refrigerated until ready to cook.

AH, SHUCKS

To shuck the oysters, place one on a cutting board and cover it with a clean tea towel. Hold the oyster firmly and slip the oyster shucker or a blunt knife blade between the top and bottom shells at the hinge of the oyster. Twist the knife slowly until the shells separate, push the knife in further and run it along the top shell to release it. Remove the top shell and use the knife to separate the oyster from the bottom shell. It would be worth doing a few practice laps before the big night.

SERVES 6

London Broil–Stuffed Yorkshires

London Broil

¾ cup (175 mL) port

2 cloves garlic, minced

1 Tbsp (15 mL) Worcestershire sauce

1 Tbsp (15 mL) soy sauce

1 Tbsp (15 mL) chopped fresh thyme, plus more for garnish

1 tsp (5 mL) freshly ground black pepper

1½ lb (750 g) flank steak (a.k.a. London Broil)

Horseradish and Dijon mustard for serving

Yorkshire Puddings

1 cup (250 mL) all-purpose flour

Pinch salt

2 eggs, beaten

1 cup (250 mL) milk

¼ cup (50 mL) vegetable shortening, cut into 12 cubes

NOTE: Many grocery stores carry frozen Yorkshire puddings and you can easily substitute these for the homemade variety if you prefer. Mini brioches or small rolls also work well.

This is like a portable roast beef dinner. It makes a fantastic hors d'oeuvre but it can also be deconstructed and served traditionally with a side of mashed potatoes and blanched asparagus—on any other night but New Year's, of course.

For the London Broil, combine the port, garlic, Worcestershire sauce, soy sauce, thyme and pepper. Pour over the steak, cover and refrigerate for at least 3 hours or overnight if possible.

Bring the steak to room temperature before broiling.

Meanwhile, for the Yorkshire puddings, sift the flour and salt together in a medium bowl and make a well in the center. Pour the beaten eggs into the well with a little of the milk and gradually whisk the flour into the center, slowly adding the milk until the batter is smooth. Cover and set aside for at least 30 minutes.

Put a cube of shortening into each cup of a 12-cup muffin tin and place in a cold oven. Heat oven to 425°F (220°C). When the oven comes to temperature and the shortening is very hot, remove the pan. Whisk the batter and divide evenly among the cups. Bake for 15 minutes, or until puffed, golden and crisp. Remove the Yorkshire puddings from the tin and cool on a wire rack.

Preheat oven to broil. Line a baking sheet with aluminum foil.

Remove the steak from the marinade, and set the marinade aside. Place the steak on the prepared baking sheet and broil on the top rack of the oven until browned, about 5 minutes. Flip, then continuing broiling until the second side is browned. Remove the steak and wrap loosely in aluminum foil.

Meanwhile, pour the reserved marinade into a small saucepan and simmer until reduced by half.

Slice the steak against the grain into thin strips. Place a couple of strips of steak in the cavity of each Yorkshire pudding and spoon over a bit of the sauce. Serve at room temperature and arrange on a serving platter alongside the horseradish and spicy mustard.

SERVES 6

Blood Orange and Champagne Sabayon

4 eggs, separated

¼ cup (50 mL) granulated sugar

½ cup (125 mL) champagne

1 tsp (5 mL) vanilla extract

5–6 blood oranges, peeled and chopped

This light dessert is perfect after all the holiday chocolate, decadent cheesecakes and heavy trifles you've consumed over the last two weeks. While it may not be low in calories, its airy texture will fool your stomach.

Whisk together the egg yolks and sugar in a large stainless steel bowl until frothy. Stir in the champagne and vanilla. Place the bowl over a pot of barely simmering water, making sure the water doesn't touch the bottom of the bowl.

Whisk the egg mixture over the water for about 10 minutes until it's extremely light and fluffy and has tripled in volume. Remove the bowl from the heat from time to time while whisking so the custard doesn't get too hot. Once the custard has thickened to the desired consistency remove from the heat and continue whisking for 2 minutes.

Meanwhile, beat the egg whites in a separate bowl until stiff peaks form. Gradually fold the egg whites into the custard mixture until just combined. Do not beat or overmix as this will deflate the mixture.

Divide the oranges among 6 dessert bowls or martini glasses (or a combo of glassware) and top with sabayon. Cover and refrigerate until ready to serve.

NOTE: Substitute ¾ cup (175 mL) heavy (35%) cream beaten until soft peaks form for the beaten egg whites if you're serving this to anyone who shouldn't consume raw egg.

FIZZ FACTOR

Drink the champagne within a few hours of opening the bottle to maintain the highest fizz factor. Urban legends abound about inserting the end of a silver spoon into the neck of the bottle to hold the carbonation, but we've never found it to work even remotely well. Suction wine stoppers are your best bet—or a batch of mimosas.

SERVES 6

Baked Brie with Lobster, Mushrooms and Madeira

1½ lb (750 g) live lobster

2 lb (1 kg) wheel double-cream brie

1 Tbsp (15 mL) butter

2 shallots, minced

1 cup (250 mL) sliced button mushrooms

¼ cup (50 mL) Madeira wine

1 baguette, thinly sliced

A tribute to our French cousins. If you can get your hands on a black truffle, grate some over this dish just before serving, then wait smugly for the applause.

Steam the lobster in the top of a double-boiler for 10–15 minutes, or until bright red and cooked through. Remove from the double-boiler and cool. Crack the lobster, remove the meat from the tail and claws and chop into 1-inch (2.5 cm) pieces.

Preheat oven to 425°F (220°C).

Place the brie on a large ovenproof plate and bake for 5–8 minutes, or until heated through.

Meanwhile, heat the butter in a medium nonstick frying pan until foaming. Add the shallots and mushrooms and sauté until softened, about 3 minutes. Add the Madeira and cook until reduced by half. Add the lobster meat and toss with the mushroom mixture until heated through. Pour the lobster mixture over the baked brie and serve with baguette slices.

REMINDS ME OF MY SAFARI IN AFRICA. SOMEBODY FORGOT THE CORKSCREW AND FOR SEVERAL DAYS WE HAD TO LIVE ON NOTHING BUT FOOD AND WATER.

W. C. Fields

CHAPTER 2

Intimate Meals

MY DAD USED TO HAVE TO OPEN THE SECOND BOTTLE OF WINE IN THE LOO IN CASE MUM HEARD THE CORK COMING OUT.

Hugh Grant

SERVES 2

The Perfect Romantic Dinner

Menu

Butternut Squash Bisque with Lobster and Cognac

Haricots Verts with Almonds and White Wine

Châteaubriand with Béarnaise Sauce

Bourbon Caramel and Cream Profiteroles

WINE PAIRING

Start the evening by popping a bottle of bubbly. For such a special occasion only real champagne will do, so buy the most expensive bottle you can afford. Look for the words "sec" or "extra sec" on the label—these wines have just a hint of sweetness that pairs wonderfully with the Butternut Squash Bisque. "Brut" champagnes are too dry for the sweet lobster meat.

COFFEE

Brew a fresh pot of coffee for dessert—believe us, if everything goes according to plan, the extra hit of caffeine will come in handy.

This menu sounds fancy, but that's due more to the ingredients than to the skill required to make the dishes. We've taken our cues for this menu from the French as they tend to have their priorities straight: wine, food and love, in no particular order.

No need to freak yourself out with mixing cocktails—this menu and the evening ahead are better suited to champagne and red wine. Easy to open, easy to drink and perfectly suited to the French theme.

Wine Pairing

The Châteaubriand has a milder flavor than other cuts of beef so serve a medium-bodied red such as Grenache or Merlot.

Setting the Mood

Pull out all the stops: buy a new outfit (wear an apron in the kitchen), and dress the table with a freshly pressed tablecloth, linen napkins and a simple bouquet of fresh flowers. Don't get anything too tall or you won't be able to see your date across the table. Red roses are a bit of a cliché so ask your florist for something a bit more unusual and therefore more special. A white or off-white palette is always a safe bet.

Dim the lights, light some candles and pop some vocal jazz CDs into the stereo. Contemporary crooners like Michael Bublé, Matt Dusk and Molly Johnson should capture the right space between cool and sultry.

Serving Suggestion

For such a formal meal, plate everything in the kitchen and bring it out to the table. You don't want to clutter the space around you with soup tureens and platters of beef. You want to keep it clear for hand-holding and eye-gazing.

SERVES 2

Butternut Squash Bisque with Lobster and Cognac

½ lb (250 g) cooked lobster or lump crabmeat

1½ Tbsp (22 mL) cognac or brandy

1 Tbsp (15 mL) extra virgin olive oil

¼ cup (50 mL) diced onion

1 small carrot, diced

2 cups (500 mL) peeled and cubed butternut squash

2 cups (500 mL) vegetable or chicken stock

½ tsp (2 mL) salt

¼ tsp (1 mL) ground nutmeg

Pinch cayenne

¼ cup (50 mL) light (10%) cream

Very fancy sounding, but actually dead simple to prepare. Really. It's basically soup with a seafood garnish and a fancy name. Easy-peasy.

Chop the lobster meat into bite-sized pieces and toss with the cognac. Cover and set aside.

Heat the oil in a medium saucepan over medium heat. Add the onion and carrot and cook until softened, about 7 minutes. Add the squash, stock, salt, nutmeg and cayenne and bring to a boil. Reduce the heat and simmer, covered, for 15–20 minutes, or until the vegetables are tender.

Purée the soup with a handheld immersion blender or in a regular blender until smooth. Stir in the cream and keep the soup warm until ready to serve. Do not boil.

Pile half the lobster meat in the center of a shallow bowl and add a ladleful of the soup around it. Garnish with a sprinkle of nutmeg and some chives if desired. Repeat for the second bowl.

NOTE: You can find frozen lobster meat in the seafood section of most supermarkets. Alternatively, buy a small lobster (1 lb/500 g) and steam it in the top of a double-boiler for 7–10 minutes. Remove and submerge in a bowl of ice water to stop the cooking. Twist off the tail, cut it in half and remove the meat. Break the claws with a nutcracker, removing the meat and any pieces of shell.

SERVES 2

Haricots Verts with Almonds and White Wine

¼ cup (50 mL) white wine
2 fresh bay leaves
1½ cups (375 mL) green beans, stems trimmed
2 Tbsp (30 mL) slivered almonds
1 tsp (5 mL) grated orange zest

Steaming the beans over a water and wine mixture imparts a wonderful flavor and keeps this dish low-cal. You could sauté the beans in a little butter after steaming if you're so inclined. Depends if you're already married, or hoping to be?

Fill the bottom of a double-boiler with 1 inch (2.5 cm) of cold water. Add the wine and bay leaves and bring to a simmer. Place the beans in the steaming attachment and steam, covered, for 5 minutes, or until tender. Toss with the almonds and orange zest.

THE BEST WAY TO EXECUTE FRENCH COOKING IS TO GET GOOD AND LOADED AND WHACK THE HELL OUT OF A CHICKEN. BON APPÉTIT.

Julia Child

SERVES 2

Châteaubriand with Béarnaise Sauce

Châteaubriand

1 lb (500 g) beef tenderloin roast

¼ tsp (1 mL) salt

¼ tsp (1 mL) freshly ground black pepper

1 Tbsp (15 mL) canola oil

Béarnaise Sauce

1 small shallot, minced or 2 tsp (10 mL) minced onion

½ tsp (2 mL) chopped fresh tarragon or ¼ tsp (1 mL) dried tarragon

1 Tbsp (15 mL) white wine

1 egg yolk

1 Tbsp (15 mL) freshly squeezed lemon juice

¼ cup (50 mL) cold butter, cubed

The French are great lovers for a reason—they love their meat and their cream sauces. Wash this down with a glass of Merlot for your antioxidant fix if it makes you feel better.

Allow the roast to reach room temperature before starting to cook.

Preheat oven to 450°F (230°C).

Season the roast with salt and pepper. (Turn your oven hood fan to high—this baby's a bit of a smoker, but that only adds a sultry jazz club feeling to the room.) Heat the oil in a cast iron frying pan or other heavy-bottomed skillet over medium-high heat until smoking. Sear the roast on all sides until browned, about 1 minute per side. Transfer to a small baking sheet and continue roasting in the oven until desired doneness is reached; about 10 minutes for medium rare (130°F/55°C). Remove and cover with aluminum foil until ready to carve (see Meat Doneness Guide, page 5). Remove from the oven and cover with aluminum foil until ready to carve.

Meanwhile, make the Béarnaise Sauce. Combine the shallot, tarragon and white wine in a small bowl. Whisk together the egg yolk and lemon juice in a separate metal bowl set over a pot of gently simmering water. Add the butter a piece at a time until melted and well incorporated. Stir in the shallot mixture and remove from the heat.

Spoon the sauce onto plates and top with slices of Châteaubriand.

ALSO PICTURED: HARICOTS VERTS WITH ALMONDS AND WHITE WINE (PAGE 75)

SERVES 2

Bourbon Caramel and Cream Profiteroles

1 cup (250 mL) water

¼ cup (50 mL) butter

1 cup (250 mL) cake-and-pastry flour

4 eggs

1 cup (250 mL) heavy (35%) cream

2 Tbsp (30 mL) confectioner's sugar

¼ cup (50 mL) Bourbon Caramel Sauce, warmed (see page 116)

A traditional cream puff tower, or croquembouche, *is served instead of wedding cakes at French receptions. It's traditionally held together with hot caramel that hardens into sweet candy but this simpler (and smaller) version is equally delicious.*

Preheat oven to 400°F (200°C).

Bring the water and butter to a boil in a medium saucepan. Add the flour and stir with a wooden spoon for 1–2 minutes, or until the mixture pulls away from the sides of the pan.

Transfer to a cool bowl. Beat in the eggs, 1 at a time, with an electric mixer until completely incorporated and the mixture is smooth.

Transfer the dough to a pastry bag fitted with a large round tip (or cut the end off a large freezer bag) and pipe 1-inch (2.5 cm) rounds onto a cookie sheet. Dip your finger into cold water and tap down any peaks on the cream puffs so they don't burn in the oven.

Bake for 15 minutes, or until lightly golden and cooked through. Turn off the oven, open the door and allow the pan to cool for 10 minutes inside (this prevents the puffs from collapsing).

Meanwhile, beat the cream and sugar together with an electric mixer until stiff peaks form. Make a small hole in the bottom of each cream puff and use a pastry bag fitted with a small round tip to pipe the whipped cream into the center.

Arrange 4 puffs into a pyramid shape on a plate and drizzle with warmed Bourbon Caramel Sauce.

NOTE: The profiteroles can be made ahead and frozen before filling. Defrost in the refrigerator before making a hole in the bottom and filling with prepared cream. Filled puffs can be refrigerated for a few hours before serving.

The Perfect Suck-Up Supper

SERVES 2

Menu

Grilled Veal Chops with Lemon and Rosemary Marmalade

French Herb, Tomato and Potato Brochettes

Chocolate Cabernet Peace Offerings

Wow. You've really screwed up this time. It may take more than a little party-planning advice from us to win back your sweetheart, but we're as good a place to start as any. First things first. Go shopping. If there was ever a time to throw money at a problem it's now. Head to the most expensive store you can find, hand your credit card over and purchase three extraordinary gifts—you'll be doling one out with each course, so save the best for dessert.

Next, head to the nearest liquor store and purchase a premium bottle of vodka. Money and gifts will only get you so far.

Wine Pairing

Enjoy your appetizer and main course with the perfectly suited Rosemary and Pear Martini but for dessert your palate will want something a little sweeter. Try a tawny port or red icewine.

Setting the Mood

Clean the house, mop the floors, make the bed and iron a clean shirt. Set the table with the good stuff—we're talking china, crystal and the diamond-encrusted serving utensils you thought you'd never use. Fill the room with as many flowers and candles as it can hold. Go for something in a neutral or muted color scheme: whites, creams or pastels are especially suited for sucking up. Stay away from reds and other bright colors—you don't want to startle the bull.

Spin some ambient sounds or instrumental jazz. You want to create a pleasant atmosphere but not distract from the task at hand—winning back your lover. Stay away from anything sad or downtrodden, but nothing overly joyous or upbeat either. You should also steer clear of your wedding song and anything else with sentimental value.

Serving Suggestion

Have your gifts wrapped professionally with gorgeous paper and ribbon, and present one at the beginning of each course. A good mood always helps stimulate the appetite. And take your time. There's no need to rush this meal—not with a pitcher of martinis in the freezer.

ROSEMARY AND PEAR MARTINI

Stir up a pitcher of these apologetic martinis as an ice-breaker. Oh, and really apologize—and we do mean a real apology, not a politician's apology—if you haven't already.

- ½ cup (125 mL) water
- ½ cup (125 mL) granulated sugar
- 3 sprigs fresh rosemary, plus more for garnish
- 1½ cups (375 mL) premium vodka
- ½ cup (125 mL) pear brandy or pear liqueur
- Juice from ½ lemon, about 2 Tbsp (30 mL)

Combine the water, sugar and 3 sprigs of rosemary in a small saucepan and bring to a boil, stirring to dissolve the sugar. Reduce the heat and simmer for 2 minutes. Remove from the heat and cool. Discard the rosemary.

Combine the cooled rosemary syrup, vodka, brandy and lemon juice in a pitcher. Place in the freezer for 2 hours, or until well chilled. Add a handful of ice, stir gently then strain into martini glasses and garnish with a small piece of rosemary.

SERVES 2

Grilled Veal Chops with Lemon and Rosemary Marmalade

Lemon and Rosemary Marmalade

1 large lemon

½ cup (125 mL) water

⅓ cup (75 mL) granulated sugar

¼ cup (50 mL) gin

2 tsp (10 mL) chopped fresh rosemary leaves

Chops

Two 12 oz (350 g) veal chops, about 1 inch (2.5 cm) thick

1 Tbsp (15 mL) extra virgin olive oil

½ tsp (2 mL) salt

½ tsp (2 mL) freshly ground black pepper

Succulent veal is the best bet for this dish but you can substitute pork or chicken if you prefer. The lemon marmalade may sound unusual but it complements the meat with an herbal zing.

To make the marmalade, peel the rind from the lemon with a vegetable peeler. Remove any remaining white pith from the peel with a sharp knife. Slice the rind into thin strips. Remove the white pith from the outer layer of the fruit and chop the lemon into small chunks, discarding the seeds.

Bring the rind, fruit and water to a boil in a small saucepan. Reduce the heat, cover and simmer for 1 hour, or until very soft. Add the sugar and gin, stirring to dissolve. Bring the mixture back to a boil, reduce the heat to medium-low and simmer, uncovered, for 20 minutes. Remove from the heat, stir in the rosemary, cover and set aside.

Meanwhile, coat the chops in the olive oil and sprinkle with the salt and pepper. Cover with plastic wrap and let come to room temperature before grilling.

Preheat the grill to medium-high. Grill the chops for 6–8 minutes per side, or until the internal temperature reaches 135°F (57°C), for medium-rare. Top with a spoonful of marmalade during the last minute of cooking and serve with more marmalade at the table.

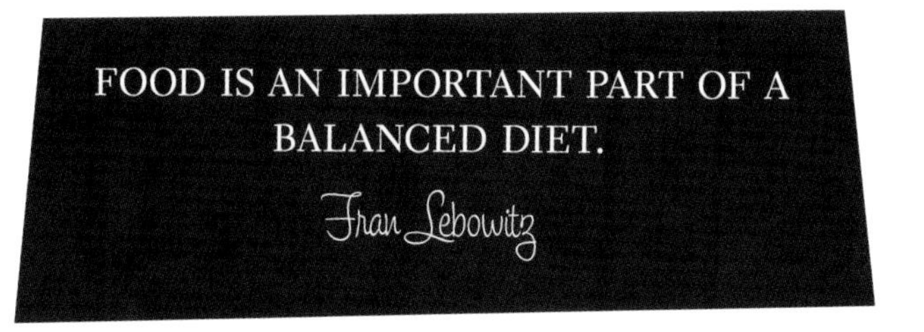

ALSO PICTURED: FRENCH HERB, TOMATO AND POTATO BROCHETTES (PAGE 84)

SERVES 2

French Herb, Tomato and Potato Brochettes

- 1 small shallot, minced
- 1 tsp (5 mL) chopped fresh thyme
- 1 tsp (5 mL) chopped fresh savory or marjoram
- ¼ tsp (1 mL) salt
- ¼ tsp (1 mL) freshly ground black pepper
- 2 Tbsp (30 mL) gin
- 1 Tbsp (15 mL) extra virgin olive oil
- 1 tsp (5 mL) Dijon mustard
- 8–10 mini new potatoes
- 8–10 cherry or grape tomatoes
- 2 large bamboo or metal skewers

If you're really in the doghouse we recommend that you take the veggies off the skewers before bringing them to the table. Your angry lover doesn't need the temptation of a ready-made weapon close at hand.

Whisk together the shallot, thyme, savory, salt, pepper, gin, olive oil and Dijon in a medium bowl. Set aside.

Bring the potatoes to a boil in lightly salted water and boil for 7–10 minutes, or until just tender. Drain and add to the gin mixture, tossing to coat well. Cool before making the skewers.

Slip the vegetables onto the skewers, being sure to end with a piece of potato so the tomato won't slide off on the grill. Place in a shallow baking dish, cover and set aside until ready to use. Reserve the marinade.

Preheat grill to medium-high.

Grill the skewers for 10–15 minutes, turning every few minutes, until the potatoes are heated through and the tomatoes are soft. Remove to a plate and drizzle with the reserved marinade.

SERVES 2

Chocolate Cabernet Peace Offerings

½ cup (125 mL) Cabernet Sauvignon

⅓ cup (75 mL) butter, plus extra for greasing

¼ cup (50 mL) granulated sugar, plus extra for dusting

4 oz (125 g) bittersweet chocolate, chopped

2 eggs, separated

1 tsp (5 mL) vanilla extract

Pinch cream of tartar

This recipe makes four deliciously intense dark chocolate soufflés with extra-gooey centers designed to melt even the most jaded of hearts. Eat them all at once or save the remainders for the morning. You can adorn one with a tiny white flag on a toothpick and present it with your third and final gift. Just try not to grovel.

Simmer the wine in a small saucepan until it's reduced to 2 Tbsp (30 mL).

Preheat oven to 400°F (200°C) and place the rack in the center of the oven. Generously butter four 6 oz (175 mL) ramekins and coat the insides with granulated sugar. Place on a baking sheet and set aside.

Melt the butter and chocolate in a bowl placed over a pot of gently simmering water. Stir in the reduced wine and set aside.

Beat the egg yolks and 3 Tbsp (45 mL) of the sugar in a medium bowl until light and fluffy, about 5 minutes. Stir in the vanilla and the chocolate mixture.

Beat the egg whites, remaining sugar and cream of tartar in a separate bowl until soft peaks form. Gently fold the egg whites into the chocolate mixture until just incorporated. Do not overmix or the batter will deflate. Pour the batter into the prepared ramekins, filling them about three-quarters full, and bake for 10–15 minutes, or until the edges appear cooked but the center remains slightly wet looking. Remove from the oven and let rest for a couple of minutes before serving.

NOTE: Store the leftover cakes in their molds, covered, in the refrigerator for up to 1 week. Microwave for approximately 30 seconds to re-soften the center.

NOTE: The batter can be prepared up to 2 hours in advance and refrigerated until ready to bake. You may lose a little leavening action—but hopefully you can make that up toward the end of the evening.

SERVES 2

Menu

Fattoush Salad with Toasted Pita

Grilled Margarita Panini

Double-Dipped Chocolate Strawberries

Cozy Beach Rendezvous

CHOCOLATE MINT ICED COFFEE

14 oz coffee

2 oz Godiva white chocolate liqueur

2 oz crème de menthe

Combine the ingredients in a cocktail shaker with ice. Shake vigorously and strain into a chilled thermos for transportation. Serve in a rocks glass.

This intimate occasion is bound to win you some points in the romance department. We've assembled a menu that's light on the stomach and the back. We've picked some dishes that are tasty, easy and travel well. The only item that needs an icepack is the whipped cream—and the boozy iced coffee, of course. If the weather looks like it might turn cool, be sure to pack extra blankets and prepare a hot version of the iced coffee.

Wine Pairing

For a delicious and romantic wine choice select a light red from France, such as a Côtes du Rhône.

Setting the Mood

For a more formal affair (and if you don't have far to carry the cargo), set up a small bistro table and chairs. For a more intimate occasion, soft cotton blankets and a couple of throw pillows are the way to go. Define your space by four lanterns to create a square border. Surprise your date with a little memento and present it during the *mandatory* long walk on the beach. The gift doesn't have to be expensive or even purchased: it could be a seashell, colorful stone or wild flower.

Let the sounds of nature be your playlist tonight—lapping waves, the breeze gently rushing through the grasses, birds and crickets combine to create a whirring symphony.

Serving Suggestion

The traditional approach to a picnic is to lay out the food in advance. This generally works well except it always ruins the anticipation of the next course. If you've prepared this to surprise your date, just reveal one course at a time to maintain the excitement. Of course, the strawberry bouquet should be reserved for the finale.

SERVES 2

Fattoush Salad with Toasted Pita

3 medium-sized pita breads (pocket type), sliced in ½-inch (1 cm) strips

⅔ cup + 1 Tbsp (165 mL) extra virgin olive oil

1 large English cucumber, peeled, deseeded and chopped into ½-inch (1 cm) wedges

12 cherry tomatoes, quartered

1 yellow pepper, diced

½ small red onion, diced (optional)

⅓ cup (75 mL) chopped Italian parsley

⅓ cup (75 mL) fresh coriander

⅓ cup (75 mL) chopped fresh mint

1 clove garlic, minced (optional)

3 Tbsp (45 mL) freshly squeezed lemon juice

2 Tbsp (30 mL) Pernod

Salt

Freshly ground black pepper

This Middle Eastern salad combines toasted strips of pita bread with a crunchy assortment of crisp veggies and fresh herbs. It's almost the perfect summer salad by itself, but of course we just couldn't leave well enough alone and added a tangy French-inspired dressing using Pernod—which creates herbal sophistication.

Preheat oven to 325°F (160°C). Line a baking sheet with parchment paper.

In a large bowl toss the pita strips with 2 Tbsp (30 mL) of the olive oil. Spread out the pita strips on the prepared baking sheet and bake until golden brown (about 10 minutes). Remove the pita from the oven and transfer to a wire rack to cool. Pack in a resealable plastic bag.

In a large salad bowl mix together the cucumber, cherry tomatoes, yellow pepper, onion, parsley, coriander and mint. Store in a plastic container with a tight-fitting lid and refrigerate until ready to use.

In a small bowl whisk together the remaining olive oil, garlic, lemon juice and Pernod. Transfer to a plastic container with a tight-fitting lid.

Build the salad at your destination by transferring the cucumber mix to a salad bowl. Shake the dressing vigorously before opening and pour over the salad. Top with the toasted pita strips. Season to taste with salt and pepper.

ALSO PICTURED: GRILLED MARGARITA PANINI (PAGE 90)
DOUBLE-DIPPED CHOCOLATE STRAWBERRIES (PAGE 91)

SERVES 2

Grilled Margarita Panini

½ baguette

2 Tbsp (30 mL) extra virgin olive oil

3 Tbsp (45 mL) tomato pesto

4 large bocconcini cheese, sliced

1 ripe plum tomato, thinly sliced

12 large fresh basil leaves, chiffonade*

Freshly ground black pepper

We've borrowed a little inspiration from the most famous pie in Italy, and turned it into a picnic sandwich to go. The flavors in pizza Margarita are all about a balance between the tomato, milky bocconcini cheese, fresh basil and pepper. It's prefect served at room temperature and keeps its crunchy base. Just don't get any sand in it.

Preheat grill to high.

Slice the baguette in half lengthwise and brush each half with 1 Tbsp (15 mL) of olive oil. Place each half facedown on the grill for 2–3 minutes, or until well-defined grill marks appear but the bread is still soft. Alternatively, place the bread under the broiler until golden. Remove from the grill, close the lid and turn off the heat. Spread tomato pesto over each baguette half, layer the bocconcini and tomato slices and evenly distribute the basil leaves overtop. Generously grind over black pepper. Return to the hot grill, close the lid and leave for 6–8 minutes until the cheese has just started to melt. (Again, you can do this under the broiler if you prefer.) Remove from the heat and cool before wrapping in parchment paper and packing.

* For information on chiffonade, see page 233.

SERVES 2

Double-Dipped Chocolate Strawberries

¼ lb (125 g) white chocolate
¼ lb (125 g) dark chocolate
2 cups (500 mL) strawberries
½ cup (125 mL) heavy cream (35%), whipped to form stiff peaks
¼ cup (50 mL) crème de banane

Nothing wins more points in the romance department than fruit dipped in chocolate, except maybe fruit dipped twice in chocolate and then dunked in whipped cream. Okay, so this isn't exactly a low-calorie fruit cup, but the crème de banane in the whipped cream makes up for it in flavor. We've stuck these strawberry gems on candy sticks and wrapped them in treat bags so they can be tied together and presented like a bouquet.

Line a plate with waxed paper.

Using a double-boiler or a metal bowl over a pot of simmering water, melt the white chocolate, about 8–10 minutes. Dip the strawberries and rotate to cover them evenly. Stand them on the prepared plate to cool. Repeat with the dark chocolate, double-dipping the strawberries to create a white and dark chocolate layer effect. Skewer the berries onto long candy sticks and wrap them individually in small clear plastic treat bag wrappers tied with ribbon. (You can buy treat bags and candy sticks from a bulk food or bakery supply store.) Tie a bunch together with ribbon to form a bouquet.

Fold crème de banane into the whipped cream and chill. Use an ice pack to keep it cold. Serve as a dip for the strawberries.

OF COURSE ONE SHOULD NOT DRINK MUCH, BUT OFTEN.

Henri de Toulouse-Lautrec

SERVES 6

Do You Fondue?

Menu

Classic Swiss Fondue

White Wine and Seafood Fondue

or

Red Wine and Red Meat Fondue

White Chocolate and Berry Fondue

WINE, STRAIGHT UP

5 oz white or red wine

Pour wine into glass and garnish with 2 or 3 more bottles on the side. Enjoy.

It's incredible how many people we meet who received a fondue set as a shower or wedding gift and who subsequently abandoned it in the basement—unopened, unused and unloved. Well, no more, people. Here you have all the tools and tips you need to throw your very own fondue party—a truly simple get-together that's social, interactive and only improves with more wine.

Wine Pairing

The simplest tip to pairing wine with food is to drink the same wine that you use in preparing the dish. In the case of a fondue party, that's easy. For instance, enjoy the cheese course with either a Sauvignon Blanc or Riesling. If you absolutely must drink red go for a Beaujolais—you'll need something light and fruity to complement the rich, bubbling cheese.

Setting the Mood

The casual and social aspects of fondue call for simplicity but you can be as low-key or froufrou as you wish. If your party marks a special occasion you may want to break out the linen napkins, crystal wine glasses and your best serving platters. If it's happening on any given Saturday night, paper napkins and salad plates will suffice.

For this retro-inspired throwback you'll want to fill the room with suitably vintage tunes. Dig out those 45s and dust off the record player. Tonight the soundtrack is Simon and Garfunkel, The Guess Who and The Bee Gees, of course.

Serving Suggestion

A standard fondue pot will comfortably feed six people without creating undue reaching and straining across the table. If you're planning on eight or more guests you'll need two pots bubbling for each course.

You can find superdeluxe fondue sets that come with a built-in lazy Susan for adding various dipping sauces. They spin effortlessly so guests can reach all the boozy dips you've whipped up. Don't fret if your pot is a little less flashy, as small bowls placed strategically around the table will have the same effect.

DO YOU FONDUE?

HEADY CHEESE

FONDUE CHEESES

APPENZELLER is a hard, cow's milk cheese with a nutty or fruity flavor. Its rind is usually washed in wine or cider.

EMMENTHAL, or what North Americans usually call Swiss, is a semihard, cow's milk cheese with a piquant, yet mild flavor.

GRUYÈRE has a nutty flavor that's both sweet and salty. It's also made from cow's milk and is considered hard but it actually has a wonderfully creamy texture.

RACLETTE is also made from cow's milk. Its salty flavor and semifirm texture are ideal for melting.

Gettin' Your Fondue On!

You'll notice that no vegetables appear in the recipes for dipping—not because we don't like veggies (although we do confess a certain flesh bias), but because we're leaving the selection up to you. Use your favorites or make this an excuse to try something different. The following all work well with either of the broth fondues but if you plan to dip veggies in cheese you'll need to precook items like broccoli, cauliflower, baby carrots or asparagus. Simply blanch them in boiling water for 1–2 minutes then submerge in ice-cold water to stop the cooking.

VEGETABLES

Asparagus	Cauliflower
Baby carrots	Cherry tomatoes
Baby potatoes*	Mini corn cobs
Bell peppers	Mushrooms
Broccoli	Zucchini rounds

NOTE: Mini or Parisienne potatoes need to be cooked in boiling water for about 5 minutes, or until tender, for either cheese or broth fondues.

POT HEAD

Fondue sets come in many shapes and sizes and are made for different types of fondues. Stainless steel and cast iron are used for broth- or oil-based fondues while ceramic or enameled pots are best for cheese because they don't get as hot and so won't burn the cheese.

Chocolate sets are usually ceramic and lit only by a candle—any more heat than that and you're sure to scorch your dessert.

JET FUEL

You can either use "fondue fuel" (found in most grocery and hardware stores) or purchase single gel packs that last for 1–2 hours and are discarded afterward. Gel packs are great because you simply peel back the foil lid, insert the container into your fondue burner and light. No pouring (or spilling!) fuel on yourself or the table.

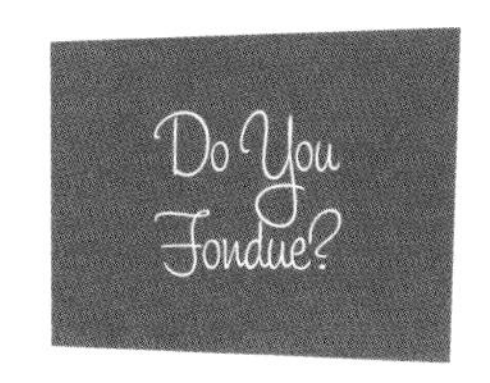

SERVES 6

Classic Swiss Fondue

"THE FRELICK CHEESE FONDUE"

- 2 cloves garlic
- 1 bottle (750 mL) Sauvignon Blanc or Riesling
- 1 lb (500 g) Gruyère cheese, shredded
- 1 lb (500 g) Emmenthal or Appenzeller cheese, shredded
- 1 lb (500 g) raclette, shredded
- 2 Tbsp (30 mL) cornstarch
- ¼ cup (50 mL) kirsch
- Freshly ground pepper
- 1–2 loaves Italian or Portuguese bread, cubed

Many things can be said about "in-laws" but when they bring fondue to the table that's as good as this, suddenly the world consists of nothing but wine and cheese. The trick to this dish is in the mix of cheeses and we don't recommend substitutions, so head to your local specialty shop—they may even grate it for you if you smile nicely. Just tell them we sent you.

Slice the garlic cloves in half and use them to rub inside the fondue pot. Discard the garlic and set the pot aside.

Heat the wine in a large saucepan over medium heat until almost simmering. Gradually add handfuls of cheese, in no particular order, stirring to melt after each addition until all the cheese has been added. Bring the mixture just to a simmer. Dissolve the cornstarch in the kirsch and add to the cheese mixture, stirring well until thickened. Stir in some freshly ground pepper then pour the cheese mixture into the fondue pot.

Serve with cubes of fresh bread and a small dish filled with kirsch for dipping.

Your flame should be warm enough to keep the fondue smooth and liquid but not so hot as to scorch the bottom. When the fondue is finished there will be a thin crust of toasted cheese at the bottom called *la religieuse*, or "the nun." This has a deliciously thin, cracker-like texture and is most excellent, especially when enjoyed with a shot of kirsch.

NOTE: Cheese fondue requires a wine with good acidity like Sauvignon Blanc or Riesling to help break down the proteins in the cheese and create a silky-smooth texture. Chenin Blanc is another good candidate, while Chardonnay should be avoided.

PEPPER PREFERENCE

Use freshly ground white pepper if you prefer a pristine pot or black pepper if you're less concerned about appearance.

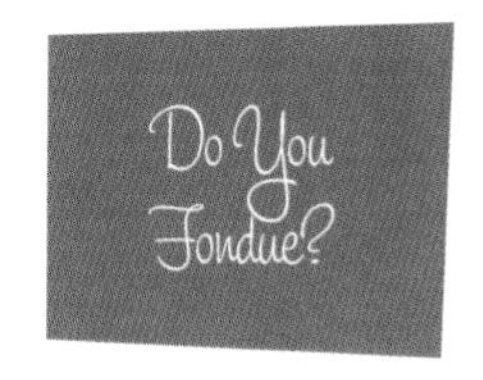

SERVES 6

White Wine and Seafood Fondue

Broth

1 Tbsp (15 mL) extra virgin olive oil

1 small onion, minced

1 clove garlic, minced

4 cups (1 L) vegetable broth

2 cups (500 mL) white wine (Chardonnay or Sauvignon Blanc)

¼ cup (50 mL) brandy

1 bay leaf

1 Tbsp (15 mL) soy sauce

1 dash hot pepper sauce

1 Tbsp (15 mL) chopped fresh tarragon

1 Tbsp (15 mL) chopped fresh parsley

Seafood

¾ lb (375 g) large or jumbo shrimp

¾ lb (375 g) bay scallops or sea scallops (quartered)

¾ lb (375 g) salmon fillet, cut into bite-sized cubes

2 lobster tails, cut into bite-sized pieces

Cooking fish and shellfish in a broth-based, rather than oil-based, fondue imparts amazing flavor and much less fat. And once the broth is simmering it can take as little as 30 seconds to cook a succulent shrimp or piece of salmon.

Heat the olive oil in a large saucepan. Add the onion and garlic and sauté for 2–3 minutes, or until softened. Add the vegetable broth, wine, brandy, bay leaf, soy sauce and hot sauce. Bring to a boil, reduce the heat and simmer uncovered for 30 minutes. Add the tarragon and parsley then pour into the fondue pot and set over the lit burner. Dip pieces of seafood into the hot broth until cooked through. Serve with slices of lemon and Béarnaise Sauce (page 76) for dipping, if desired.

SERVES 6

Red Wine and Red Meat Fondue

- 1 Tbsp (15 mL) extra virgin olive oil
- 1 small onion, minced
- 2 cloves garlic, minced
- 1 carrot, finely chopped
- 1 tsp (5 mL) freshly ground black pepper
- 1 medium tomato, finely chopped
- 4 cups (1 L) beef stock
- 2 cups (500 mL) red wine (Cabernet Sauvignon or Shiraz)
- 1 Tbsp (15 mL) Worcestershire sauce
- 1 bay leaf
- 1 Tbsp (15 mL) chopped fresh thyme
- 1 Tbsp (15 mL) chopped fresh rosemary
- 1½ lb (750 g) eye of round roast, or steaks, thinly sliced

This fondue is best served with rich meats like beef, lamb or sausage, but it also turns veggies into delicious morsels. Depending on how rare you like your beef it can take as little as 30 seconds to cook in the broth.

Heat the olive oil in a large saucepan. Sauté the onion, garlic, carrot and pepper for 2–3 minutes, or until softened. Add the tomato, beef stock, red wine, Worcestershire and bay leaf. Bring to a boil, reduce the heat and simmer, uncovered, for 30 minutes. Add the thyme and rosemary then pour into the fondue pot set over the lit burner. Dip pieces of meat into the broth and cook until desired doneness. Serve with Port, Balsamic and Honey Reduction (page 204) or Coffee Cognac Barbecue Sauce (page 50) for dipping, if desired.

SERVES 6

White Chocolate and Berry Fondue

12 oz (350 g) white chocolate, finely chopped
1 cup (250 mL) heavy (35%) cream
¼ cup (50 mL) unsalted butter
3 Tbsp (45 mL) coconut rum
1 cup (250 mL) strawberries, washed and dried
1 cup (250 mL) raspberries
1 cup (250 mL) blueberries
1 cup (250 mL) blackberries

Rich and sweet, this fondue is sure to please even the most demanding of dessert critics. Feel free to add other fruits, cubes of sponge cake or shortbread cookies if you're so inclined.

Place the chopped chocolate in a fondue pot and set aside. Bring the cream, butter and coconut rum to a simmer over medium heat. Pour the cream mixture over the chocolate, wait 30 seconds then stir until smooth. Place the pot over a candle and enjoy.

NOTE: Make berry kebabs with bamboo skewers for easy dipping and eating.

IT IS BETTER TO HIDE IGNORANCE, BUT IT IS HARD TO DO THIS WHEN WE RELAX OVER WINE.

Heraclitus

SERVES 6

It's All About Me!

Menu

Hard Cider Baba Ghanouj

Cumin Flatbread

Romaine Hearts with Haloumi Matchsticks

Coriander-Scented Chicken with White Wine and Tahini

Ciambelline with Marinated Peaches

THE MARILYN MONROE

Hire a server to hand these out to your guests as they arrive, and to tell them the drink tastes as good as the host looks.

1 tsp (5 mL) grenadine

1 oz Calvados

Sparkling wine

Spoon the grenadine into a champagne flute, add the Calvados and top with sparkling wine.

Feel like you're a rag doll being dragged around by some careless three-year-old? The demands of the job, pressure from friends, spouses, in-laws and concubines all add up and make us feel older than we are. This party is designed to help put the spotlight back where it belongs—on you. The most important ingredient for this get-together can only be provided by a doctor, the type who advertises on late-night television. So after a little nip here, tuck there and a good teeth whitening you'll be ready for your close-up.

For the unveiling ceremony we've got the perfect intimate dinner menu, packed with flavor. Top the evening off with an expensive gift to yourself.

Wine Pairing

Select an oak-aged Chardonnay or Sémillon to prepare the chicken and serve alongside the finished dish. To complement the Ciambelline with Marinated Peaches you'll need a sweet wine like Moscato d'Asti from northwest Italy—it's very low in alcohol and slightly fizzy. Served icy cold it's the ideal dessert bubbly.

Setting the Mood

The focus of this event is *you*, so make sure everyone knows it. Suggest your guests bring gifts, stack them on an homage table framed by a nice oversized portrait of you. Designate a videographer to record the event and to tape testimonials from your friends. Judiciously edit it and send out a copy with thank-you notes and the number of your surgeon.

Soul-filling music is the genre of choice for a night like tonight. Program the iPod with the likes of Xavier Rudd, Amos Lee and Nine Mile. Steer clear of anything with a heavy beat or rhythm. You don't want to shake those staples loose.

Serving Suggestion

Bring out all your silver dinnerware—chargers, platters, goblets and anything else with a reflective surface. You want to be able to catch a peek of your new face while nibbling salad greens or savoring the last ciambelline.

SERVES 6

Hard Cider Baba Ghanouj

1 large (or 2 medium) eggplant
¼ cup (50 mL) hard pear cider
¼ cup (50 mL) tahini
¼ cup (50 mL) extra virgin olive oil
3 cloves garlic, chopped
½ tsp (2 mL) ground cumin
⅓ cup (75 mL) chopped cilantro
¼ tsp (1 mL) salt
Freshly ground black pepper

Baba Ghanouj and hummus are cousins: Baba Ghanouj uses roasted eggplant where hummus uses chickpeas. The trick to this recipe is roasting the eggplant until it's slightly charred. So set your oven to "blazing inferno" and keep your paws off the eggplant until it looks good. Then use the same approach at the tanning salon.

Preheat oven to 450°F (230°C). Line a baking sheet with parchment paper.

Pierce the eggplant skin with a fork or toothpick to allow steam to escape during roasting. Roast the eggplant on the prepared baking sheet for about 25–35 minutes, or until soft, wrinkled and slightly charred. Transfer the eggplant to a large bowl filled with ice water. When cool enough to handle, remove the eggplant, slice it into quarters and peel off the skin.

Blend together the pear cider, tahini, olive oil, garlic and cumin in a blender or food processor. Add the eggplant, cilantro, salt and pepper and lightly pulse until well mixed. Cover and refrigerate until ready to serve. Serve in a bowl with the Cumin Flatbread (facing page).

SERVES 6

Cumin Flatbread

2 cups (500 mL) all-purpose flour
½ cup (125 mL) whole wheat flour
1 tsp (5 mL) granulated sugar
1 tsp (5 mL) salt
½ tsp (2 mL) ground cumin
2 egg whites, in 2 separate bowls, lightly whisked
3 Tbsp (45 mL) extra virgin olive oil
2 Tbsp (30 mL) sesame seeds, toasted

This Armenian-style flatbread (or lavosh) uses a good hit of cumin and some sesame seeds to pump up the flavor. You can make this dish in advance and warm it before you serve it, or you can serve it cool. The best part about lavosh is that you can just nibble on it like an obsessed mouse without having to open your mouth wide.

Preheat oven to 400°F (200°C). Line 2 baking sheets with parchment paper.

Sift the all-purpose flour, whole wheat flour, sugar, salt and cumin together in a large bowl. Stir in ⅔ cup (150 mL) water, 1 egg white and the oil, mixing well to form a stiff dough. Knead until the dough is smooth, about 5 minutes.

Divide the dough into 8 balls. Roll out each ball on a lightly floured surface until paper thin. Place on the prepared baking sheets and slice lengthwise into 3-inch-wide (8 cm) bands. Brush with the remaining egg white and sprinkle with the sesame seeds. Bake until golden, about 8–10 minutes. Remove from the heat and place on a rack to cool. Break into large pieces and serve with the Hard Cider Baba Ghanouj (facing page).

SERVES 6

Romaine Hearts with Haloumi Matchsticks

- ¼ cup (50 mL) extra virgin olive oil
- ½ lb (250 g) Haloumi cheese, sliced into ½-inch (1 cm) matchsticks
- 3 Tbsp (45 mL) walnut oil
- 1 Tbsp (15 mL) sambuca
- 1 Tbsp (15 mL) white balsamic vinegar
- 1 head romaine hearts (6 large leaves)
- 1 Tbsp (15 mL) grated orange zest
- Freshly ground black pepper

And for the feel-good portion of this meal, we've prepared a light appetizer of individual servings of romaine hearts. But to ensure your system doesn't go into shock, they're decorated with fried cheese sticks. Life's all about balance.

Heat the oil in a small saucepan over medium-high heat. Fry the cheese sticks until golden brown on all sides, about 6–7 minutes, working in batches if necessary. Remove from the pan and drain on paper towel.

Whisk together the walnut oil, sambuca and vinegar in a small bowl.

Arrange the romaine leaves on salad plates, place some cheese sticks on top of each romaine leaf and drizzle over some sambuca dressing. Sprinkle with orange zest and pepper, to taste.

HALOUMI-MI-MI

Native to Cyprus, Haloumi is a spongy cheese made from a combination of goat's and sheep's milk. It has a high melting point, making it ideal for frying or grilling.

I ONLY DRINK TO MAKE OTHER PEOPLE SEEM MORE INTERESTING.

George Jean Nathan

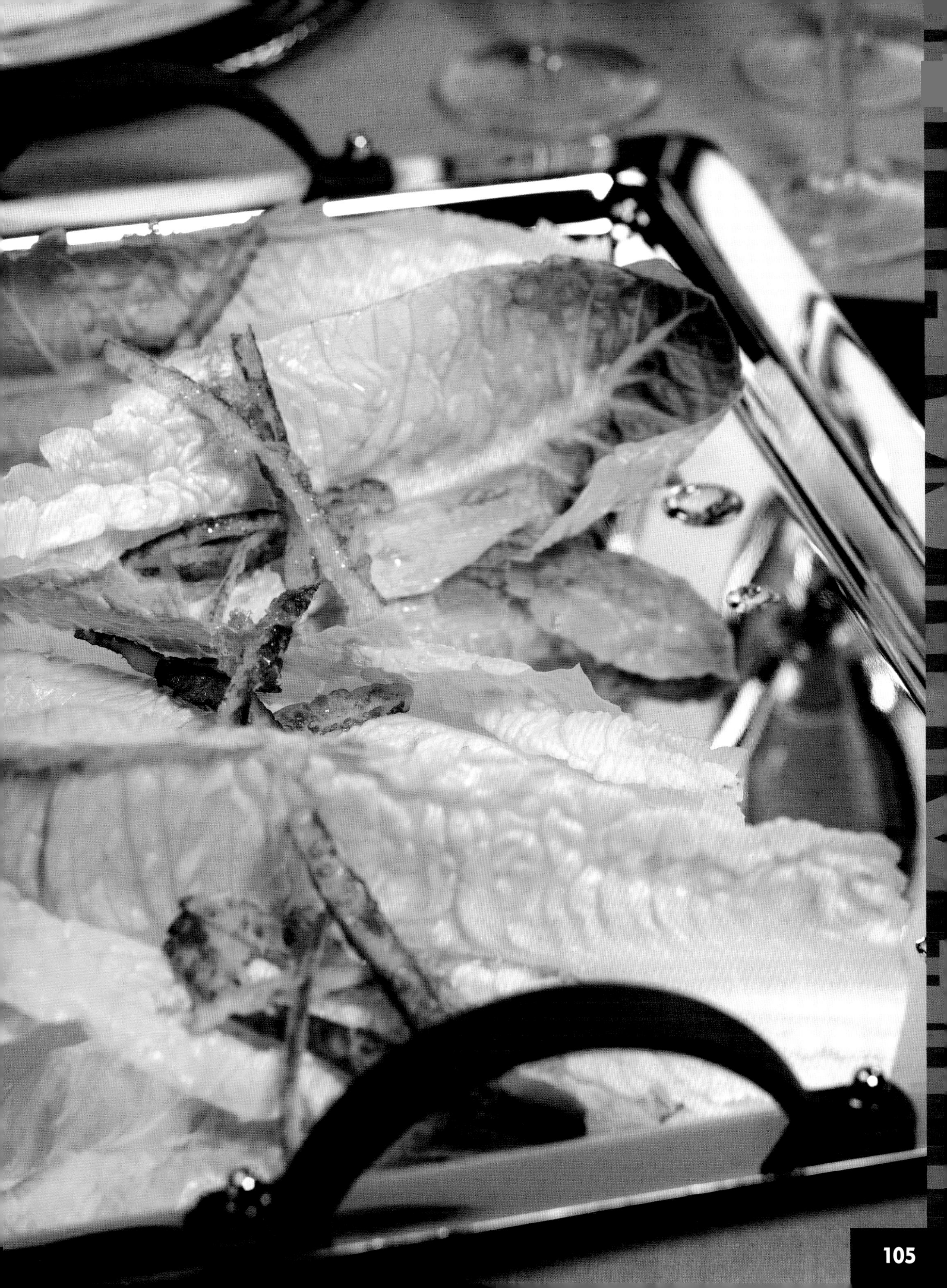

SERVES 6

Coriander-Scented Chicken with White Wine and Tahini

1½ Tbsp (22 mL) coriander seeds, crushed
3 shallots, minced
3 Tbsp (45 mL) extra virgin olive oil
6 bone-in chicken breasts, skin on
Salt
Freshly ground black pepper
2 garlic cloves, minced
½ cup (125 mL) tahini
½ cup (125 mL) Sémillon or Chardonnay
3 Tbsp (45 mL) freshly squeezed lemon juice
2 tsp (10 mL) honey

Whole coriander seeds have a magical fragrance and create the best feel-good chicken you can imagine. We recommend spreading the mixture right under the skin, but be sure to pull it tight—we don't want to see any wrinkles. Give it a quick shot of Botox if you run into trouble.

Preheat oven to 450°F (230°C).

Combine the coriander, shallots and 1½ Tbsp (22 mL) of the olive oil in a small bowl. Lift the skin of the chicken and run your fingers between the skin and flesh. Divide the coriander mixture among the breasts and spread evenly under the skin. Brush the breasts with the remaining olive oil and season to taste with salt and pepper.

Bake the chicken for 25–30 minutes (depending on size), or until the internal temperature reaches 165°F (75°C) and the juice runs clear.

Meanwhile, heat the garlic, tahini, wine, lemon juice and honey in a small saucepan over medium-low heat, stirring occasionally. Slowly stir in 1 cup (250 mL) of water and bring to a simmer, stirring constantly. Reduce the heat to low, stirring occasionally until ready to serve.

Drizzle some sauce over each chicken breast or get fancy and spoon a circle of sauce over a large dinner plate and serve the roast chicken on top with additional flatbread on the side. Garnish each plate with a wedge of lemon, if desired.

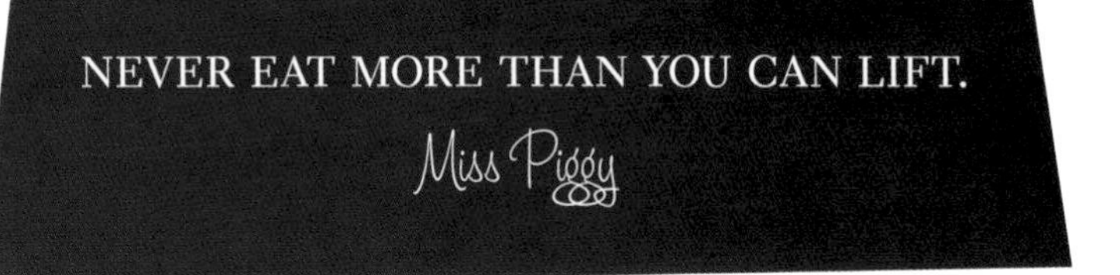

ALSO PICTURED: HARD CIDER BABA GHANOUJ (PAGE 102)
CUMIN FLATBREAD (PAGE 103)

SERVES 6

Ciambelline with Marinated Peaches

1 cup (250 mL) granulated sugar
1⅓ cups (325 mL) Pinot Grigio
⅓ cup (75 mL) extra virgin olive oil
½ tsp (2 mL) vanilla extract
2 cups (500 mL) all-purpose flour
4 large peaches
1 tsp (5 mL) freshly squeezed lemon juice
2 cups (500 mL) vanilla ice cream

You can call these "little crunchy wine doughnuts" if you have trouble with the Italian name. It's your night, so call them whatever you please. We call them the perfect cookie.

Mix together the sugar, 1 cup (250 mL) of the wine, olive oil and vanilla in a large bowl. Add the flour a little bit at a time until the dough is smooth and elastic, about 5 minutes. Turn out onto a floured work surface, and knead by hand for 1 minute. Cover with a clean dish towel and let rest for 30 minutes.

Preheat oven to 325°F (160°C). Line a baking sheet with parchment paper.

Roll the dough into a ½-inch-thick (1 cm) disk and cut out rounds using a 2½-inch (6 cm) cookie cutter. Cut out a hole in each round with a ½-inch (1 cm) cookie cutter, place the biscuits on the prepared baking sheet and bake for 20 minutes, or until light golden brown. Remove from the oven and cool for 5 minutes before transferring to wire racks to cool completely.

Meanwhile, submerge the peaches in a large pot of boiling water for 10 seconds. Transfer to a large bowl of ice water until cool. Remove the skin from the peaches and cut into sections. Toss the peaches in the lemon juice and pour over the remaining ⅓ cup (75 mL) wine. Cover with plastic wrap and refrigerate until ready to use, or for up to 6 hours.

Scoop ice cream into bowls and spoon over the peaches and syrup. Serve with the ciambelline.

CHAPTER 3

A Drink for All Seasons

IF YOU DRINK, DON'T DRIVE.
DON'T EVEN PUTT.

Dean Martin

SERVES 8

Menu

Barbecued Oysters with Champagne Mignonette

Southern Jalapeño Cornbread

Crab and Shrimp Étouffée

Pecan Banana Cream Pie with Bourbon Caramel Sauce

Get-Fat Tuesday

HURRICANE

This is the reason most people fall in love with New Orleans—this and the street-front flashes of nudity. Keep an eye on your guests and yourself and encourage everyone to sip slowly. The Hurricane, as the name suggests, can wreak havoc.

1 oz Bacardi 151 Proof Rum

1 oz white rum

1 oz dark rum

½ oz grenadine

3 oz orange juice

3 oz pineapple juice

Shake the rums, grenadine, orange juice and pineapple juice together in a cocktail shaker filled with ice. Strain into a hurricane or collins glass filled with ice and garnish with an orange wheel and a maraschino cherry, if desired.

If you can't afford to celebrate Mardi Gras in one of the cities known for throwing a raucous party—namely Venice, Rio or New Orleans—then throwing your own can be the next best thing. This menu is influenced by The Big Easy, as it best represents the hedonistic nature of the day, so indulge, indulge, indulge. If you're Christian and observe Lent, you've got 40 days ahead of you to diet and detox.

Wine Pairing

Gewürztraminer or a slightly sweet Riesling (off-dry) pair beautifully with the gentle heat of the étouffée and help cut through the richness of the sauce.

Setting the Mood

Beads, feathered masks and a bucket of gold doubloons are a good start for your décor. Greet your guests at the door by placing a few strands of beads around their necks and offering a feather mask. They can decide whether or not to hide behind it.

Accent these items with linens, flowers and even tableware in shades of purple, green and gold. Set the sound stage with a mix of southern blues, jazz and zydeco (a type of up-tempo roots music with prominent accordion and washboard sounds). Putumayo World Music has some great New Orleans compilations of brass, jazz and zydeco that are perfect for Fat Tuesday as they provide ample variety—the spice of life, right?

Serving Suggestion

Present the oysters on a serving platter covered with coarse salt—this is not only attractive but the salt helps keep the oysters level and secure. Shallow soup bowls or dinner plates work best for the étouffée as they give you the surface area needed for sopping up the sauce with pieces of cornbread.

SERVES 8

Barbecued Oysters with Champagne Mignonette

Champagne Mignonette

¼ cup (50 mL) champagne or white wine

2 Tbsp (30 mL) white wine vinegar

1 shallot, minced

1 tsp (5 mL) fresh parsley, finely chopped

Dash Pernod

Dash hot pepper sauce

Oysters

32 fresh oysters in the shell

4 cups (1 L) coarse salt

lemon wedges for serving

The heat from the grill poaches the oysters in their own liquid, resulting in tender, fresh-from-the-sea flavor. The champagne mignonette adds a little more zing without dominating. Just try to find a laid-back dominatrix in Nawlins. Go on, we dare you.

For the mignonette, stir the champagne, vinegar, shallot, parsley, Pernod and hot pepper sauce in a small dish to combine.

Preheat grill to medium-high.

Rinse the oysters under cold water, discarding any broken or open shells—an indication the oyster may be dead.

Place the oysters, cup side down, on the hot grill. Close the lid and cook for 8–10 minutes, depending on their size, or until the shells begin to open—when that happens they're done. Remove all the oysters when the first one opens, being careful not to spill their juices. Some shells will not be opened, so some prying will be necessary.

Cover the end of the oyster with a tea towel to protect your hand then pry open the shells with an oyster knife or other blunt knife. Discard the top shell. Run the knife under the oyster, along the bottom shell, to release it.

Pour the salt onto a serving platter to make a bed for the oysters. Add the oysters and serve with the mignonette, lemon wedges and hot sauce.

SERVES 8

Southern Jalapeño Cornbread

1½ Tbsp (22 mL) bacon drippings or 1 Tbsp (15 mL) butter + ½ Tbsp (7 mL) vegetable oil

⅓ cup (75 mL) boiling water

1 cup (250 mL) yellow cornmeal

¾ cup (175 mL) buttermilk, or 1 Tbsp (15 mL) white vinegar mixed with ¾ cup (175 mL) milk

1 egg, lightly beaten

1 jalapeño pepper, seeded and finely chopped

2 tsp (10 mL) granulated sugar

1 tsp (5 mL) salt

1 tsp (5 mL) baking powder

¼ tsp (1 mL) baking soda

Pinch cayenne pepper

Pouring the batter into a hot cast iron frying pan gives this bread a thin, crisp crust. You can make it in a 9-inch (23 cm) round or square cake pan simply by doubling the recipe and pouring the batter into the lightly buttered pan at room temperature. Increase the baking time to 25–30 minutes.

Place an 8-inch (20 cm) cast iron frying pan (with ovenproof handle) containing the bacon fat on the lower-middle oven rack and preheat oven to 450°F (230°C).

Pour the boiling water over ⅓ cup (75 mL) of the cornmeal in a medium bowl, stirring to form a stiff mush. Gradually stir in the buttermilk, breaking up any lumps, until smooth. Stir in the egg and jalapeño. Set aside until the oven comes to temperature.

Combine the remaining cornmeal, sugar, salt, baking powder, baking soda and cayenne in a small bowl. Stir the dry ingredients into the mush mixture just until combined.

You'll need oven gloves for this part. Carefully remove the now-hot frying pan from the oven and pour the bacon fat into the batter, stirring to incorporate (the batter will bubble and squeak so be careful). Quickly pour the batter into the frying pan and bake until golden, 15–20 minutes. Remove from the oven and instantly turn the cornbread out onto a wire rack. Cool for 5 minutes before serving.

NOTE: Eight strips of bacon will give you about 1½ Tbsp (22 mL) of drippings.

NOTE: If using a 9-inch (23 cm) cast iron frying pan, reduce the cooking time to 10–12 minutes.

SERVES 8

Crab and Shrimp Étouffée

- 1½ lb (750 g) medium-sized shrimp
- 2 cups (500 mL) vegetable stock
- ½ cup (125 mL) butter
- ⅓ cup (75 mL) all-purpose flour
- 1 Spanish onion, chopped
- 1 rib celery, chopped
- 3 cloves garlic, sliced
- ½ red bell pepper, finely chopped
- ½ green bell pepper, finely chopped
- 1 Tbsp (15 mL) paprika
- 1¼ tsp (6 mL) salt
- 1 tsp (5 mL) freshly ground black pepper
- ¼ tsp (1 mL) cayenne
- 1 Tbsp (15 mL) chopped fresh thyme leaves
- 1 Tbsp (15 mL) chopped fresh oregano leaves
- 1 Tbsp (15 mL) chopped fresh basil
- ½ cup (125 mL) white wine
- 2 Tbsp (30 mL) brandy
- 6 green onions, chopped
- ¼ cup (50 mL) chopped fresh parsley
- 1½ lb (750 g) jumbo lump crabmeat
- 2 cups (500 mL) long-grain white rice, cooked according to package directions

The sister dish to gumbo, étouffée is a Cajun stew made with a blond roux instead of a brunette one. Étouffée is most famously made with crawfish but they can be difficult to come by north of the Mason-Dixon Line. If you can find them, use them. And no, crayfish are not the same thing.

Remove the shells and tails from the shrimp and place them in a medium saucepan. Place the shrimp in a bowl, cover and refrigerate. Pour the vegetable stock over the shrimp shells, heat and simmer for 1 hour.

Meanwhile, melt the butter in a large frying pan or stockpot over medium-high heat. Add the flour, stirring constantly until the foam subsides and the mixture turns a light caramel color, about 8–10 minutes. Reduce the heat to medium, add the onion, celery and garlic and cook, stirring often, until the vegetables are soft and the roux is deep caramel, about 15 minutes. Add the bell peppers, paprika, salt, pepper, cayenne, thyme, oregano and basil and cook, stirring occasionally, for 5 minutes.

Pour the stock through a sieve to remove the shells then add half the stock to the frying pan, stirring the mixture until smooth. Add the remaining stock, white wine and brandy, bring to a boil, reduce the heat and simmer until thickened, 10–12 minutes. Add the shrimp and cook, stirring occasionally, for 3–5 minutes, or until the shrimp turn pink. Add the green onions and parsley, stirring to combine. Drop in the crabmeat. Do not stir or you'll break up the crabmeat. Cover, and simmer for 5 minutes. Turn off the heat and let it rest (with the lid on) for 5 minutes before serving.

Serve in shallow bowls over cooked rice with cornbread.

NOTE: To make ahead, add everything but the shrimp, crabmeat, green onions and parsley. Right before serving, heat the étouffée, add the shrimp and cover until cooked, 4–5 minutes. Stir in the fresh herbs, green onions and crabmeat and heat through.

ROUX OF THUMB

A roux is a thickening and flavoring agent made from fat and flour. Étouffées use flour cooked for a short time in butter to create a blond roux. Gumbos are made from dark brown roux, made from flour and usually vegetable oil cooked for up to 1 hour. The darker the roux the less thickening power it has, but the smokier and more complex flavor it adds.

SERVES 8

Pecan Banana Cream Pie with Bourbon Caramel Sauce

Crust

⅓ cup (75 mL) melted butter

1¼ cups (300 mL) graham cracker crumbs

Bourbon Caramel Sauce

3 Tbsp (45 mL) water

½ cup (125 mL) sugar

½ cup (125 mL) heavy (35%) cream

Pinch salt

2 Tbsp (30 mL) butter

2 Tbsp (30 mL) bourbon

½ cup (125 mL) toasted pecans, chopped

Filling

⅓ cup (75 mL) sugar

2 Tbsp + 1 tsp (35 mL) cornstarch

Pinch salt

3 large egg yolks, lightly beaten

1 cup (250 mL) milk

¼ cup (50 mL) evaporated milk

1 Tbsp (15 mL) butter

3 Tbsp (45 mL) crème de banane liqueur

1–2 bananas thinly sliced

Topping

1 cup (250 mL) heavy (35%) cream

1 Tbsp (15 mL) confectioner's sugar

1 tsp (5 mL) vanilla extract

¼ cup (50 mL) chopped pecans

If anything, New Orleans is a city of indulgence and this over-the-top dessert will satisfy any sugary craving.

Preheat oven to 350°F (180°C).

For the crust, combine butter and graham crumbs in a bowl. Press onto the bottom and up the sides of a 9-inch (23 cm) pie plate. Bake for 8–10 minutes, or until golden. Cool on wire rack.

For the sauce, pour the water into a medium saucepan. Add sugar to the center and bring to a boil over high heat while stirring. Reduce heat to medium-high and boil for 5–8 minutes, stirring until sugar reaches a deep golden color and registers 350°F (180°C) on a candy thermometer.

Meanwhile, heat the cream and salt in a small saucepan until it just simmers.

Remove sugar mixture from heat and add one-third of the cream mixture to it, stirring to combine. (Be careful: caramel will boil rapidly and dangerously.) Pour remaining cream and bourbon into caramel. Return to the heat and boil 2–3 minutes longer or until mixture reaches 215°F (100°C). Remove from heat, whisk in butter and set aside for 10 minutes.

Sprinkle pecans in the bottom of pie shell and pour caramel sauce over. Refrigerate for 1 hour.

To make the filling, whisk the sugar, cornstarch and salt together in a medium saucepan. Whisk in the egg yolks, then gradually whisk in the milk and evaporated milk until smooth. Cook over medium heat until foaming subsides and mixture thickens, about 8–10 minutes, whisking constantly. Remove from heat and whisk in the butter and banana liqueur. Cool 5 minutes, whisking periodically to prevent a skin from forming.

Place 1 layer of sliced bananas over caramel and pour filling over. Cover surface with plastic wrap and cool completely before refrigerating for 3 hours or until chilled.

To serve, beat the heavy cream, sugar and vanilla together until stiff peaks form. Spread whipped cream over filling, top with pecans and cut into slices.

SERVES 12

Menu

Snapped Snapper Ceviche

Tequila-Poached Chorizo Tostadas

Ole Mole Guacamole

Kahlúa Caramel Flan

Cinco de Mayo

WATERMELON AND CUCUMBER MOJITO

To keep your hands free, we've prepared a recipe for mojitos by the pitcher. If you have several pitchers you can make this *en masse*, or by the bucketload if you're feeling particularly enthusiastic.

1 cup (250 mL) watermelon, cubed with rind removed

3 bunches fresh mint

12 slices English cucumber

1 cup (250 mL) granulated sugar

¼ cup (50 mL) freshly squeezed lime juice

3 cups (750 mL) white rum

Ginger ale

Combine the watermelon, mint, cucumber slices, sugar and lime juice in a large pitcher and muddle until fragrant (3–4 minutes), then add the rum. To serve, strain into rocks glasses half-filled with ice and top up with the ginger ale. Garnish with watermelon chunks and cucumber slices, if desired.

On occasion we may have exploited the celebrations of other cultures as an excuse to throw a party. There was the Guy Fawkes "Great English Parliament Building Extravaganza" with its cute dynamite-stick napkin rolls. Then there was the funky rendition of the Swedish all-night festival Midsommar. We jammed our friends into a stark white airport lounge, cranked up ABBA and served meatballs in lingonberry sauce. However, in our own defense, Cinco de Mayo is an honest reason to celebrate. Not only does it lead into summer, it's also the anniversary of an outstanding Mexican victory over the French at the battle of Puebla on May 5, 1862. Ay, caramba!

Wine Pairing

Pairing wine with Mexican food is tricky. Avoid reaching for a big buxom red, and instead try a light white such as a Pinot Grigio, or a dry Riesling.

Setting the Mood

Draw inspiration from the colors of the Mexican flag—red, white and green, or go for a tropical color scheme of bright blues, turquoise, washed-out greens and faded yellows. Accent your linens and tableware with fresh flowers that complement your theme and throw in a few palm fronds or large tropical leaves for interest. Serving the ceviche in an old sombrero should be avoided, though hiring a Mariachi band to perform is a festive idea.

There are lots of styles of traditional music but when Mexicans party they listen to the upbeat rhythms of Jarocho or Tropical, with its heavy Latin and African influences. Try *Music of Mexico: Conjunto Alma Jarocha "Sones Jarochos."*

Serving Suggestion

Greet your guests with a freshly poured mojito and a ceviche appetizer. It's easiest to prepare the tostadas first and serve them fresh since they are easy to assemble and quick to heat up.

SERVES 12

Snapped Snapper Ceviche

2 lb (1 kg) fresh red snapper fillets, finely chopped

½ cup (125 mL) freshly squeezed lime juice

½ cup (125 mL) pineapple juice

½ cup (125 mL) white rum

½ red onion, minced

½ cup (125 mL) finely chopped cilantro

1 hot Thai chili, seeded and finely diced

2 tsp (10 mL) salt

1½ lb (750 g) red, white and green tortilla chips

Spring means fresh, and nothing is fresher than fish cured in citrus juice. In ceviche, the acid from the citrus actually cooks the fish, turning it from translucent to solid white. We've added a healthy dose of rum to let the flavors pair perfectly with the mojito. It's absolutely essential to use fresh fish for this dish. Be sure to tell your seafood purveyor that you intend to make ceviche. Don't be afraid to put your nose right up into the fish to take a good sniff. If it smells fishy, walk away, hombre.

This recipe can be prepared the night before.

Combine the fish, lime juice, pineapple juice, rum, onion, cilantro, chili and salt in a glass or ceramic bowl (it needs to be nonreactive). Cover and refrigerate for at least 6–8 hours, stir once, halfway through.

To serve, use a slotted spoon to lift the fish out of the citrus juice and spoon into serving bowl. Serve with tortilla chips.

I LIKE THE ODD GLASS OF WINE, A COFFEE AND A CIGARETTE. AS YOU GET OLDER YOU CAN'T SEE THE WRINKLES.

Jerry Hall

SERVES 12

Tequila-Poached Chorizo Tostadas

- 10 chorizo sausages (casing removed)
- 2 Spanish onions, chopped
- 5 cloves garlic, minced
- 3 chipotle peppers, minced
- ½ cup (125 mL) gold tequila
- 2 Tbsp (30 mL) chili powder
- 1 Tbsp (15 mL) dried oregano
- 24 corn tostadas
- 4 cups (1 L) shredded Manchego cheese
- 8 plum tomatoes, chopped
- 2 cups (500 mL) chopped cilantro

This recipe combines the spicy heat of chipotle peppers with chorizo sausage and a good hit of tequila. It's also easy to make and can be reheated if prepared in advance, which eliminates stress and allows you to enjoy your party.

Brown the sausage meat, onions and garlic over medium-high heat until the onions become translucent and the chorizo is browned, about 12–15 minutes. Drain off any excess renderings and stir in the chipotle peppers, tequila, chili powder and oregano. Cover, reduce the heat and simmer for 10 minutes. Uncover and cook for an additional 6–8 minutes, or until the mixture has thickened.

Preheat oven to 450°F (230°C).

Arrange the tostadas on a large baking sheet (you may need to do this in 2 batches) and top with a spoonful of chorizo mixture. Sprinkle each tostada with a little cheese and bake for 5 minutes, or until the cheese is melted and bubbly. Garnish with chopped tomatoes and cilantro and serve warm with a side of Ole Mole Guacamole (facing page).

MANCHEGO AMIGO

Manchego is a sheep's milk cheese from Spain with a slightly salty taste and creamy texture. Its flavor and texture change depending on how long it's aged. Fresh Manchego is almost white with a mild taste and texture similar to crumbled feta. Manchego that's aged from 3 to 6 months is semifirm and light in color, with a sweet, nutty flavor. If aged longer than 6 months Manchego turns a deep golden color and has a rich, piquant flavor. Any type works well in this recipe. If unavailable, Monterey Jack or aged cheddar can be substituted.

SERVES 12

Ole Mole Guacamole

3 ripe avocados
3 Tbsp (45 mL) fresh squeezed lime juice
2 Tbsp (30 mL) gold tequila
1 tsp (5 mL) salt
2 plum tomatoes, seeds removed and diced
½ cup (125 mL) red onion, diced
¼ cup (50 mL) chopped cilantro
Pinch cayenne pepper
1 clove garlic, minced (optional)

A hit of tequila puts this avocado dip on the holy-moly end of guacamole. It's great by itself as a dip with tortilla chips or served with the Tequila-Poached Chorizo Tostadas (facing page).

Cut the avocados in half with a sharp knife, remove the pit and scoop the flesh into a bowl. Add the lime juice, tequila and salt and mash with a fork or potato masher. Stir in the tomatoes, onion, cilantro, cayenne and garlic (if using). Cover and refrigerate for at least 1 hour before serving.

SERVES 12

Kahlúa Caramel Flan

¾ cup (175 mL) granulated sugar
2 egg yolks
6 egg whites
½ cup (125 mL) Kahlúa
one 10 oz (300 mL) can sweetened condensed milk (not evaporated)
½ tsp (2 mL) vanilla extract
1 tsp (5 mL) instant coffee granules
Pinch salt

This recipe may seem a bit complex, but don't be intimidated. The result is a creamy and smooth, almost crème brûlée–like flan with its own runny caramel sauce baked right in. You'll be like Speedy Gonzales, racing back for seconds. Note that this needs to be made the night before you plan to serve it.

Preheat oven to 350°F (180°C).

Gently melt the sugar in a medium nonstick frying pan over medium heat. This may take a while, but be patient and keep an eye on it so it doesn't burn. When the sugar has melted and turned light brown, carefully pour it into a 9-inch (23 cm) round pie plate, evenly coating the base of the dish.

In a separate bowl, beat together the egg yolks, egg whites, Kahlúa, condensed milk, vanilla, coffee, salt and 1½ cups (375 mL) of water. Pour the mixture over the caramel.

Create a *bain-marie* (see below) and bake on the center rack of the oven for about 1 hour, or until the outside edges are firm, but the center is still a little loose and jiggly.

Remove from the oven and cool on a wire rack. Refrigerate overnight.

To serve, allow the dish to come to room temperature and slide a knife around the outside edge. Place a large, lipped serving plate on top and carefully (but quickly) flip the dish upside down. It helps if you cross your fingers and hold your breath at this stage.

GIVE MARIE A BATH

A *bain-marie* is fancy chef talk for creating a water bath and it's used in recipes like crème brûlée and other custards to ensure even, slow cooking. To create a *bain-marie* take the dish with your ingredients in it and place it in a casserole dish that's at least 1 inch (2.5 cm) larger all the way around. Place both dishes on the rack of your oven and slowly fill the outer dish with hot water at least three-quarters of the way up the side of the inner dish. We're not particularly religious, but we've been told that this type of cooking dates back to biblical times and was named after Marie, wife of Moses. Apparently that whole family has a real thing for water.

Menu

Mojito Lamb Popsicles

Prosciutto-Wrapped Scallops with Maple Bourbon Glaze

Slow-Smoked Brisket with Chimichurri Sauce

Pineapple Cherry Bombs

SERVES 8

Christening the Q

BOURBON ICED TEA

½ cup (125 mL) granulated sugar

½ cup (125 mL) fresh mint leaves

3 cups (750 mL) brewed black tea, chilled

1 cup (250 mL) lemonade

1 cup (250 mL) bourbon

½ cup (125 mL) triple sec

1 orange, sliced into wheels

In a large glass pitcher gently muddle together the sugar and mint leaves, then add the tea, lemonade, bourbon and triple sec. Chill until ready to serve. Pour into collins glasses filled with ice and garnish with orange wheels.

The barbecue is an unsung hero. It sits all winter in the frigid cold, waiting silently for that moment when you call it to duty. This year when you pull off its cover, why don't you recognize just how special it is? Treat it to new lava rocks or a fancy new tank, perhaps? Christening the barbecue is a rite of passage for summer and this varied menu has you grilling everything from fruit and veggies to scallops, lamb and beef. Set "Propane Elaine" to sub-nuclear and put the heat to the meat.

Wine Pairing

A voluptuous red like a Zinfandel or its close cousin Primitivo goes great with a big beef dish like the brisket.

Setting the Mood

Hopefully you'll be celebrating outdoors, but we know there are those of you who'll gladly "pan-climate barbecue." No matter the weather, channel midsummer's hazy-glow atmosphere and toss in a little Mary Ann from *Gilligan's Island*: red gingham tablecloth dressed with dark denim napkins and fresh flowers, like tulips, daffodils and hydrangea. Dixieland jazz, with its toe-tapping clarinet, banjo and brassy "whoop-whoop," will help fill in the audio atmosphere.

Serving Suggestion

Barbecues tend to be stand-up-and-chew affairs, which fits this get-together perfectly. Treat the barbecue as your altar and serve your guests the appetizer directly from its flaming glory. Set up a table where your guests can help themselves to the extra chimichurri sauce, utensils, plates, napkins and whatever else they might need. Be sure to add some salads or veggies to this menu. Try our Grilled Zucchini with Feta and Mint at www.cookingwithbooze.com. The brisket should be served pre-sliced on a platter or wooden cutting board and drizzled with a thick ribbon of chimichurri. For added effect, elect someone to parade the meat around "steak house-style" (whole, on a bed of lettuce) and have your guests ogle at your barbecue mastery. Dessert can be served hot off the grill into individual bowls. Let your guests open their own little foil pouches themselves—this will save your fingertips.

SERVES 8

Mojito Lamb Popsicles

2 racks of lamb (1½ lb/750 g each), frenched

1 cup (250 mL) fresh mint

⅓ cup (75 mL) brown sugar, lightly packed

4 limes, quartered

5 cloves garlic, minced

½ cup (125 mL) dark rum

In our story today, Mary's little friend opts to go out in a blaze of glory, instead of being eaten by the clichéd old wolf. In honor of this courage, we present a chic appetizer that's bound to class up your next backyard culinary adventure. Inspired by the refreshing summer cocktail, this rum-based gem makes a great light snack or appetizer. Sophisticated finger-food made with a boozy twist!

Slice between each bone of the lamb to form individual popsicles. Muddle the mint and brown sugar together in a small bowl until fragrant. Add the lime quarters and continue to muddle to release their juice. Add the garlic and rum, stirring to combine well. Place the lamb in a large resealable plastic freezer bag and pour in the rum mixture. Refrigerate for 3 hours, or overnight if possible.

Preheat grill to high.

Grill the popsicles over indirect heat by turning the cooking side of the grill down to medium-low and leaving the opposite side of the grill on high. Close the lid and allow the lamb to cook for 4–5 minutes, flip it onto the hot side of the grill and reduce the heat to medium-low. Close the lid and allow it to cook for an additional 4–5 minutes. Check the doneness by testing the firmness of the meat—when cooked, the lamb will be firm to the touch but not completely resilient. The center should reach 130°F (55°C).

FRENCHED? *MAIS OUI!*

Frenched is just fancy chef talk for the way the rack of lamb is prepared at the butcher. A frenched rack of lamb means the butcher has removed the excess meat or sinew from the top portion of the ribs, leaving them exposed and clean. This provides a convenient stick for guests to hold onto, especially when the lamb is served on a buffet table.

ALSO PICTURED: PROSCIUTTO-WRAPPED SCALLOPS WITH MAPLE BOURBON GLAZE (PAGE 130)

SERVES 8

Prosciutto-Wrapped Scallops with Maple Bourbon Glaze

8 large bamboo skewers
16 large sea scallops
16 slices prosciutto
2 Tbsp (30 mL) extra virgin olive oil
3 Tbsp (45 mL) maple syrup
2 Tbsp (30 mL) brown sugar
3 Tbsp (45 mL) bourbon
Pinch cayenne pepper

A twist on a classic, this recipe uses prosciutto instead of traditional bacon so there's no need to worry about the possibility of undercooking the bacon while overcooking the scallop. The addition of a glaze balances the salty with a quick hit of sweet and smoky.

Soak the bamboo skewers for at least 30 minutes in warm water.

Preheat grill to medium-high.

Wrap each scallop in a slice of prosciutto, allowing any excess to overlap. Secure 2 scallops onto each bamboo skewer. Lightly brush them with olive oil and set aside.

Whisk together the maple syrup, brown sugar, bourbon and cayenne pepper in a small bowl and set aside.

Grill the skewers for 3–4 minutes, then flip and brush with glaze. Grill the second side for another 3–4 minutes, or until the center of the scallops is opaque. Brush once more with glaze and serve.

MOM, CAN WE GO CATHOLIC SO WE CAN GET COMMUNION WAFERS AND BOOZE?

Bart Simpson

SERVES 8

Slow-Smoked Brisket with Chimichurri Sauce

Brisket

10 lb (4.5 kg) beef brisket

¼ cup (50 mL) paprika

3 Tbsp (45 mL) brown sugar, packed

2 Tbsp (30 mL) chili powder

2 Tbsp (30 mL) ground cumin

2 Tbsp (30 mL) salt

1 Tbsp (15 mL) ground oregano

1 Tbsp (15 mL) garlic powder

1 Tbsp (15 mL) freshly ground black pepper

2 tsp (10 mL) cayenne pepper

8 cups (2 L) hardwood chips, such as mesquite

Beer Mop

two 12 oz (341 mL) bottles coffee porter or stout

½ cup (125 mL) balsamic vinegar

¼ cup (50 mL) maple syrup

1 Tbsp (15 mL) Worcestershire sauce

½ medium onion, minced

2 cloves garlic, minced

This is an all-day recipe but it's worth every minute. Once you've mastered the art of smoking with your barbecue, a whole new world of possibilities opens up. You'll be smoking everything: fish, game, old hockey equipment. This takes about eight hours to smoke, so make sure you have enough beer to last you until reinforcements arrive. Once this starts you need to keep an eye on it, just like babysitting. You don't want it ending up in the pool. We should point out that this recipe makes way more than your guests should be able to eat. Leftovers are a good thing.

Trim any excess fat from the brisket, but leave about ¼ inch (5 mm). Set aside.

Combine the paprika, brown sugar, chili powder, cumin, salt, oregano, garlic powder, pepper and cayenne in a medium bowl. Rub this mixture over all the sides of the brisket and wrap tightly in plastic wrap. Refrigerate for at least 12 hours.

Preheat gas grill to medium and remove the brisket from the plastic wrap.

Soak the wood chips in water for at least 10 minutes. Drain off the excess water and spread half the chips evenly over a large sheet of aluminum foil. Cover with an additional sheet of foil, crimping the edges to form a pouch. Poke the foil a few times with a fork to create rows of vents on top. Repeat with the remaining chips to make a second pouch.

Place 1 smoker pouch on 1 side of the grill, turn the heat to low on this side and turn off the opposite side of the grill. Cook the brisket using indirect heat by placing it on the side of the grill opposite to the side with pouch. Cook the brisket for 3 hours with the lid closed before turning.

Meanwhile, make the beer mop by combining the beer, balsamic vinegar, maple syrup, Worcestershire sauce, onion and garlic in a small saucepan over medium heat, stirring until the mixture comes to a rolling boil.

CONTINUED ON NEXT PAGE

CONTINUED FROM PREVIOUS PAGE

Chimichurri Sauce

1 cup (250 mL) chopped Italian parsley

1 cup (250 mL) chopped cilantro

1 Tbsp (15 mL) dried oregano

1 Tbsp (15 mL) dried chilies

1 Tbsp (15 mL) lemon zest

6 cloves garlic, minced

1 shallot, minced

⅓ cup (75 mL) balsamic vinegar

2 Tbsp (30 mL) sweet vermouth

3 Tbsp (45 mL) freshly squeezed lemon juice

1 cup (250 mL) extra virgin olive oil

Salt and freshly ground black pepper

Brush the brisket with the beer mop and change the smoke pouch if the smoke has run out. Cook for an additional 3–5 hours, mopping regularly, until the center of the brisket has reached 140°F (60°C). Remove from the heat, tent in aluminum foil and rest for 30 minutes. Carve the brisket across the grain into thin strips. Serve alone or on lightly toasted rolls topped with Chimichurri Sauce.

For the Chimichurri, pulse together the parsley, cilantro, oregano, chilies, lemon zest, garlic and shallot in a food processor or blender. Add the vinegar, vermouth and lemon juice then slowly pulse in the olive oil. Season to taste with salt and pepper.

TIPS FOR DELICIOUSLY MOIST BRISKET

1. Start with a well-marbled brisket with a thin layer of fat.
2. Don't trim all the fat away—keep a thin layer for flavor and moisture.
3. Keep the fat between the meat and the fire as much as possible.
4. Baste frequently with beer mop.
5. Flip and rotate your brisket at least once during the smoking to even out the exposure to heat.
6. Keep the heat in the smoker low, under 250°F (120°C).
7. Cover the brisket with foil and let it rest for at least 30 minutes before carving.

SERVES 8

Pineapple Cherry Bombs

1 cup (250 mL) granulated sugar
1 cup (250 mL) all-purpose flour
1½ tsp (7 mL) baking powder
3 eggs
⅓ cup (75 mL) milk
1 tsp (5 mL) vanilla extract
8 fresh pineapple slices, ¾ inch (2 cm) thick
3 Tbsp (45 mL) butter, melted
¼ cup (50 mL) brown sugar, packed
2 tsp (10 mL) cinnamon
¼ cup (50 mL) cherry brandy
Vanilla ice cream
Chopped fresh or dried cherries

Much like booze at breakfast, barbecued desserts are highly underrepresented in the culinary world. Our inspiration for this recipe came from friends who invented the campfire version. This dessert is a great way to prove yourself as lord-of-the-grill. For the campfire version, just substitute an old-fashioned doughnut for the cake and cook it on the edge of the fire until tender.

Preheat oven to 350°F (180°C). Line a baking sheet or jellyroll pan with parchment paper.

Sift together the sugar, flour and baking powder into a large mixing bowl. Combine the eggs, milk and vanilla in a medium bowl and beat with an electric mixer until fluffy. Mix the wet ingredients into the dry ingredients and beat the batter until smooth (about 4–5 minutes). Pour batter onto the prepared baking sheet or jellyroll pan and bake for about 12–15 minutes or until a toothpick inserted in the center comes out clean. Remove from the heat and turn out on a wire rack to cool. Cut the cake into 8 pieces, using a round 3½-inch (9 cm) pastry cutter.

Preheat grill to high.

Brush 1 side of the pineapple slices with half the melted butter. Grill, buttered side down, until well-defined grill marks appear (about 3–5 minutes), flip the pineapple, brush the top side with butter and grill until evenly cooked. Remove from the heat and place each pineapple slice on an individual piece of aluminum foil large enough to completely wrap round it. In a small bowl combine the brown sugar, cinnamon and cherry brandy, stirring until well integrated. Spoon this mixture evenly across each pineapple slice (about 1 Tbsp/15 mL each) and top with a cake round. Wrap in the aluminum foil and grill pineapple side down over medium heat for 8–10 minutes, or until the pineapple is soft and tender. Carefully turn out of the foil pouches into individual bowls (pineapple side up) and serve hot with vanilla ice cream. Garnish with chopped cherries.

SERVES 8

Summer Whites Garden Party

Menu

Gin-Bathed Cucumber Sandwiches

Chilled Parsnip and Strawberry Soup

Tea-Poached Trout

Empire Biscuits with Rosewater Icing

When summer's heat makes you sweat in your shoes, it's time to take a leaf from the British book of remaining cool, calm and collected. For this party it's important to have a nice garden. If yours is more scrub than chic, hijack a local garden, like one at a museum, gallery or historical house, for example. (This nefarious activity is in no way condoned by the authors or the publisher of this book.)

Wine Pairing

Take your cues from the food and serve the same Sauvignon Blanc as you use to poach the fish. For variety, have some Früli Strawberry beer on hand as well.

Setting the Mood

Have your guests dress in shades of white and off-white—light cottons and linens always look chic. Ladies can accessorize with wide-brimmed hats and parasols while gentlemen look the part in cool fedoras and Panama hats. Light colors keep you cool as you work up a sweat playing high-impact sports like lawn bowling and croquet.

Keep the table setting white and accent it with natural materials like grass mats and bamboo cutlery. Create drama with flowers by using freshly cut hydrangeas placed in galvanized metal watering cans. Set up a croquet pitch and post the rules to encourage play. Hire a jazz quartet to play favorites from the likes of Louis Armstrong and Benny Goodman—or buy a couple of compilations and spin those through your outdoor speakers.

Serving Suggestion

Set up your buffet in the shade—stack the sandwiches on a large platter to create a formidable pile. Present the soup in a suitably fussy lidded tureen and serve slightly chilled, removing it from the refrigerator 30 minutes before serving. Lay the trout side-by-side on an elegant serving platter and rest it on a large baking dish filled with ice and wrapped in linen. Provide a fish knife and a serving utensil. Doilies provide the perfect base for the empire biscuits, and you may wish to pick up some mesh covers to keep pesky little critters from ruining your serene English setting.

ELDERFLOWER SPRITZER

2½ oz Elderflower Presse (or ½ oz Elderflower cordial + 2 oz club soda)

2 oz chilled Sauvignon Blanc or Pinot Grigio

Combine the ingredients in a wine glass filled with ice. Stir gently and garnish with an edible flower or sprig of mint.

RESPECT YOUR ELDERS

Elderflower cordial or carbonated elderflower soda is available at most grocery stores in the fizzy aisle. It's made from little squished British flowers and when it's mixed with the gooseberry quality of a Sauvignon Blanc it creates a remarkably refreshing and delicious drink.

SERVES 8

Gin-Bathed Cucumber Sandwiches

1 large English cucumber, thinly sliced
¼ cup (50 mL) gin (Hendricks is a good choice)
2 cups (500 mL) cream cheese, softened
½ cup (125 mL) mayonnaise
¼ tsp (1 mL) garlic powder
24 slices white bread
Freshly ground black pepper

Cucumber sandwiches are about as British as the Mini. We've given these pale-faced gems a big red nose with a boozy bath that turns them into something refreshing and just a wee bit tipsy.

Combine the cucumber and gin in a medium-sized bowl and marinate for 1 hour, tossing occasionally.

Whip the cream cheese with an electric mixer, slowly working in the mayonnaise until it's very smooth. Add the garlic powder and blend well. Spread the cream cheese mixture over 1 side of all 24 slices of bread, using about 1½ Tbsp (22 mL) per slice. Sprinkle generously with the freshly ground black pepper.

Remove the cucumber slices from the gin and pat dry with paper towel. Distribute the cucumber slices evenly over 12 slices of the bread. Close each sandwich with the remaining 12 slices of bread. Square up the sandwiches and trim off the crusts with a serrated knife. Slice each sandwich into thirds. Cover and refrigerate until ready to serve.

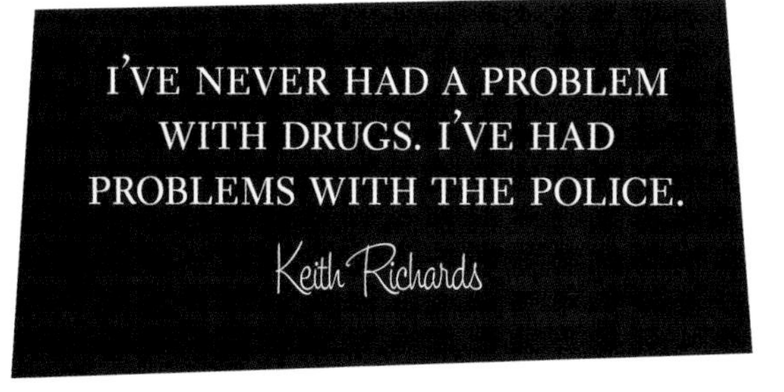

ALSO PICTURED: EMPIRE BISCUITS WITH ROSEWATER ICING (PAGE 141)

SERVES 8

Chilled Parsnip and Strawberry Soup

- 1½ lb (750 g) parsnips, peeled and diced
- 2 Tbsp (30 mL) vegetable oil
- ½ large sweet onion, diced
- 4 cups (1 L) vegetable stock
- ½ tsp (2 mL) salt
- Pinch nutmeg
- one 8 oz (250 mL) bottle Früli strawberry beer
- 1 cup (250 mL) milk
- White pepper

This veggie-friendly soup can be served hot or cold and it even freezes well. When served chilled it's the perfect refresher on a hot summer day. The strawberry flavor comes from the Früli beer, which as far as we're concerned is just about the best way to preserve those little ruby gems.

Toss the parsnips in oil and sauté in a large frying pan or stockpot over medium-high heat until lightly golden around the edges, about 10 minutes. Add the onion and cook until transparent, about 3–4 minutes. Deglaze the pan by adding vegetable stock and stirring in any caramelized bits that have stuck to the bottom of the pan. Bring the mixture to a simmer and cook over medium-high heat until the parsnips are soft, about 10 minutes. Purée the ingredients with a handheld immersion blender, or work in batches with a regular blender. Pour the soup back into the frying pan, add the salt, nutmeg, beer and milk and season to taste with pepper. Bring to a gentle simmer, adding additional stock or milk to reach the desired consistency, if required. Remove from the heat and cool before refrigerating.

Spoon into bowls and garnish with a sprig of watercress or a sliver of strawberry if desired.

ALSO PICTURED: TEA-POACHED TROUT (PAGE 140)

SERVES 8

Tea-Poached Trout

1 Tbsp (15 mL) butter
3 shallots, minced
4 cups (1 L) silver needle tea
1 cup (250 mL) Sauvignon Blanc
1 cup (250 mL) vegetable stock
2 bay leaves
1 Tbsp (15 mL) fresh tarragon, chopped
1 lemon, thinly sliced
½ tsp (2 mL) salt
¼ tsp (1 mL) freshly ground black pepper
2 large trout fillets (about 1 lb/500 g) each

What's better than water for a fish? Well, if it was a British fish and it could talk, it might just say "tea." Of course, if the fish you have is talking, it might be time to put down this book and go to bed. This recipe uses silver needle tea, which is a Chinese tea made from the most revered leaves of the tea plant. You may prefer to substitute your favorite unflavored black tea, but check with the fish first.

Melt the butter in a large frying pan with a lid over medium-high heat. Add the shallots and sauté until translucent, about 4–5 minutes. Add the tea, wine, stock, bay leaves, tarragon, 4 slices of lemon, salt and pepper. Cover the frying pan, reduce the heat to medium and simmer for about 15 minutes. Add 1 trout fillet, skin side down, and fully immerse. Reduce the heat to medium-low and poach the trout with the lid on for about 8–10 minutes, or until the center of the flesh is opaque.

Carefully remove the fillet from the frying pan and place on a plate, tent with aluminum foil and allow to cool. Repeat with the second fillet. Cover and refrigerate until ready to serve. Serve the fillets on a large platter and garnish with the remaining lemon slices.

SERVES 8

Empire Biscuits with Rosewater Icing

1 cup (250 mL) unsalted butter, softened

½ cup (125 mL) granulated sugar

2 cups (500 mL) all-purpose flour, sifted

½ cup (125 mL) raspberry jam

¼ cup (50 mL) Chambord

2 cups (500 mL) confectioner's sugar

3 Tbsp (45 mL) rosewater

David grew up in Scotland and it was his next-door neighbor who first got him involved in food. She taught him how to bake bread from scratch, make the crumbliest scones and create the most angelic angel food cake. She also taught him how to knit . . . By the age of six David was a full-fledged homemaker. Alas, he lost most of these life skills by the age of 12. The one thing that did persist was his love for British sweets—while chocky-bickies, Jaffa cakes and those enrobed marshmallow puffy things were high on the list, nothing outdid these jam-filled marvels.

Preheat oven to 350°F (180°C). Line a baking sheet with parchment paper.

Beat the butter and sugar together in a large bowl until smooth. Gradually blend in the flour until it's completely incorporated. Cover and refrigerate for 1 hour.

Roll out the dough to ¼-inch (5 mm) thickness on a lightly floured surface. It should be cool enough to be pliable, but not so cold that it crumbles. Re-chill the dough if it becomes sticky. Cut into 2-inch (5 cm) rounds with a cookie cutter.

Bake the biscuits on the prepared baking sheet for 8–10 minutes, or until the edges are lightly golden. Cool the biscuits on the baking sheet for 5 minutes before transferring to a wire rack.

Meanwhile, combine the raspberry jam and Chambord in a small saucepan and heat until bubbling. Pour the mixture through a mesh sieve to remove the seeds. Set aside to cool.

To make the icing, combine the confectioner's sugar and rosewater in a medium bowl and whisk gently until the icing is soft enough to spread, adding a couple of drops of water if necessary.

Sandwich 1 tsp (5 mL) of jam mixture between 2 biscuits and spread with icing. Allow the icing to set before serving.

Garnish with a piece of maraschino cherry, if desired.

SERVES 4

Put Your Friends to Work Party

Menu

Spiced Tomato Chutney

Tuscan Grilled Chicken

80 Proof Rum Pot

Sweet Balsamic Cherries

Dark Chocolate Semifreddo

We should really call this the "Lazy Canner's Preserving Party" as all the canning recipes will hold up for extended periods in the refrigerator without processing in a water bath. You gotta love the preserving powers of booze. However, to cover all bases—because that's the kinda guys we are—we've also included instructions for proper processing. It's our nod to all those by-the-book kinda cooks out there.

Wine Pairing

Match the Tuscan chicken with a Chianti for the red wine drinkers or a Pinot Grigio to satiate the appetites of the white wine crowd.

Setting the Mood

Set your work station up with bushel baskets filled with everything you and your friends will need for the afternoon: canning jars, colorful aprons and all your fresh ingredients. Present utensils, measuring cups and spoons in clean tin cans or old jam jars. A fresh bouquet of flowers from your garden will play nicely off the bright colors of the local produce.

Some good ol' working music like bluegrass or roots should provide ample inspiration. The soundtrack to *O Brother, Where Art Thou?* or Earl Scruggs's *Foggy Mountain Breakdown* are good places to start.

Serving Suggestion

Simply grill some asparagus and brush it with a mixture of equal parts Dijon mustard and honey for a simple side dish to pair with the chutney and chicken. Accompany both with a pot of boiled new potatoes tossed with butter and chopped fresh chives. That should provide enough fuel for your guests to keep working through the night, if necessary.

STRAWBERRY BASIL MOJITOS

Plump, ripe strawberries fresh from the field are like Viagra and a willing partner; they offer welcome relief during long, unfulfilled dry spells. Unfortunately neither lasts forever. It's best to pounce when either opportunity presents itself.

4 limes, juiced and quartered

1 cup (250 mL) fresh strawberries, hulled and quartered

½ cup (125 mL) fresh basil leaves, torn

¼ cup (50 mL) granulated sugar

1 cup (250 mL) amber rum

1 cup (250 mL) sparkling water

Muddle together the limes, strawberries, basil and sugar in the bottom of a large pitcher until the sugar dissolves and the mixture is very fragrant. Add the rum and stir. Strain into 4 ice-filled glasses and top with sparkling water. Garnish with a sprig fresh basil or sliced strawberry, if desired.

MAKES 4 JARS

Spiced Tomato Chutney

- 2 Tbsp (30 mL) canola oil
- 1 Spanish onion, finely chopped
- 2 Tbsp (30 mL) minced fresh ginger
- 2 Tbsp (30 mL) mustard seeds
- 1 Tbsp (15 mL) cumin seeds or ground cumin
- 1 Tbsp (15 mL) paprika
- 1 tsp (5 mL) crushed red pepper flakes
- 1 tsp (5 mL) salt
- 1 cup (250 mL) red wine vinegar
- 1 cup (250 mL) gin
- 1 cup (250 mL) granulated sugar
- 8 cups (2 L) skinned, seeded and chopped tomatoes

This is ketchup for grown-ups and you'll want to use it on everything from sandwiches to Indian curries. Serve it with a cheese plate or in lieu of cranberries with roast turkey. You can still squeeze some Heinz on your mac 'n' cheese, if you insist.

Heat the oil in the bottom of a large stockpot over medium heat. Add the onion and ginger and cook for 5 minutes, or until soft. Add the mustard seeds, cumin seeds, paprika, crushed red pepper flakes and salt, stirring until they become fragrant, about 1–2 minutes. Add the vinegar, gin and sugar, bring to a boil and simmer, uncovered, for 10 minutes. Add the tomatoes, mashing large chunks against the side of the pot with a wooden spoon, and cook, stirring, until thickened, about 15 minutes.

Pour into 4 sterilized medium-sized canning jars with tight-fitting lids, filling to within ½ inch (1 cm) of the rim. Wipe the rims clean, seal tightly and cool completely before refrigerating for up to 1 year.

NOTE: For water bath processing see page 149.

ALSO PICTURED: SWEET BALSAMIC CHERRIES (PAGE 149)

SPICED TOMATO CHUTNEY
SWEET

SERVES 4

Tuscan Grilled Chicken

- ¼ cup (50 mL) extra virgin olive oil
- 6 green onions, chopped
- 2 cloves garlic
- 1 tsp (5 mL) dried basil
- 1 tsp (5 mL) dried oregano
- 1 tsp (5 mL) dried marjoram
- 1 tsp (5 mL) salt
- 1 tsp (5 mL) freshly ground black pepper
- ½ cup (125 mL) white wine
- 3 Tbsp (45 mL) freshly squeezed lemon juice
- 1 Tbsp (15 mL) lemon zest
- 4 bone-in, skin-on chicken breasts

When served with the Spiced Tomato Chutney (page 144) this fresh-tasting chicken transforms into an exotic and smoky entrée. Ask yourself if you can handle the heat.

Blend together the olive oil, green onions, garlic, basil, oregano, marjoram, salt, pepper, white wine, lemon juice and zest in a food processor or blender until smooth. Pour this mixture over the chicken, breast side down, in a shallow baking dish and refrigerate for 3 hours.

Preheat grill to medium-high.

Remove the chicken from the marinade and grill, breast side down, for 5–10 minutes, or until the skin starts to crisp. Turn the chicken, close the lid and continue cooking for 10–15 minutes, checking occasionally to prevent flare-ups, or until the internal temperature reaches 160°F (70°C) and the juices run clear.

I'M LIKE OLD WINE. THEY DON'T BRING ME OUT VERY OFTEN, BUT I'M WELL PRESERVED.

Rose Fitzgerald Kennedy

MAKES 1 GALLON (4 L)

80 Proof Rum Pot

2 cups (500 mL) strawberries
7 cups (1.75 L) superfine sugar
8 cups (2 L) (approximately) rum, bourbon or brandy (or a combination)
2 cups (500 mL) cherries
2 cups (500 mL) raspberries
2 cups (500 mL) blueberries (wild are best)
8 plums
6 medium peaches
6 pears

This classic European vat of boozy fruit is a work in progress and not for the impatient.

Start your rum pot in June when local strawberries are in season, then add your favorite fruits as they become available, finishing with pears in the early fall. By Christmas you'll have the most decadent dessert topping and liqueur this side of the Alps.

Use only fresh, unblemished fruits that are just ripe and the best booze you can afford. This will yield the best results. And feel free to substitute other fruits such as currants, blackberries, melon, grapes or pineapple.

You'll need a 1-gallon (4 L) glass canister with a tight-fitting lid for your rum pot.

Wash and pat dry the strawberries. Remove the tops and cut any large berries in half. Sprinkle with 1 cup (250 mL) of the sugar and let stand for 1 hour. Put in the canister and cover the strawberries with rum, making sure the fruit is submerged under 1 inch (2.5 cm) of rum.

Cover with the tight-fitting lid and store the rum pot in a cool, dark place until ready to add the next fruit.

Cut the cherries in half, remove the pits and sprinkle with 1 cup (250 mL) of the sugar. Let stand for 1 hour before adding them to the rum pot. Pour in enough bourbon to cover the layered fruit by 1 inch (2.5 cm). Cover and store.

Sprinkle the raspberries with 1 cup (250 mL) of the sugar and let stand for 1 hour before adding them to the rum pot. Pour in enough brandy to cover the fruit by 1 inch (2.5 cm). Cover and store.

Sprinkle the blueberries with 1 cup (250 mL) of the sugar and let stand for 1 hour before adding them to the rum pot. Pour in enough rum to cover the fruit by 1 inch (2.5 cm). Cover and store.

Cut the plums into slices, discard the stones, sprinkle with 1 cup (250 mL) of the sugar and let stand for 1 hour before adding to the rum pot. Pour in enough bourbon to cover the fruit by 1 inch (2.5 cm). Cover and store.

CONTINUED ON NEXT PAGE

CONTINUED FROM PREVIOUS PAGE

Drop the peaches into boiling water for 30 seconds then immerse in cold water. Peel and slice then sprinkle with 1 cup (250 mL) of the sugar and let stand for 1 hour before adding to the rum pot. Pour in enough brandy to cover the fruit by 1 inch (2.5 cm). Cover and store.

Peel and core the pears then chop them into bite-sized pieces. Dissolve the remaining 1 cup (250 mL) sugar in 1 cup (250 mL) water in a medium saucepan. Add the pears and bring to a boil. Remove from the heat and let stand for 1 hour. Strain the pears out of their syrup and discard the syrup. Add the pears to the rum pot and pour in enough rum to cover the fruit by 1 inch (2.5 cm). Cover and store the pot in a cool, dark place for at least 2 months.

Check the pot occasionally to make sure that there is sufficient rum to keep the mixture covered; add more when necessary.

Enjoy on ice cream, waffles or pancakes. Ladle the liqueur into glasses and enjoy as a digestif or mix with soda for a refreshing aperitif.

NOTE: If the fruit starts to float you can weigh it down with a saucer or small plate to ensure it stays submerged.

NOTE: If your rum pot doesn't have a tight-fitting lid, cover the opening with plastic wrap before replacing the lid. This will prevent evaporation. Store in a cool, dark place.

MAKES 4 JARS

Sweet Balsamic Cherries

- 4 cups (1 L) fresh black cherries, pitted
- ¼ cup (50 mL) granulated sugar
- ¼ cup (50 mL) balsamic vinegar
- ¼ cup (50 mL) water
- ¼ cup (50 mL) kirsch or brandy

The great thing about this recipe is that the vinegar and booze mixture helps preserve the cherries so the jars don't need to be processed, but they do need to be kept in the fridge. If you don't plan to send your guests home with a souvenir jar and want to store the extras in the pantry, you'll need to process them properly. Instructions follow.

Place the cherries in 4 small canning jars with tight-fitting lids. Boil the sugar, vinegar and water in a small saucepan, stirring to dissolve the sugar. Add the kirsch and pour over the cherries to within ½ inch (1 cm) of the rim. Wipe the rims clean, seal tightly and refrigerate. Cherries will keep for up to 1 year after opening

Serve with cheese courses, on roast duck breasts and other game meats or to finish off a decadent sundae.

WATER BATH PROCESSING

Fill canning jars with preserves and affix lids tightly. Submerge the jars completely in a large pot of boiling water and boil for 15 minutes. Remove with tongs to a wire rack to cool. You may hear popping or burping sounds coming from the jars as they cool—this is good as it indicates the vacuum seal is underway. Store the jars in a dark, cool and dry place.

SEAL OF APPROVAL

After 12–24 hours you can test to see if the jars are properly sealed. Press down on the center of the lid. If there's no movement or popping sound the jar is sealed.

THE PITS

If you don't have a cherry pitter, don't fret. Use a chopstick to poke the pits out or cut the cherries in half to remove the pits.

SERVES 4

Dark Chocolate Semifreddo

½ lb (250 g) bittersweet chocolate, chopped

2 Tbsp (30 mL) cocoa powder

3 eggs + 2 egg yolks

¾ cup (175 mL) superfine sugar

1¾ cups (425 mL) heavy (35%) cream

We love semifreddos because they pack the creamy and palate-cleansing benefits of ice cream without all the work and special gadgets. This one is especially wonderful when topped with Sweet Balsamic Cherries.

Melt the chocolate and cocoa together in a bowl over a pot of gently simmering water, stirring until smooth. Set aside until completely cooled.

Whisk the whole eggs, yolks and sugar together in a large bowl over a pot of gently simmering water for 5 minutes, or until heated through and frothy. Remove from the heat and beat with an electric mixer for another 5 minutes, or until doubled in size and very pale. Cool completely before gently folding in the melted chocolate. Set aside.

Beat the cream in a large bowl with an electric mixer until soft peaks form. Gently fold in the chocolate and egg mixture then pour into a 9- × 13-inch (3.5 L) pan. Cover with aluminum foil and freeze for at least 4 hours, or until completely firm.

Scoop into bowls and serve with a few Sweet Balsamic Cherries (page 149).

ALSO PICTURED: SWEET BALSAMIC CHERRIES (PAGE 149)

SERVES 8

Menu

Beer Pretzel Sticks

Alsatian Choucroute Garnie

Weissbier Mussels with Coriander and Orange

Apple Strudel with Fiery Cinnamon Icing

Oktoberfest

THE DEER HUNTER

Beer is the drink of choice for Oktoberfest, but when in Germany do as the Germans do and provide your guests with a Jägermeister chaser.

2 oz Jägermeister

1 oz vodka

3 oz root beer

Splash freshly squeezed lemon juice

Combine Jägermeister and vodka in a shaker with ice. Strain into a highball glass with ice, top with root beer and a squeeze of lemon.

No other country embraces October quite like Germany. For two weeks each year Munich is transformed from a cosmopolitan city to a beer-swilling, polka-playing party venue. This is a great excuse to try some of the country's most exciting exports, excluding sleek sports cars. Pick up a good assortment of beers from the fruity weiss (white) beers to the dark dunkels, and throw in some pilsners for good measure.

Wine Pairing

A wine pairing for Oktoberfest? There's always one, isn't there? Explore some of the world's most underrated wines like German Rieslings or wines from the French border region of Alsace. Both are great choices and they won't empty your wallet.

Setting the Mood

Resist the temptation to don some lederhosen and decorate the entire venue with Bavarian farm equipment. Instead, let some fun German-inspired music along with subtle décor cues provide the main theme. Oktoberfest is held outdoors in a beer garden–type venue; large picnic tables with checkered tablecloths serve as the communal eating and drinking areas. If the weather holds up, this is the ideal afternoon party for saying *auf Wiedersehen* to your outdoor space before winter.

Oktoberfest hats and large glass beer steins (they hold 4 cups/1 L) are a great touch. Drop by a garden center and find a small wooden barrel. With a little jury-rigging and a mini-keg, this can serve as your very own tap and barrel.

Weird Al is the son of the Frank Yankovic, "America's Polka King" and polka is perfect for Oktoberfest. Check out some great hits from the Yankovic family: Weird Al's montage, *Polka Your Eyes Out*, and his father's, *Songs of the Polka King*.

Serving Suggestion

Serve your food in large, steaming bowls and provide guests with small bowls so they can help themselves. The strudel can be served warm on a wooden cutting board.

OKTOBERFEST

OKTOBERFEST

Oktoberfest dates back to 1810 when Crown Prince Ludwig married his high school sweetheart, Princess Therese of Saxony-Hildburghausen. He was madly in love and had some extra cash to burn, so instead of blowing it at the all-night royal casino, he decided to throw a party for the people of Munich. Which, in 1810, was a really smart way to keep one's head firmly attached to one's neck.

SOME OF THE BEERS OF GERMANY

SELECT BRANDS

If you want the complete list, head to the Fatherland—and take notes.

BOCK—an amber, heavy-bodied, bittersweet lager. Many varieties exist in this category including Dunkels Bock (dark and heavy) and Eisbock (ice beer or freeze-distilled). Try Holsten Festbock with its deep amber color and sweet, roasted malt and coffee flavors.

DUNKEL—a dark lager that comes in two main varieties. Munich-style is sweet and malty while the Franconian varieties are drier with a more hoppy taste. Try Warsteiner Dunkel, a Munich-made lager with sweet and rich, malty aromas.

PILSNER—a pale lager with a light body and a hoppy flavor. Two-thirds of all the beer consumed in Germany is pilsner. Try Konig Pilsner with its rich floral aromas, medium body and full-hop flavor.

RAUCHBIER—the use of smoked malts give Rauchbier its signature dark color and smoky (duh!) flavor. Try Aecht Schlenkerla Rauchbier (say that quickly three times) for a true beer adventure. Almost black, and smoky, chewy and formidable—this is not a beer for the timid.

WEISSBIER/WEIZEN—wheat beer or white beers. Weissbier can vary greatly in flavor and texture depending on how it's made and where it's from. Try Paulaner Hefe-Weissbier, a pale and cloudy amber ale with great balance and a slightly spicy character.

FIRST CLASS GLASS

The darker the beer the wider the glass; the lighter the lager the taller and more narrow the vessel. Don't ask questions, just follow the instructions.

SERVES 8

Beer Pretzel Sticks

one 12 oz (341 mL) bottle dark German beer

2 Tbsp (30 mL) brown sugar, packed

¼ oz (8 g) package active dry yeast (not instant yeast)

3 cups (750 mL) all-purpose flour

1 cup (250 mL) bread flour

1 tsp (5 mL) salt

1 Tbsp (15 mL) olive oil

2 Tbsp (30 mL) baking soda

1 egg white

2 Tbsp (30 mL) sesame seeds (or coarse salt)

It makes sense that the country known best for its beer is also responsible for the pretzel. These soft-centered, bread-like pretzels are great by themselves or dipped in melted butter or mustard. They're also great for soaking up all the flavors of the Weissbier Mussels (page 158) and Choucroute Garnie (page 156).

Heat the beer and sugar in a small saucepan until the temperature registers about 110°F (43°C) on a candy thermometer. Remove from the heat, sprinkle in the yeast and stir to dissolve. Set aside for about 10 minutes, or until foamy.

Combine the all-purpose flour, bread flour and salt in a large bowl and form a well in the center. Add the beer mixture to the well and mix by hand, slowly incorporating flour into the well until a dough forms.

Knead the dough on a lightly floured surface until it's smooth and elastic, about 8 minutes. Coat a large mixing bowl with the 1 Tbsp (15 mL) olive oil, transfer the dough to a bowl, cover with plastic wrap and store in a warm place for about 1 hour to rise.

Punch down the dough once it's doubled in size and cut into 12 equal pieces. Roll each piece into an 18-inch (45 cm) length, allow the dough to relax for 5–6 minutes, then roll each piece into a pencil-thin length about 3 feet (1 m) long. Cut these into 12-inch (30 cm) sections.

Line a baking sheet with parchment paper.

Combine 2 cups (500 mL) warm water and the baking soda in an 8-inch square (2 L) pan and dip each piece of dough in the water for 2–3 seconds. Place on the prepared baking sheet, cover and set in a warm place to rise for 30 minutes.

Preheat oven to 450°F (230°C).

Whisk together the egg white and ¼ cup (50 mL) water. Brush over the dough and sprinkle with sesame seeds or coarse salt.

Bake for 8–10 minutes, or until golden brown.

Serve pretzels with melted butter or grainy Dijon mustard, if desired.

SERVES 8

Alsatian Choucroute Garnie

¼ lb (125 g) bacon, cut into 1-inch (2.5 cm) pieces

1 large onion, sliced

2 cups (500 mL) dry Riesling

8 smoked pork sausages, such as bratwursts

¼ cup (50 mL) Jägermeister

2 cups (500 mL) chicken stock

1 cup (250 mL) sauerkraut

1 lb (500 g) parsnips or white potatoes, cut into ½-inch (1 cm) slices

2 red apples, cored, peeled and cut into ½-inch (1 cm) slices

2 Tbsp (30 mL) granulated sugar

3 bay leaves

½ tsp (2 mL) freshly ground black pepper

Choucroute is the French term for "sauerkraut," and this traditional dish from the border region between Germany and France makes for a delicious fall warm-up. It's hearty and has a perfect balance of sweetness between the apples and the wine. Good sausages are essential here. If you can't find smoked sausages, precooked fresh ones will work just fine. To serve this to a crowd, slice up the sausages into three pieces each. This dish can be made ahead, covered and reheated as needed.

Preheat oven to 375°F (190°C).

Cook the bacon in a large frying pan over medium-high heat until tender. Add the onion and cook until it becomes translucent and slightly browned on the edges, about 6–7 minutes. Deglaze the pan with 1 cup (250 mL) of the wine. Transfer to a large roasting pan or ovenproof casserole dish. Add the sausages, remaining wine, Jägermeister, stock, sauerkraut, parsnips, apple, sugar, bay leaves and pepper to the casserole dish. Bake, uncovered, for 1 hour, or until the parsnips are tender. Transfer to a warmed soup tureen and serve.

ALSO PICTURED: BEER PRETZEL STICKS (PAGE 155)

SERVES 8

Weissbier Mussels with Coriander and Orange

1 lb (500 g) mussels, scrubbed and de-bearded

1 Tbsp (15 mL) extra virgin olive oil

1 medium onion, minced

2 cloves garlic, minced

1 Tbsp (15 mL) coriander seeds, crushed

one 12 oz (341 mL) bottle weissbier (white beer)

⅓ cup (75 mL) Jägermeister

1 red Thai chili pepper, seeds removed and minced

1 Tbsp (15 mL) orange zest

½ cup (125 mL) freshly squeezed orange juice

½ tsp (2 mL) salt

This easy-to-make recipe combines the citrus notes of a weissbier with the sweet honey notes of coriander seed and just a splash of anise for balance. Your guests will be using their pretzel sticks to fight their way for more.

In a colander, shake and rinse the mussels under cold water, discarding any that remain open.

Heat the oil in a large stockpot over medium-high heat. Add the onion and garlic and cook for 2–3 minutes, until softened. Add the coriander, beer, Jägermeister, chili, orange zest, juice and salt. Bring the mixture to a boil then add the mussels. Cook for 5–7 minutes, or until the mussels have opened. Transfer to a serving bowl, discarding any unopened mussels. Garnish with Italian parsley and orange wedges, if desired.

A TELEPHONE SURVEY SAYS THAT 51 PERCENT OF COLLEGE STUDENTS DRINK UNTIL THEY PASS OUT AT LEAST ONCE A MONTH. THE OTHER 49 PERCENT DIDN'T ANSWER THE PHONE.

SERVES 8

Apple Strudel with Fiery Cinnamon Icing

½ cup (125 mL) butter

¾ cup (175 mL) brown sugar, packed

2 lb (1 kg) red apples, peeled, cored and sliced

¼ tsp (1 mL) ground cinnamon

¼ cup (50 mL) dark rum

½ cup (125 mL) dried cherries, chopped

½ cup (125 mL) gingersnap cookie crumbs

¼ cup (50 mL) chopped toasted hazelnuts

1 tsp (5 mL) lemon zest

10 sheets phyllo pastry

1 egg white

2 Tbsp (30 mL) Goldschläger

½ cup (125 mL) confectioner's sugar

Pinch cayenne pepper

This dessert combines the best flaky pastry with a sweet and smooth apple filling. Chopped dried cherries add a jewel-like quality and tangy flavor. Then, like Lucifer rising, top it with a spicy cinnamon icing.

Melt 2 Tbsp (30 mL) of the butter in a large frying pan set over medium heat. Add ½ cup (125 mL) of the brown sugar, the apples, cinnamon and rum. Reduce the heat to medium-low and simmer until the apples soften and the liquid has thickened, about 15–20 minutes. Stir in the cherries, remove from the heat and set aside.

Preheat oven to 375°F (190°C). Line a baking sheet with parchment paper.

Combine the cookie crumbs, hazelnuts, lemon zest and remaining brown sugar in a small bowl. Melt the remaining butter in a saucepan and set aside.

Assemble the strudel by placing a dry kitchen towel on a flat work surface. Place 1 sheet of phyllo on the towel, keeping the remaining phyllo covered with a damp towel. Brush the phyllo lightly with melted butter, top with a second sheet of phyllo, then lightly brush with more butter. Sprinkle about ¼ cup (50 mL) of the nut and cookie mixture over the second sheet of phyllo. Repeat this process 3 more times, layering 2 sheets of phyllo, followed by the nut and cookie mixture each time. Top with 2 final layers of phyllo pastry. Using a sharp knife, lightly score the top of the pastry 2 or 3 times.

Spoon the apple mixture over half the pastry (lengthwise), about 2 inches (5 cm) from all the edges. Fold in the short ends of the phyllo stack then carefully roll up the whole stack like a jelly roll. Brush with more butter and turn out (seam side down) onto the prepared baking sheet. Bake for 30 minutes. Remove from oven. Whisk together the egg white with 2 Tbsp (30 mL) water. Brush over the strudel and bake for a further 15 minutes, or until golden.

Meanwhile, combine the Goldschläger, icing sugar and cayenne pepper in a small bowl, stirring until smooth. Drizzle this icing over the warm strudel and sprinkle with additional chopped dried cherries if desired. Serve with vanilla ice cream or whipped cream.

SERVES 8

Comfort Food to Cure the Winter Blues

Menu

Mini Grilled Cheese

Herb-Roasted Poutine with Applewood Smoked Cheddar

Pancetta-Wrapped Meatloaf with Cognac Red Currant Glaze

Rum Baba

CREAM SODA

2 oz vanilla vodka

½ tsp (2 mL) grenadine

Club soda

Combine the vodka and grenadine in a fountain or collins glass. Fill with ice and top with club soda. Serve with a straw.

Comfort food is unpretentious and wholesome—the culinary equivalent of a hug. This celebration is perfect after a long day of snow shoveling, skiing or watching people shovel snow and ski. Start a big fire (in the fireplace) and serve up some piping hot love.

Wine Pairing

Comfort food requires comfort wine, so crack open a big bottle of your coziest Merlot. It's mouth-filling fruit flavor (say that three times fast) and low tannins are ideally paired with the Pancetta-Wrapped Meatloaf.

Setting the Mood

Get inspired by the 1950s diner style and work from a theme of black, white and chrome. Accent this with hints of turquoise or candy-apple red. Accessorize the table with a chrome napkin holder or gumball machine. Of course, a retro jukebox, if you happen to have one lying around, makes a gorgeous and useful adornment to this meal. Play music from the golden era of rock 'n' roll: Elvis, Buddy Holly and The Big Bopper will get you started.

Serving Suggestion

Most of the items on this menu can be made in advance. Prep the grilled cheese in morning so they're ready to grill on demand. The meatloaf can be made the day before and easily reheated in the pan. The roast potatoes can be made up to a day before and re-roasted until crisp, and the Rum Baba can also be made a day ahead.

ALSO PICTURED: MINI GRILLED CHEESE (PAGE 162)

SERVES 8

Mini Grilled Cheese

1 loaf rye bread, sliced

⅓ cup (75 mL) extra virgin olive oil

¼ cup (50 mL) Dijon mustard

¼ lb (125 g) Gruyère cheese, sliced

¼ lb (125 g) Gouda cheese, sliced

Fresh rosemary

There are three tricks to making the world's best grilled cheese sandwich (other than using good cheese). The first is the bread. If you can find it, use white rye, but make sure to get a square loaf. The second trick is the rosemary. It infuses flavor though the sandwich when it cooks. The third trick is a little hit of Dijon mustard, for some sophistication. Your guests will think they've gone to diner heaven.

To make a single grilled cheese sandwich brush 1 side of 2 slices of bread with olive oil to form the outside top and bottom of each sandwich. Spread the Dijon mustard over the inside of the slices and layer a slice of each cheese on top. Close the sandwich and trim off the crusts. Stick 4 small sprigs of rosemary in the center of each quarter of the sandwich (avoid thick stalks). Grill the sandwich on an electric grill or in a large frying pan over medium-high heat for 3–5 minutes per side, or until golden.

Remove from the heat, cool for 1–2 minutes and cut into 4 mini-sandwiches, using the rosemary sprigs as guides. Stack on a serving plate and garnish with a sprig of rosemary. Repeat to make as many sandwiches as you need.

I SPENT 90 PERCENT OF MY MONEY ON WOMEN AND DRINK. THE REST I WASTED.

George Best

SERVES 8

Herb-Roasted Poutine with Applewood Smoked Cheddar

2 lb (1 kg) mini red potatoes
¼ cup (50 mL) olive oil
1 tsp (5 mL) dried rosemary
1 tsp (5 mL) dried thyme
½ tsp (2 mL) garlic powder
¼ cup (50 mL) butter, softened
3 Tbsp (45 mL) corn starch
½ cup (125 mL) minced cremini mushrooms
2¼ cups (550 mL) beef stock
¼ cup (50 mL) port
Salt
Freshly ground black pepper
½ lb (250 g) Applewood Smoked Cheddar, crumbled

Poutine is a national comfort food and at least three towns in Quebec claim to be its original source. We've traded the french fries for herb roasted mini-potatoes and given the gravy an elegant twist with some port. While the origin of poutine is steeped in controversy, there'll be no controversy in the minds of your guests when you feed them this new classic.

Preheat oven to 450°F (230°C). Line a baking sheet with parchment paper.

In a large stockpot bring 6 cups (1.5 L) of salted water to a boil over high heat. Add the potatoes and cook on high for 8–10 minutes.

Remove from the heat, drain the potatoes then return the potatoes to the pot and fill it with cold water. Once the potatoes are cool enough to handle, drain them in a colander and allow them to dry completely. With a sharp knife, quarter the potatoes into mini-wedges and transfer to a large mixing bowl. Toss the potatoes in the olive oil then add the rosemary, thyme and garlic powder. Toss vigorously.

Pour the potatoes out onto the prepared baking sheet in a single layer, cut side down.

Roast for 25 minutes, or until the underside is golden, then turn the potatoes and roast them for another 15–20 minutes. Remove from the oven and season generously with salt and pepper.

To make the gravy, combine the butter and cornstarch in a small bowl. Transfer the butter mixture to a large saucepan, add the mushrooms and cook over medium-high heat until slightly browned, about 5–7 minutes. Slowly add the beef stock a little at a time, stirring constantly and bringing the gravy up to a rolling boil before adding more stock. Add the port and continue to cook, stirring constantly until the gravy thickens and coats the back of a spoon, about 5–7 minutes. Maintain on low heat, and season to taste with salt and pepper.

To assemble the poutine, use a rectangular strip of parchment paper about 6 inches (15 cm) wide to form a paper cone and fasten it with a toothpick. Place the cone in a highball glass and fill half-full with roasted potatoes. Add 1 Tbsp (15 mL) of cheese, then more potatoes and top with an additional 1 Tbsp (15 mL) of cheese. Pour over 3–4 Tbsp (45–60 mL) gravy. Top with freshly ground black pepper and serve.

SERVES 8

Pancetta-Wrapped Meatloaf with Cognac Red Currant Glaze

- 2 Tbsp (30 mL) sesame oil
- 1 large onion, chopped
- 3 cloves garlic, minced
- 3 slices whole wheat bread, shredded
- 1 large egg
- ½ cup (125 mL) sour cream
- ½ tsp (2 mL) dried thyme
- ½ tsp (2 mL) freshly ground black pepper
- 2 lb (1 kg) lean ground beef
- 1 beef bouillon cube, crushed
- 1 tsp (2 mL) Worcestershire sauce
- ¼ cup (50 mL) Jägermeister
- ¼ lb (125 g) round pancetta slices
- ½ cup (125 mL) red currant jelly
- ¼ cup (50 mL) cognac

We've classed this old girl up by draping her in thin pancetta slices. It's a trick we learned from our heroes, the Two Fat Ladies, who lived by the credo "wrap it in streaky bacon." We also topped this diner classic with a boozy-berry sauce. We guarantee you'll be digging in the fridge for this during a late-night raid.

Preheat oven to 350°F (180°C).

Heat the sesame oil in a large frying pan over medium-high heat, and sauté the onion until translucent. Add the garlic and continue cooking for an additional 3–4 minutes, or until the onions are lightly browned. Remove from the heat and set aside.

Pulse together the bread, egg, sour cream, thyme and black pepper in a food processor or in a large bowl with a fork. Set aside.

In a large bowl combine the beef, bouillon cube, Worcestershire and Jägermeister. Add the onion mixture and wet ingredients and mix well.

Line the inside of an 8½- × 4½-inch (1.5 L) loaf pan with pancetta slices and fill with the meat mixture. Bake for about 1 hour, drain any excess liquid and cook for another 15–20 minutes, or until the center temperature reaches 140°F (60°C) on a meat thermometer. Remove from the oven, drain and tent with aluminum foil for 10–15 minutes.

Meanwhile, melt the jelly in a small saucepan over medium heat. Add the cognac and bring just to a boil. Remove from the heat and set aside.

Cut the meatloaf flat using the top edge of the loaf pan as a guide. Cover the pan with a large plate or cutting board and invert to turn the meatloaf out. Brush liberally with the red currant glaze and serve sliced on a platter with the remaining glaze on the side.

SERVES 8

Rum Baba

Cake

1¾ cups (425 mL) cake-and-pastry flour

2 Tbsp (30 mL) granulated sugar

1½ Tbsp (22 mL) instant yeast

2 eggs

⅔ cup (150 mL) milk

¼ cup (50 mL) melted butter

2 Tbsp (30 mL) dark rum

1½ Tbsp (22 mL) grated orange zest

Syrup

1 cup (250 mL) granulated sugar

⅓ cup (75 mL) Cointreau or triple sec

⅓ cup (75 mL) dark rum

1 tsp (5 mL) vanilla extract

Glaze

½ cup (125 mL) apple jelly

2 Tbsp (30 mL) Goldschläger

Garnish

⅓ cup (75 mL) chopped dried cranberries (optional)

1 cup (250 mL) whipping cream (optional)

A rum baba or Baba au Rhum was a traditional Polish dish made popular by the French. Baba *means "dizzy," and with the soak this cake takes, you might be a little baba, too. The boozy syrup makes this cake deliciously moist, a cooking technique we think should be used more often—perhaps to quell insolent children.*

Make sure all your ingredients are at room temperature—this helps the rising process.

Grease a Bundt pan, or seek out a nonstick one.

For the cake, sift together the flour, sugar and yeast in a large bowl and make a well in the center. Add the eggs, milk, butter and rum to the well and beat with an electric mixer for 5 minutes, or until the batter is smooth. Stir in the orange zest. Pour the batter into the Bundt pan, cover with a damp cloth and set in a warm place to rise for about 1 hour, or until doubled in size.

Preheat oven to 375°F (190°C).

Bake the cake for about 45 minutes, or until a toothpick inserted into the center comes out clean.

Meanwhile, make the syrup. Heat the sugar, Cointreau, rum and vanilla in a small saucepan, stirring to dissolve the sugar. Remove from the heat and cool for 5 minutes.

Remove the cake from the oven and allow to cool in the pan for about 10 minutes before turning it out onto a serving platter or plate. Slowly and evenly drizzle the syrup onto the cake, allowing it to be fully absorbed.

Combine the apple jelly and Goldschläger in a small saucepan over low heat and stir until it becomes a liquid. Remove from the heat and allow to thicken slightly. Using a pastry brush, glaze the cake to give it an even luster.

Slice and serve with dried cranberries and whipped cream, if desired.

CHAPTER 4

Excuses for Booze

WORK IS THE CURSE OF
THE DRINKING CLASSES.

Oscar Wilde

SERVES 6

Breakfast at Wimbledon

Menu

Strawberries with Amarula Cream

Apricot-Stuffed French Toast

Sticky Breakfast Bangers

Refreshing Watermelon and Mint Skewers

One of the great things about Wimbledon is that it's an international event—meaning you can create your party around the players' countries of origin. The brunch menu below borrows its inspiration from two rival nations—Britain and France. Let the games begin.

Wine Pairing

Champagne or sparkling wine is most suitable for this event as it sets the appropriate tone but also brings out the flavor of the strawberries and watermelon. The main course is best paired with the Cucumber Lemonade.

Setting the Mood

Even though the rules on the court have changed, donning your tennis whites (and that goes for your linens, as well) is always in style. A crisp, white tablecloth, pressed linen napkins and ivory dishes set an appropriate standard worthy of the monarch. Break up the monotony with flowers and glassware in the game's official colors of green and purple.

Keep the music to a minimum or you might rattle the attentions of any die-hard tennis fans.

Serving Suggestion

Break out the gold- and silver-plated platters. What? No precious metals in your hutch? In that case gold- or silver-colored chargers (those big decorative plates that go under dinner plates) will suffice, as they play off the grandeur of the Wimbledon trophies.

CUCUMBER LEMONADE

This refreshing twist on lemonade is so wonderful you'll find yourself making it regularly during the dog days of summer. And (are we really admitting this?) it's equally delicious without the gin.

⅔ cup (150 mL) freshly squeezed lemon juice

¼ cup (50 mL) granulated sugar

6 cups (1.5 L) water

½ English cucumber, sliced

1 oz gin

Stir together the lemon juice, sugar and water in a large pitcher until the sugar dissolves. Add the cucumber slices and refrigerate until needed. Add gin to ice-filled collins glasses, top with the lemonade and garnish with a cucumber slice.

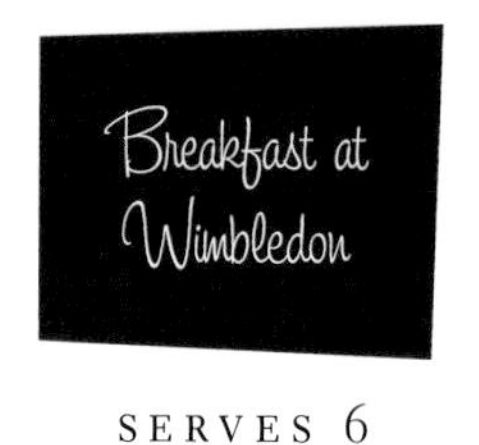

SERVES 6

STRAWBERRIES WITH AMARULA CREAM

6 cups (1.5 L) fresh strawberries
1 cup (250 mL) heavy (35%) cream
3 Tbsp (45 mL) Amarula
1 Tbsp (15 mL) confectioner's sugar

Traditional tennis fare taken to the next level. Amarula is a cream liqueur made from the African marula fruit, which is favored by elephants. Its sweet and rich flavor is wonderful with fresh strawberries. Try it once and you'll remember it forever.

Rinse the strawberries under cold water and pat them dry with paper towels.

Combine the cream, Amarula and sugar in a medium bowl and beat with an electric mixer until very soft peaks form. Spoon the cream into serving dishes and arrange the strawberries all around. Dip and enjoy.

YOU'RE NOT DRUNK IF YOU CAN LIE ON THE FLOOR WITHOUT HOLDING ON.

George Best

ALSO PICTURED: APRICOT-STUFFED FRENCH TOAST (PAGE 173)

SERVES 6

Apricot-Stuffed French Toast

- 8 oz (250 g) package cream cheese, softened
- ½ cup (125 mL) apricot preserves
- 1 Tbsp (15 mL) Grand Marnier or Cointreau
- ½ tsp (2 mL) ground nutmeg
- six 2-inch (5 cm) thick slices French bread
- 3 eggs
- ⅔ cup (150 mL) milk
- 2 tsp (10 mL) vanilla extract
- ¼ cup (50 mL) butter, divided in 2
- 2 cups (500 mL) sliced fresh apricots, optional

Raspberries, blueberries, strawberries, or any other fruit you can think of, can be substituted if apricots aren't your thing—their fuzzy wee skins, hard stones and sweet disposition can be very offensive, we know.

Preheat oven to 200°F (95°C).

Beat the cream cheese, preserves, Grand Marnier and nutmeg together in a medium bowl until smooth. Cut a pocket into each slice of bread by making an incision along the edge and cutting into the slice without going all the way through. Divide the cream cheese mixture evenly between the bread slices and spoon into the pockets. Set aside.

Meanwhile, whisk together the eggs, milk and vanilla in a clean bowl until just blended. Dip each sandwich into this egg mixture, turning to coat but without soaking it through.

Melt half the butter in a large frying pan over medium heat. Cook half the sandwiches until golden, about 2 minutes per side. Place on an ovenproof platter and keep warm in the oven. Repeat with the remaining sandwiches. Top each serving with sliced apricots (if using) and serve with pure maple syrup.

ALSO PICTURED: STICKY BREAKFAST BANGERS (PAGE 174)

SERVES 6

Sticky Breakfast Bangers

1½ lb (750 g) breakfast sausages (about 18)

⅓ cup (75 mL) pure maple syrup

3 Tbsp (45 mL) Canadian whisky

Adapted from our Sticky Bacon recipe from Cooking with Booze, *this sweet-meat treat is our new favorite. No, you're our new favorite. Yes, you are. Really.*

Cook the sausages in a large frying pan over medium heat until browned on all sides. Pour off the fat and reduce the heat to medium-low. Add the maple syrup and whisky and cook until the liquid thickens, about 1 minute. Cover and keep warm until ready to serve.

MARRIAGE IS LIKE WINE. IT IS NOT TO BE PROPERLY JUDGED UNTIL THE SECOND GLASS.

Douglas William Jerrold

SERVES 6

Refreshing Watermelon and Mint Skewers

½ seedless watermelon
2 Tbsp (30 mL) chopped fresh mint
¼ cup (50 mL) vodka
2 Tbsp (30 mL) Grand Marnier
24 bamboo skewers

This is ideal after a hot game on the courts, or if you've worked up a sweat during the final moments of any Grand Slam.

Cut the watermelon into 1-inch (2.5 cm) slices and remove the rind. Chop the slices into cubes and place them in a large bowl. Toss with the mint then pour over the vodka and Grand Marnier. Place about 4 pieces of watermelon onto each skewer and arrange on a serving platter. Pour the boozy mixture from the bottom of the bowl overtop the skewers and serve.

NOTE: These skewers can be refrigerated for up to 4 hours.

SERVES 8

Menu

Crispy Parmesan and Rosemary Crackers

Apricot and Jalapeño Preserves

Caramelized Pear and Onion Pastries

Spiced Plum Galette with Whipped Ricotta and Red Wine Jus

Cheese, Please

NIAGARA GOLD

We first created this cocktail with icewine and sparkling wine from Ontario and so the name was appropriate. It's doubly suited for this party as it's also the name of an amazing wash-rind cheese from the Upper Canada Cheese Co. Crazy, eh?

¼ oz icewine

4 oz sparkling wine

Pour the icewine into the bottom of a champagne flute and top with sparkling wine.

DID YA KNOW?

If you're lactose intolerant, goat and sheep's milk cheese are easier to digest than cow's milk cheeses.

Knowing how to assemble a great cheese platter isn't complicated but there are a few things that will help you pull off your next wine and cheese party with gracious ease—and no, we're not talking about Valium and hired help. Not this time, anyway.

Wine Pairing

This depends on the cheese you use. See Jeez Curds! on page 179.

Setting the Mood

Wine and cheese call out for jazz, lounge or upbeat ambient. Your guests will be mingling and milling about so you want to spin tunes that add a little rhythm to their movements. *Frequent Flyer*, *Hotel Costes* and the *Buddha Bar* series all fit the bill nicely with cool Latin and World sounds.

Serving Suggestion

Unwrap your cheese at least 1 hour before serving, allowing it to come to room temperature. This will unleash more flavor and will especially help the texture of soft and semisoft cheeses.

Use a cake stand to display your cheese or stack two different sizes together for added drama. Place the tiered stand on your table with low bowls, plates and other serving dishes to add interest to the table. Adorn each cheese with a name tag to help your guests make what's going to be a very tough decision.

Wineglass charms are a good idea to help your guests keep track of their glasses. Cocktail plates and graphic print napkins will round out your dinnerware needs.

PARTY PLANNER

How Much Is Too Much?

You'll need about ½ lb (250 g) of cheese per person—a little less, a little more, depending on appetites. If you plan to serve a cheese course as part of a dinner party you'll need much less, about 2 oz (65 g) for each guest.

Odd Couple

For some reason things always look better in odd numbers (unless you're a symmetry freak) so display either three or five different types of cheese and be sure to vary them in terms of flavor (mild to pungent), texture (hard to soft) and milk variety (cow, sheep or goat). This will keep your guests' taste buds alert and will make for an interesting sampling.

Eat the Rind

Unless it's wax (used on cheeses like Gouda, for example) you can eat it. Really. The rind is produced naturally, or with a little help from the cheese maker, but it's generally just a firmer and dryer outer portion of the cheese itself. Much of the flavor is concentrated in the rind so don't cut around it, eat it.

Who Cut the Cheese?

I did, I did! Unless you're serving small amounts of cheese as a pre- or post-dinner course, it's a good idea to cut all the cheeses in half when building your platter. This way you can replenish your cheese spread halfway through the evening, thus sprucing it up and making it look attractive again for your guests. It's also a good way to cut down on waste as you can determine what needs to be replenished and what doesn't. You'll also know for next time what was a hit and what was a miss.

Side Sister

Fresh slices of baguette and water crackers are always welcome on a cheese platter, but don't stop there. Artisanal flatbreads, olives, fruit chutneys or preserves, berries and shards of dark chocolate are also wonderful additions. Of course, apples, pears and grapes are also much-loved veterans of the cheese plate. Avoid citrus fruit because the high acid content tends to overpower the wine—and really, what's cheese without wine?

JEEZ CURDS!

Lucky us! We have friends like Gurth Pretty, author of *The Definitive Guide to Canadian Artisanal and Fine Cheese*. His book is not only a romp across Canada's cheese country but is also a much-needed source of answers to many of our cheese-related questions. Here's a very condensed list of terms to help you shop — complete with wine recommendations.

CHEESE TYPE	EXAMPLE	WINE PAIRING
FRESH CHEESE All cheese begins this way — young, full of moisture and subtly flavored.	• Cream cheese, ricotta, etc.	Serve with dry sparkling wines or light-bodied whites such as Riesling or Pinot Grigio.
SOFT CHEESE Fresh curds are placed into molds and their moisture naturally drained.	• Brie, chèvre, etc.	Try these with dry white wines that have low acidity, like Chardonnay or Pinot Blanc.
SEMISOFT A few sub categories here depending on how it's ripened: unripened, interior ripened and surface ripened.		
UNRIPENED — cheese is cut and stretched after draining.	• Bocconcini, mozzarella, etc.	Pair these with full-flavored whites like oaked Chardonnays or light-bodied reds like Gamay and Pinot Noir. All these wines work well with these more strongly flavored cheeses.
INTERIOR RIPENED — curds are pressed, cooked and then ripened.	• Monterey Jack, Casata, etc.	
SURFACE RIPENED — cheese is turned, washed and aged in cold rooms. Ripening occurs from the surface to the center.	• Oka, Limburger, etc.	
FIRM Fresh curds are drained and heavily pressed to remove more moisture. Some may be cooked.	• Provolone, cheddar, Gouda, etc.	Serve these fuller-flavored cheeses with more flavorful red wines such as Merlot or Cabernet Sauvignon blends.
HARD Cooked and pressed cheese, usually strong flavored.	• Parmesan, Romano, etc.	Serve with stronger wines still. Try Valpolicella or Shiraz.
BLUE Cheese is injected with a bacterial culture, such as *Penicillium roquefortii*, either on the rind or inside the cheese to produce veining or surface mold.	• Gorgonzola, Stilton, etc.	These cheeses call out for sweet, high-alcohol wines to put them in their place. Try Madeira, icewine, port or sherry.

MAKES 32 CRACKERS

Crispy Parmesan and Rosemary Crackers

8 oz (250 g) fresh Parmesan cheese, grated

1 Tbsp + 1 tsp (20 mL) finely chopped fresh rosemary

These are always a big hit, as they provide a cheesy platform for piling on even more cheese. They could probably be topped with other things as well, such as pâté or preserves.

Preheat oven to 350°F (180°C). Line a large baking sheet with parchment paper or a silicone mat.

Spoon 1 Tbsp (15 mL) of the cheese into a 1-inch (2.5 cm) circle. Repeat until the sheet is full, leaving 1 inch (2.5 cm) between each cracker. Sprinkle each cracker with a pinch of rosemary and bake for 3–5 minutes, or until bubbling and golden. Cool completely before removing.

ALSO PICTURED: APRICOT AND JALAPEÑO PRESERVES (PAGE 182)
CARAMELIZED PEAR AND ONION PASTRIES (PAGE 183)

SERVES 8

Apricot and Jalapeño Preserves

1 cup (250 mL) finely chopped dried apricots

1 jalapeño pepper, finely diced

1 star anise

⅓ cup (75 mL) granulated sugar

1-inch (2.5 cm) piece ginger, peeled

1 cup (250 mL) white wine vinegar

½ cup (125 mL) triple sec

For a bigger hit of spice, use the flesh and *seeds of the jalapeño pepper.*

Combine the apricots, jalapeño, star anise, sugar, ginger, vinegar and triple sec in a small saucepan and bring to a boil, stirring to dissolve the sugar. Reduce the heat and simmer for 20 minutes until the mixture thickens (the preserves will continue to thicken as they cool). Discard the ginger and star anise. Cool before serving with cheese.

Any leftovers can be stored in the refrigerator for up to 3 months.

FROM WINE WHAT SUDDEN FRIENDSHIP SPRINGS!

John Gay

SERVES 8

CARAMELIZED PEAR AND ONION PASTRIES

2 Tbsp (30 mL) butter

1 Spanish or Vidalia onion, thinly sliced

1 medium-sized pear, peeled, cored and finely chopped

½ tsp (2 mL) salt

¼ cup (50 mL) Calvados or brandy

1 sheet (½ lb/250 g) frozen puff pastry, thawed

4 oz (125 g) smoked cheddar cheese, crumbled

1 Tbsp (15 mL) chopped fresh thyme

Smoked cheddar is superb on a cheese platter but is also wonderful for cooking, adding a deep and rich flavor to the accompanying dish. You can use other smoked cheeses like Gouda in this recipe, though many are processed and contain lots of filler ingredients like emulsifiers and extra salt.

Melt the butter in a medium-sized nonstick frying pan over medium heat. Add the onion and cook until translucent, about 10 minutes. Reduce the heat to medium-low, cover and cook until golden in color, stirring occasionally, about 10 minutes. Add the pear and salt, stirring to combine. Increase the heat to medium and cook for 5 minutes. Add the Calvados and continue cooking until almost all the liquid has evaporated. Remove from the heat and set aside.

Preheat oven to 400°F (200°C).

Unfold the pastry sheet on a lightly floured surface. Roll the sheet into a 12-inch (30 cm) square. Cut the sheet in half, then cut each half lengthwise into 2 long strips. Cut each strip into eight 1- × 3-inch (2.5 cm × 8 cm) rectangles. Gently press your thumb into the center of each rectangle to make a small indentation.

Spoon the onion mixture into the cavities and sprinkle with a couple of pieces of smoked cheddar and some fresh thyme. Bake for 15 minutes, or until golden. Serve warm.

SERVES 8

Spiced Plum Galette with Whipped Ricotta and Red Wine Jus

Filling

1 cup (250 mL) Cabernet Sauvignon or Zinfandel

¾ cup (175 mL) granulated sugar

½ vanilla bean

3-inch (8 cm) piece orange peel

5 green cardamom pods

7 cups (1.75 L) sliced black or red plums

⅓ cup (75 mL) crushed gingersnap cookies

3 Tbsp + 1 tsp (50 mL) cornstarch

Pastry

2½ cups (625 mL) all-purpose flour

2 Tbsp (30 mL) granulated sugar

¼ tsp (1 mL) salt

¾ cup (175 mL) cold butter

¾ cup (175 mL) ice water

1 egg

Whipped Ricotta

2 cups (500 mL) smooth ricotta cheese

⅓ cup (75 mL) confectioner's sugar

¼ cup (50 mL) heavy (35%) cream

This rustic-style pie from France is meant to look homemade and is ideal for the novice pastry maker. Soaking the plums in the red wine marinade imparts fantastic flavor and a deep, rich color.

For the filling, heat the wine and sugar together in a small saucepan until sugar dissolves. Slice the vanilla bean down the center and scrape out the seeds with the back of your knife. Add the pod and seeds to the wine mixture with the orange peel and cardamom pods. Bring the mixture to a boil, reduce the heat and simmer for 5 minutes. Remove from the heat, cool for 5 minutes then pour the wine mixture over the plums and set aside.

Make the pastry by whisking together the flour, sugar and salt in a large bowl. Cut in the butter with a pastry cutter until the mixture resembles coarse meal. Add the ice water all at once, let stand for 30 seconds then mix with a fork just until the dough comes together. Shape the dough into a disk and cover with plastic wrap. Refrigerate for at least 30 minutes or until chilled.

Preheat oven to 375°F (190°C).

Roll the dough into a 17-inch (43 cm) circle on a lightly floured piece of parchment paper then transfer it to a large baking sheet. Sprinkle the center with the crushed cookies, leaving a 4-inch (10 cm) border all around. Remove the plums from the wine mixture, reserving this for later, and toss the plums with the cornstarch. Place them on top of the cookies and fold over the edges of the pastry, leaving about a 4-inch (10 cm) opening in the center of the pie. Whisk the egg with 1 Tbsp (15 mL) water and lightly brush the pastry with this egg wash. Sprinkle with sugar and bake for 50–60 minutes or until the center is bubbly and the crust is golden. Cool on a wire rack.

While the pastry is cooling, bring the wine mixture to a boil in a small saucepan, reduce the heat and simmer until the mixture is reduced to ½ cup (125 mL). Discard the vanilla pod, orange peel and cardamom. Set aside.

For the whipped ricotta, beat together the ricotta, sugar and heavy cream in a medium bowl for 1 minute or until fluffy. Refrigerate until ready to serve.

Slice the galette and serve with a dollop of whipped ricotta and a drizzle of the reduced wine mixture.

Menu

Cashew and Tamarind Chicken Kebabs

Sweet Potato and Chickpea Curry

Lamb Tajine with Port and Cinnamon

Almond and Cardamom Baklava

SERVES 8

Smokin' Hookah Party

This Middle Eastern–inspired get-together is a great excuse to go hookah shopping, push the furniture aside and throw some pillows on the floor. After all, inviting the neighborhood busybody over for afternoon tea would be far more interesting with a four-foot hookah on the mantel, don't you think?

Wine Pairing

Try a rich and flavorful red like Ripasso or Amarone.

Setting the Mood

The focus of this party is the floor, the food and, of course, the hookah. Pick up some richly colored fabric ends from your local fabric store to help inspire a Middle Eastern feeling and wrap your existing throw pillows in bright oranges, magentas and purples. Fez hats are always a welcome treat. If your local party supply store doesn't have them, ask your neighbor the Shriner (you can spot him by his little car). Hang a beaded or a tasseled curtain at the entrance to your entertaining room. Assign one of your friends (preferably an athletic man or woman) the role of belly dancer. Ask them to collect money for a mutually acceptable charity. (This is a great way to hook them into doing it.) You may need to help them a little with their costume, which should consist of many light fabric scarves that can be removed individually without ever revealing too much.

The perfect ambience for this get-together is music you can belly dance to. Crank up the iTunes and let your fingers do the walking. Intermix this with some psychedelic hits from the 1960s and your neighbors will think you've lost it completely. Wait until they see the hookah.

Serving Suggestion

Tajines are the best way to serve both the main dishes for this party. They look cool and keep food nice and hot. If you don't have a tajine or two kicking around, large shallow bowls can also be used. The baklava will look great stacked high on a turquoise or azure platter with some additional pistachios or almonds sprinkled overtop.

ROSEWATER LEMONADE

⅓ oz Campari

1 tsp (5 mL) grenadine

½ tsp (2 mL) rosewater

6 oz lemonade

Pour the ingredients over ice in a collins glass and stir lightly. Garnish with a lemon twist.

HELLUVA HOOKAH

The hookah was originally an Indian creation derived from a hollowed-out coconut shell. While it's still popular in India, Iran launched the smoking vessel into worldwide superstardom and now hookahs can be found in chic clubs and restaurants worldwide. The true culture of the hookah is very communal and social, a time to ponder, reflect and relax.

Shisha is the tobacco blend used in hookahs. It comes in small, tightly packed medallions, which are placed directly over a hot coal that burns inside the hookah. Shisha is made from tobacco and molasses, honey or sugar, and comes in various flavors, like apple, rose and cappuccino. It's light and aromatic (unlike cigarette and cigar smoke), and is enjoyed for its flavor rather than for a buzz or high.

SERVES 8

Cashew and Tamarind Chicken Kebabs

- ⅔ lb (350 g) package pure tamarind
- ½ cup (125 mL) vegetable oil
- 3 cloves garlic, minced
- 3 Tbsp (45 mL) brown sugar, packed
- 1 Tbsp (15 mL) chili powder
- 2 tsp (10 mL) salt
- 1 tsp (5 mL) cayenne pepper
- ¼ tsp (1 mL) nutmeg
- 12 boneless skinless chicken thighs (cut into bite-sized pieces)
- ¼ cup (50 mL) cashews, crushed
- 8 bamboo skewers

Our good friend Gord has become something of a pest. Not only does he regularly invite himself over for Sunday dinner, but now he's started dictating the menu. To date, these tamarind chicken skewers are his favorite. Maybe we shouldn't encourage him.

First of all, you need to transform the tamarind into a paste. Bring 2 cups (500 mL) of water to a boil in a medium saucepan over medium-high heat. Add the tamarind, reduce the heat to medium-low and simmer for 15 minutes. Using the end of a wooden spoon, or stiff rubber spatula break apart the tamarind as much as possible. Continue to simmer for another 10 minutes. Remove from the heat, mash thoroughly with a potato masher and strain through a sieve. Set aside to cool.

To prepare the marinade, combine 1 cup (250 mL) of the tamarind paste, oil, garlic, sugar, chili powder, salt, cayenne and nutmeg in a large bowl, add the chicken and stir to coat thoroughly. Transfer to a large resealable plastic freezer bag and allow to marinate for at least 3–4 hours.

Soak the bamboo skewers in water for at least 20 minutes.

Preheat grill to medium-high.

To prepare the kebabs, evenly distribute the marinated chicken onto the 8 skewers. Grill over direct heat for about 8 minutes, turning every 2 minutes. Remove from the heat, tent in aluminum foil and rest for 5 minutes. Serve with crushed cashews sprinkled overtop.

THE 'IN' ON TAMARIND

You may not be familiar with tamarind, but you've undoubtedly tasted it more than you think. This exotic pulp is derived from the seed pod of the tamarind tree found in India, the Middle East and most tropical countries. Tamarind imparts a slightly sour flavor with citrus notes as well as a caramel undertone. It is one of the key ingredients in Phad Thai, as well as being used to flavor steak sauce, chutney and even cola. Pure tamarind is generally sold in a hard, concentrated paste that resembles a small block. You can look for it in the exotic spice aisle of your superstore and if you can't find it there, any Caribbean or Indian grocery should carry it.

SERVES 8

Sweet Potato and Chickpea Curry

Sweet Potato Stock

2 Tbsp (30 mL) olive oil
1 Spanish onion, chopped
3 sweet potatoes, peeled and cubed
1 jalapeño pepper, minced
8 cups (2 L) vegetable stock
1½ Tbsp (22 mL) tomato paste
1 Tbsp (15 mL) salt

Curry

2 Tbsp (30 mL) butter
1 Tbsp (15 mL) olive oil
3 shallots, minced
½ Tbsp (7 mL) coriander seeds, whole
1½ Tbsp (22 mL) coriander seeds, crushed
1 Tbsp (15 mL) black mustard seeds
2 Tbsp (30 mL) ground cumin
⅓ cup (75 mL) sweet vermouth
two 19 oz (540 mL) cans chickpeas, rinsed
3 Tbsp (45 mL) grated fresh ginger
6 green onions, sliced

Our vegetarian friends are all girls, and unfortunately at least one of them has a black belt in karate. We were told it would be in our best interest to have some vegetarian dishes in this book. We would like to take this opportunity to formally apologize to the vegetarian community for making comments like "if God had wanted us to be vegetarians, he wouldn't have made animals out of meat." This was clearly insensitive. We present this dish as a peace offering for everyone to enjoy.

For the sweet potato stock, heat the oil in a large stockpot over medium-high heat. Add the onion and sauté until it becomes translucent, about 5–8 minutes. Add the sweet potatoes, jalapeño, stock, tomato paste and salt and bring to a boil. Reduce the heat to medium-low and simmer uncovered for 1 hour. Purée this mixture using a handheld immersion blender or work in batches with a regular blender. Cover and keep on low heat, just below a simmer.

Meanwhile, to make the curry, melt the butter in a medium frying pan over medium-high heat. Add the olive oil and shallots and sauté until the shallots are slightly golden. Add the coriander seeds (whole and crushed), mustard seeds and cumin and cook until for about 5–6 minutes. Stir in the vermouth and transfer this into the sweet potato stock. Add the chickpeas and ginger and bring to a gentle simmer. Cover the pot and cook for about 30–45 minutes. Garnish with the green onions and serve.

SERVES 8

LAMB TAJINE WITH PORT AND CINNAMON

1 Tbsp (15 mL) cumin
1 Tbsp (15 mL) turmeric
1 Tbsp (15 mL) cinnamon
1 tsp (5 mL) green cardamom seeds
1 tsp (5 mL) ground ginger
1 tsp (5 mL) cayenne
¼ cup (50 mL) vegetable oil
5 cloves garlic, minced
4 large carrots, sliced
2 onions, diced
2 lb (1 kg) lamb, cubed
1 cup (250 mL) dried figs, chopped
1½ cups (375 mL) port
1 Tbsp (15 mL) miso paste (or 1 Tbsp/15 mL soy sauce + 1 tsp/5 mL Worcestershire sauce)
1 Tbsp (15 mL) salt (or to taste)
1 Tbsp (15 mL) freshly ground black pepper
1 cup (250 mL) loosely chopped cilantro
¾ cup (175 mL) chopped cashews

A tajine *is the name for both a North African meal and the dish it's cooked in. Tajines are the original slow cooker and have a trademark conical lid that allows evaporated water to condense, run down the side and back into the dish. If you don't have a tajine, go get one. Its shape will mystify your guests and makes for great presentation and conversation. If you're light on cupboard space a slow cooker, stockpot or Dutch oven will also work.*

Using a mortar and pestle or a spice grinder, blend the cumin, turmeric, cinnamon, cardamom, ginger and cayenne. In a large pot (or stovetop tajine) heat the oil over medium-high heat. Sauté the garlic, carrots and onions until the onions become translucent. Add the spice blend and cook for 1–2 minutes until the aromas are released. Add the lamb, figs, port and miso paste. Cover the tajine, reduce the heat to low and simmer for 3–4 hours. Add the salt and black pepper. Remove from the heat and stir in ½ cup (125 mL) cilantro. Serve in a large bowl garnished with the remaining cilantro and cashews.

SERVES 8

Almond and Cardamom Baklava

Filling

2 cups (500 mL) slivered almonds, lightly toasted and chopped

2 cups (500 mL) unsalted pistachios, chopped

1 tsp (5 mL) ground green cardamom

¼ cup (50 mL) brown sugar, packed

1 tsp (5 mL) ground cinnamon

Pastry

24 sheets phyllo pastry

½ cup (125 mL) butter, melted

Syrup

2 cups (500 mL) granulated sugar

1 cup (250 mL) honey

¼ cup (50 mL) amaretto

1 Tbsp (15 mL) lemon juice

1 tsp (5 mL) grated orange zest

Topping

¼ cup (50 mL) slivered almonds, toasted

If you've ever wandered (or staggered) into a late night Middle Eastern takeout joint, you've likely seen the overwhelming assortment of baklava piled high on platters and under cake domes. There's no substitute for its crisp layered pastry, sweet-honey varnish and green pistachio filling. This is your time to create the same awe-inspiring effect. It's really not difficult and this recipe makes a pile—guaranteeing your guests will think you were a pastry chef in a past life. Takeout boxes recommended.

Preheat oven to 325°F (160°C). Line a baking sheet with parchment paper.

For the filling, in a large bowl combine the almonds, pistachios, cardamom, brown sugar and cinnamon. Set aside.

To prepare the pastry, place 1 sheet of phyllo on the prepared baking sheet, keeping the remaining phyllo covered with a damp towel. Brush the phyllo lightly with melted butter, top with a second sheet of phyllo and lightly brush this sheet with butter, too. Repeat this process with 5 more sheets of phyllo.

Top this stack with half the nut mixture, then layer with 3 sheets of phyllo, each brushed with melted butter. Top with the remaining nut mixture and an additional 6 sheets of phyllo, each brushed with butter. Using a large pastry wheel, pizza cutter or large knife, cut the baklava in half lengthwise and into 3 strips widthwise to form 6 large squares. Cut each square on the diagonal to form triangles. Lightly sprinkle the top of the pastry with water to prevent curling and bake for 35–40 minutes. Meanwhile, prepare the syrup.

For the syrup, heat 1¼ cups (300 mL) of water in a medium-sized saucepan over medium-high heat. Combine the sugar, honey, amaretto, lemon juice and orange zest, cook, stirring constantly, until the mixture foams up and becomes syrupy, about 10 minutes. Reduce the heat to low, stirring occasionally if sugar crystals form. Remove from the heat and spoon syrup over the hot pastries. Allow to cool.

Garnish with the slivered almonds and allow to rest for about 4 hours at room temperature before serving.

SERVES 8

Menu

Wishing Trees with Strawberry Sambuca Vinaigrette

Pecan-Crusted Chicken with White Wine and Maple Reduction

Carrot and Goat Cheese Mash

Pear Tarte Tatin

Bookworms and Booze

A friend of the Cooking with Booze *team told us that her "book club" was really just an excuse to get away from her husband and kids. She also told us that the wine consumed during the evening usually took precedence over the literature being discussed. If any of this sounds familiar, read on.*

Wine Pairing

An off-dry Riesling—one with a bit of residual sugar—is an ideal match for the chicken dish (especially if you use the same wine as you cook with). For red, choose a light and fruity Cabernet Franc, Pinot Noir or Gamay (a.k.a. Beaujolais).

Setting the Mood

Dim lighting creates instant warmth, though in this case it probably doesn't provide enough light for discussing fine works of literature. Unless you're reading direct passages from certain chapters, though, you can certainly get away with softer lighting than your local library uses.

Keep things casual by rolling silverware in decorative paper napkins and presenting everything on serving platters so guests can dish out their own dinner.

Instrumental jazz is most appropriate for such a cerebral event as this, though you'll want to keep the volume at a minimum so as to not interfere with the dynamic literary theories being thrown around. Chick Corea and the Wayne Shorter Quartet make wonderfully inspiring music perfect for lively debates.

Serving Suggestion

Haul out your hardcover collection to create a lively buffet table by stacking volumes next to, or under, your prepared dishes. Tasseled bookmarks make great food labels and mini versions can be used as wine glass identifiers. Assign this craft to the kids while you prepare the meal.

MAYAN COFFEE

You can begin the evening with this drink or serve it with dessert, where it's best suited. We're best suited to a lifestyle of private jets and vintage champagne, though you're more likely to find us on the subway drinking out of brown paper bags.

1 oz Kahlúa

½ oz Goldschläger

Freshly brewed coffee

Whipped cream

Cinnamon

Combine the Kahlúa and Goldschläger in a specialty coffee glass and top with hot coffee. Finish with a dollop of whipped cream and sprinkling of cinnamon, if desired.

WINE MATCHING 101

Always drink a wine that's sweeter than the food it's paired with. For this menu the wine and maple marinade add ample sugar to the chicken so it calls for something with a residual sugar level of at least (1).

SERVES 8

Wishing Trees with Strawberry Sambuca Vinaigrette

½ cup (125 mL) fresh or frozen strawberries, washed, dried and hulled

¼ cup (50 mL) extra virgin olive oil

2 Tbsp (30 mL) sambuca

2 Tbsp (30 mL) balsamic vinegar

1 Tbsp (15 mL) Dijon mustard

1 Tbsp (15 mL) honey

½ tsp (2 mL) salt

½ tsp (2 mL) freshly ground black pepper

1 English cucumber

8 cups (2 L) mixed salad greens, washed and dried

2 cups (500 mL) snow peas, trimmed

¾ cup (175 mL) thinly sliced radish

A simply impressive salad, especially when dressed in our favorite flavor combo—strawberries and sambuca—something the Brontë sisters would have enjoyed, we're sure.

Purée the strawberries, olive oil, sambuca, vinegar, Dijon, honey, salt and pepper in a blender or food processor until smooth.

Trim the ends off the cucumber and slice lengthwise into 8 long strips with a vegetable peeler. (If you're adept at this you might end up with half of the cucumber left over. If not, you might use all of it to get 8 nice strips.) Arrange 1 cup (250 mL) of greens along half the length of the cucumber strip and roll tightly. (Moisture from the cucumber should hold it together.) Continue with the remaining greens to make the Wishing Trees.

Arrange the Wishing Trees in the center of a large platter, toss snow peas and radish slices around the base and spoon over the vinaigrette.

I ALWAYS KEEP A SUPPLY OF STIMULANT HANDY IN CASE I SEE A SNAKE—WHICH I ALSO KEEP HANDY.

W. C. Fields

SERVES 8

Pecan-Crusted Chicken with White Wine and Maple Reduction

8 boneless, skinless chicken breasts
1 cup (250 mL) off-dry Riesling
¾ cup (175 mL) maple syrup
⅓ cup (75 mL) extra virgin olive oil
3 cloves garlic, minced
2 Tbsp (30 mL) Dijon mustard
1 tsp (5 mL) salt
½ tsp (2 mL) freshly ground black pepper
1½ cups (375 mL) finely chopped pecans
¼ cup (50 mL) chopped fresh thyme leaves

Bookworms love this recipe as it features all the elements of good character development. A bland, nondescript protagonist goes skinny-dipping in murky waters, rolls around in the sand with danger-loving hooligans, bakes all day in the sun and emerges forever changed: sweeter, slightly spicy and full of crunch.

Arrange the chicken in a single layer in a 9- × 13-inch (3.5 L) glass baking dish.

Whisk together the wine, maple syrup, olive oil, garlic, Dijon, salt and pepper. Pour over the chicken, cover and refrigerate for at least 1 hour, or overnight if possible.

Preheat oven to 375°F (190°C).

Combine the chopped pecans and thyme leaves on a plate. Remove the chicken from the marinade, reserving the marinade, and coat 1 side of the chicken in the pecan mixture. Place the chicken breasts, nut side up, on a large baking sheet and bake for 20–30 minutes, or until the juices run clear.

Meanwhile, pour the marinade through a fine mesh sieve to remove any bits of garlic, bring to a boil in a small saucepan and reduce by half. Transfer to a gravy boat.

Arrange the chicken on serving platter and let your guests help themselves to the sauce.

ALSO PICTURED: CARROT AND GOAT CHEESE MASH (PAGE 200)

SERVES 8

Carrot and Goat Cheese Mash

6 cups (1.5 L) peeled and chopped carrots
2-inch (5 cm) piece of ginger, sliced
1 Tbsp (15 mL) granulated sugar
1 tsp (5 mL) salt
¼ cup (50 mL) butter
¾ cup (175 mL) soft goat cheese

Sweet and tangy, this side dish is a superb alternative to potatoes and complements the chicken wonderfully. It's like a side of Schroeder to a somewhat crusty Sally.

Cover the carrots, ginger, sugar and salt with water in a large saucepan and bring to a boil. Reduce the heat and simmer for 20 minutes, or until the carrots are soft. Drain and remove the ginger slices.

Mash the carrots with the butter until well combined, then add the goat cheese and stir until completely incorporated. Transfer to a serving dish and keep warm until ready to serve.

WHEN I READ ABOUT THE EVILS OF DRINKING, I GAVE UP READING.

Henny Youngman

SERVES 8

Pear Tarte Tatin

6 large Bosc pears, peeled, cored and sliced into eighths

2 Tbsp (30 mL) freshly squeezed lemon juice

⅓ cup (75 mL) butter

½ cup (125 mL) brown sugar, packed

¼ tsp (1 mL) nutmeg

¼ cup (50 mL) Calvados or brandy

½ package of puff pastry dough (½ lb/250 g)

Every good book party needs to reference the classics, and since the only thing we read is raving book reviews, our classic reference has to come in the form of a recipe. Read on.

Preheat oven to 375°F (190°C).

Toss the pears in the lemon juice to prevent browning and set aside.

Melt ¼ cup (50 mL) of the butter in a medium-sized frying pan over medium-high heat until it begins to bubble. Stir in the brown sugar and cook until it begins to dissolve, about 1–2 minutes. Add the nutmeg and Calvados (the mixture should bubble up and foam). Cook for an additional minute, then remove from the heat and pour the caramel into a 9-inch (23 cm) round, nonstick cake pan. Overlap the pears in a circular pattern over the caramel in the cake pan.

Roll out the pastry on a lightly floured surface until it's large enough to cover the pan. Place the pan on top of the pastry and trim it into a circle with a sharp knife, then place the pastry on top of the pears. Melt the remaining butter and brush it over the pastry.

Place the pan on a baking sheet and bake for 25–30 minutes, or until the crust is golden. Remove from the oven and cool for 30 minutes. Place a large serving plate on top of the cake pan and invert onto the plate. Cut into wedges and serve warm.

Menu

SERVES 6

Port, Balsamic and Honey Reduction

Potatoes Lyonnaise

Crispy Duck Breasts with Sweet Balsamic Cherries

Sautéed Rapini with Pumpkin Seeds

Brandied Apple and Cheddar Crumble

Fall Harvest

ROYAL HARVEST

We created this drink for the Royal Agricultural Winter Fair and it quickly became one of our favorites. It's even packed with potassium and vitamin C to help boost the immune system for the long, cold winter ahead.

2 oz port

4 oz fresh-pressed apple juice (cider)

Cinnamon stick

Add the port and apple juice to a rocks glass filled with ice and garnish with the cinnamon stick.

NOTE: Use a ruby or late vintage port as they're less expensive than tawny and have a lovely garnet color.

Somehow the feel of crisp, fall air and the crunching sound of leaves underfoot stirs our appetites. It's a good thing Mother Nature's bounty is ready for the reaping—we'll take a pound of potatoes, a few locally raised ducks and a basket of Ontario apples. Thanks, Momma N! Douse that in some port, a dram of kirsch and just a splash of brandy and you'll have some very happy dinner guests. So happy, in fact, they may wish to spend the night.

Wine Pairing

Serve the duck with a fruity Pinot Noir—like one from Ontario or BC.

Setting the Mood

Decorating a table this time of year couldn't be easier. Take inspiration from the grocery store and even your own backyard. A natural centerpiece composed of figs and kumquats, or dried flowers and seed pods, or even a large bowl of mixed nuts in their shell will add rustic charm. Gourds can be hollowed out and used to hold tea lights, act as condiment dishes or even placecard holders.

Put away the stark white tablecloth and instead opt for cream or ochre and accent it with chocolate brown or rust-colored napkins. Paper napkins in a graphic print can add a splash of interest to the table and help keep things looking modern.

Spin Neil Young for the soundtrack, starting with 1972's *Harvest*, featuring backing vocals by Linda Ronstadt on the ethereal "Heart of Gold," then spin the 20-year follow-up, 1992's *Harvest Moon*. Linda makes another back-up appearance on this album of steel guitar and country melodies.

Serving Suggestion

Show off all your hard work by plating each serving and delivering it to each guest. Fan slices of duck breast out around a good helping of potatoes and rapini then spoon some cherries over the duck. Keep everything compact in the center of the plate and wipe any drips from the rim before serving. Then pat yourself on the back and say "aren't I fancy!?"

SERVES 6

Port, Balsamic and Honey Reduction

¼ cup (50 mL) port
¼ cup (50 mL) balsamic vinegar
2 Tbsp (30 mL) honey

Ryan's Aunt Carolyn is a fantastic cook, and she made this dip for him one Christmas. It's wonderful any time of year and is best served with a selection of hard Italian cheeses for dipping. Parmigiano Reggiano, Asiago, Romano and pecorino are all wonderful choices. Add a few stems of blanched asparagus and some fresh foccacia to complete this simply amazing appetizer.

Combine the port, vinegar and honey in a small saucepan and bring to a simmer over medium heat. Reduce the heat to low and continue cooking until the mixture reduces by one-third. Remove from the heat and cool.

I DISTRUST CAMELS, AND ANYONE ELSE WHO CAN GO A WEEK WITHOUT A DRINK.

Joe E. Lewis

SERVES 6

Potatoes Lyonnaise

6 Yukon Gold potatoes, peeled
8 strips bacon
2 Spanish onions, thinly sliced
2 Tbsp (30 mL) butter
1 Tbsp (15 mL) chopped fresh parsley or thyme
Salt
Freshly ground black pepper

Purists will have our heads for "bastardizing" this traditional dish, made originally from only four ingredients—potatoes, onion, butter and parsley. We don't mind, though, because this version is better and we defend it wholeheartedly. We also prefer thyme or rosemary instead of the parsley. Release the hounds.

Cut the potatoes into ¼-inch (5 mm) slices. Cook in a large pot of boiling water for 2 minutes then transfer to a large bowl of ice water to stop the cooking. Drain, pat dry and refrigerate.

Meanwhile, cook the bacon in a large, nonstick frying pan until crisp. Drain on paper towel, crumble and set aside.

Pour off all but 1 Tbsp (15 mL) of the bacon renderings (reserving the extra fat). Add the onions to the frying pan and sauté over medium heat until softened, about 5 minutes. Cover the frying pan, reduce the heat and cook until caramelized, about 20–25 minutes. Remove the onions from the frying pan and set aside.

Heat the reserved bacon renderings and butter in a frying pan over medium-high heat. Add the potatoes and cook until brown and crispy, turning so they cook evenly, about 20 minutes. Toss with the reserved bacon and onions until just heated through, sprinkle with parsley and season generously with salt and pepper.

NOTE: Cook the potatoes in 2 batches, using half the bacon renderings and butter for each batch if you don't have a large enough frying pan to accommodate them all at once. They'll cook faster and be easier to handle. Put the first batch of crisp potatoes in a shallow baking dish, uncovered, in the oven to keep them warm, then toss all the potatoes together with the bacon, onions, parsley, salt and pepper.

SERVES 6

Crispy Duck Breasts with Sweet Balsamic Cherries

3 large Magret or Muscovy duck breasts (about 1–1½ lb/ 500–750 g each)

1 tsp (5 mL) salt

1 cup (250 mL) Sweet Balsamic Cherries (page 149)

Freshly ground black pepper

Getting crispy skin on a duck while achieving medium-rare meat is an art form. The best method is to dry the skin until it's translucent—though this can take up to three days in the refrigerator. If you've got the time, by all means do it this way, but if you're like the rest of us and you've purchased your duck breasts the day you plan to cook them, then the technique below will give you the best results on such short notice.

Dry the duck breasts with paper towel then sprinkle the skin side with the salt. Cover and refrigerate for at least 1 hour, but preferably as long as possible—this helps expedite the drying process.

Preheat oven to 425°F (220°C).

Rinse the duck breasts with cold water to remove the salt then pat them dry with paper towel. Cut the skin in a cross-hatch pattern to prevent shrinking when cooked. Be careful not to cut into the meat.

Place the duck breasts on a rack in the sink, skin side up, and pour a kettleful of boiling water overtop. Dry with paper towel again then sprinkle with black pepper.

Heat a large, ovenproof frying pan to medium. Sear the duck breasts skin side down for 4–5 minutes, or until they turn deep brown. Turn and cook meat side down for 1–2 minutes, or until just beginning to color. Transfer to the oven and roast for 10–12 minutes, or until the skin is crisp and the meat is medium-rare. Tent with aluminum foil and let rest for 15 minutes.

Meanwhile, pour off the excess fat from the pan and place the pan over medium heat. Pour in the cherries, stirring to deglaze the pan, and simmer for 5 minutes.

Slice the breasts thinly and spoon over the cherry sauce.

SERVES 6

Sautéed Rapini with Pumpkin Seeds

½ cup (125 mL) pumpkin seeds

2 bunches rapini

2 garlic cloves, thinly sliced

1 Tbsp (15 mL) extra virgin olive oil

¼ cup (50 mL) Riesling or Sauvignon Blanc

Salt

Freshly ground black pepper

Be careful not to cook the rapini too long or it will become overly bitter and jaded, like struggling writers and out-of-work actors.

Toast the pumpkin seeds in a large frying pan over medium heat until golden and fragrant, shaking the pan frequently to prevent scorching. Remove from the pan and set aside.

Trim any large stems from the rapini and discard. Rinse with cold water and shake off the excess. Cook the garlic in the oil over medium heat until golden. Add the wine and rapini and sprinkle with salt. Cook for 5 minutes, or until tender, stirring every minute or so. Arrange on a serving platter and sprinkle with pepper and the toasted pumpkin seeds.

SERVES 6

Brandied Apple and Cheddar Crumble

- 6 medium red apples, peeled, cored and sliced
- 1 tsp (5 mL) cinnamon
- 1 tsp (5 mL) freshly grated nutmeg
- 2 Tbsp (30 mL) brandy
- ⅔ cup (150 mL) brown sugar, packed
- ½ cup (125 mL) all-purpose flour
- ½ cup (125 mL) rolled oats
- ⅓ cup (75 mL) cold butter, cut into small cubes
- ½ cup (125 mL) crumbled extra-old cheddar

We like to prepare and serve this dessert in individual ramekins but it can easily be made in a casserole dish with portions spooned out at the table. It depends on the formality of your dinner party—will your guests be dressed in black tie or plaid flannel?

Preheat oven to 375°F (190°C).

Toss the apples with the cinnamon, nutmeg and brandy and place in a 9-inch (1.5 L) round casserole dish or among six 6 oz (175 mL) ramekins.

Combine the brown sugar, flour and oats. Cut in the butter with a pastry blender or by hand until the mixture resembles coarse meal. Stir in the crumbled cheddar. Distribute this evenly over the apples and bake for 45 minutes for 1 dish, or 25 minutes for individual servings. You'll know it's done when the topping is brown and the center is bubbling. Serve warm with crème fraîche, if desired.

NOTE: If you can't find crème fraîche you can make your own by combining 1 cup (250 mL) heavy (35%) cream with ½ cup (125 mL) sour cream or 2 Tbsp (30 mL) buttermilk in a jar with a tight-fitting lid. Shake ingredients together then seal and let sit at room temperature for 24 hours or until very thick, stirring twice during that time. Refrigerate after opening.

NOTE: Crumble cheddar into small pieces by breaking it up with your fingers.

SERVES 4

Bottling BBQ: Making the Good Stuff at Home

Menu

Stone Fruit Liqueur

Caribbean Spiced Rum

Sizzling Pork Kebabs with Grilled Pineapple

Limoncello

Frozen Lemon and Vanilla Sabayon

Okay, so you'll need to plan three months in advance for this one. Gotcha! Well, not really. Bottling the good stuff takes time and to make an infused fruit liqueur we're talking at least a few months. We suggest the host gets busy about a week in advance and kickstarts the homemade limoncello—a lip-smacking liqueur made with lemons and vodka. Have it bottled and ready to go on the day of your barbecue so you can make the accompanying frozen sabayon for dessert. Spiced rum is quick to make. Simply infuse it at least one day before using and you're good to go.

The Stone Fruit Liqueur is a little more time-driven so make it a sort of adult craft project. Invite your guests over to sample the good stuff you've already made and then organize it so you have all the ingredients ready for your friends to make their own booze to take home. You might just become known as the best party host ever. Maybe.

Wine Pairing

Try the pork with a refreshing Sauvignon Blanc or a light-bodied and fruity red like an Ontario Pinot Noir.

Setting the Mood

Draw your inspiration from the spiced rum recipes and mix a playlist of reggae, Afro-Cuban beats and calypso—the perfect feel-good, high-energy music for serious work like bottling your own booze. Set up your work station with all the tools and ingredients you and your bottling partners will need, like fresh fruit, large jars or containers, knives, cutting boards, etc. Have an apron for everyone to wear and send them home with copies of the recipes so they'll be able to finish off the brewing process and bottle their own efforts in a short time.

Serving Suggestion

Source attractive bottles from specialty shops or become a packrat and start keeping fancy store-bought booze bottles for these occasions. Get crafty and make Martha-like labels from rare Japanese paper and strands of mermaid hair, or design your own booze label on your computer and print them out on labels.

SPICED RUM PUNCH

With subtle hints of cinnamon, clove, anise and other tropical spices there's more depth to this drink than you might expect. You can use store-bought spiced rum if you like, but just don't expect the same fulfilling relationship. Money can't buy the kind of depth required here.

1 cup (250 mL) Caribbean Spiced Rum (page 214)

2 cups (500 mL) orange juice

2 cups (500 mL) pineapple juice

Juice from 1 lemon, about 3 Tbsp (45 mL)

Grenadine

Combine the rum, orange juice, pineapple juice and lemon juice in a large pitcher and refrigerate until ready to use. Put a dash of grenadine into the bottom of 4 red wine glasses, fill with ice and pour in the punch. Garnish with some freshly grated nutmeg and an orange wheel, if desired.

ALSO PICTURED: SIZZLING PORK KEBABS WITH GRILLED PINEAPPLE (PAGE 215)

MAKES 1 BOTTLE

Stone Fruit Liqueur

- 2 lb (1 kg) stone fruit
- 2 cups (500 mL) granulated sugar
- 2 cups (500 mL) vodka
- ½ cup (125 mL) brandy

This recipe does not teach you how to get your booze "high." Instead, the stone in "stone fruit" refers to any type of fruit with a pit—you can use plums, peaches, cherries, apricots, etc., to create this sweet and easy sipping liqueur. Of course, you can also make this with stone-less fruit and serve it at your next pity party.

Cut the fruit in half and remove the pits. (If you're using peaches or large fruit you'll want to cut them into quarters.) Place the fruit in a large clean container with a tight-fitting lid. Sprinkle the sugar over the fruit, then pour in the vodka and brandy, stirring to dissolve the sugar. Place the container in a cool, dark place for 2 months, stirring the contents every 2 weeks.

Strain the fruit mixture through a mesh sieve, discarding the pulp. For extra clarity, you should then strain the liqueur through a few layers of cheesecloth or a coffee filter. Pour it into a clean bottle, cork and age for another month for best results. Serve straight-up or mixed with a little sparkling water.

ALWAYS DO SOBER WHAT YOU SAID YOU'D DO DRUNK. THAT WILL TEACH YOU TO KEEP YOUR MOUTH SHUT.

Ernest Hemingway

ALSO PICTURED: LIMONCELLO (PAGE 216)
CARIBBEAN SPICED RUM (PAGE 214)

MAKES 1 BOTTLE

Caribbean Spiced Rum

2 whole cloves

2 whole allspice berries

1 cinnamon stick

1 whole star anise

½ vanilla bean (optional)

one 26 oz (750 mL) bottle amber rum

Try to find a brand of rum with a built-in plastic pourer as this prevents the spices from flowing out into your drinks. Alternatively, you can wrap the spices in cheesecloth and tie it shut with a piece of butcher's twine so you can remove them after the rum is sufficiently spiced.

Drop the cloves, allspice, cinnamon stick, star anise and vanilla (if using) into the rum. You may need to break the star anise into a few pieces to get it into the bottle. Seal and infuse for at least 1 day before using.

SERVES 4

Sizzling Pork Kebabs with Grilled Pineapple

Kebabs

1½ lb (750 g) pork loin, cut into cubes

¾ cup (175 mL) Caribbean Spiced Rum (facing page)

¼ cup (50 mL) freshly squeezed orange juice

2 Tbsp (30 mL) olive oil

1 Tbsp (15 mL) chopped fresh thyme

1 Tbsp (15 mL) chopped fresh chives

1 clove garlic, minced

1 Tbsp (15 mL) orange zest

1 tsp (5 mL) salt

1 tsp (5 mL) freshly ground black pepper

4 large bamboo or metal skewers

Grilled Pineapple

1 pineapple

2 tsp (10 mL) granulated sugar

Pinch ground cinnamon

If you've never grilled pineapple and served it with meat before, watch out. It's like your first sexual tryst. No, not clumsy and disappointing—sweet and memorable. You'll find yourself doing it (grilling pineapple, that is) all the time.

For the kebabs, combine the pork, rum, orange juice, oil, thyme, chives, garlic, zest, salt and pepper in a shallow dish. Cover and marinate in the refrigerator for at least 3 hours, or overnight.

Preheat grill to medium-high.

Skewer the pork and grill for 15–20 minutes, rotating as required, until cooked through.

For the grilled pineapple, first remove the crown and bottom of the fruit. Cut lengthwise into quarters then cut out the center from each quarter to remove the core. Run the knife between the rind and fruit to separate them. Slice each quarter into 2 or 3 spears. Combine the sugar and cinnamon in a small bowl, sprinkle the spears lightly with the sugar mixture and grill for 2–3 minutes per side.

Serve with grilled corn, asparagus and a leafy green salad.

MAKES 2 BOTTLES

LIMONCELLO

8 lemons

one 26 oz (750 mL) bottle vodka

2 cups (500 mL) granulated sugar

We first tried this in Dave's mom's backyard. We were heading to a local restaurant to promote Cooking with Booze *and this delicious liqueur put us in the best of moods, so Helen generously offered up the recipe. Keep it in the fridge and serve it like Helen does: with mini ice cubes, made by filling the tray only one-third full before freezing. Moms know best.*

Peel the rind from the lemons with a sharp vegetable peeler, being careful to remove only the yellow zest. Cut the lemons in half and squeeze the juice (you'll have approximately 2 cups (500 mL) into a clean jar through a mesh sieve to catch the pulp and seeds. Seal the jar and refrigerate. Place the zest in a large bowl and pour over the vodka. Cover and place in a cool, dark place for 5 days.

Add enough water to the lemon juice to bring the total volume to 2½ cups (625 mL). Combine the water and lemon juice with the sugar in a medium saucepan over medium heat, stirring to dissolve the sugar. Remove from the stovetop and cool completely.

Remove the rind from vodka and pass the vodka through a mesh sieve to remove any lemon bits if necessary. Combine the vodka and cooled sugar mixture. Pass the final mixture through a coffee filter for extra clarity. Pour into clean bottles, cork and enjoy. Limoncello will keep for up to a year if stored in a cool, dark place.

NOTE: Insert a fork into the lemon halves and squeeze tightly to extract the most amount of juice.

SERVES 4

Frozen Lemon and Vanilla Sabayon

1 vanilla bean
or 1 tsp (5 mL) vanilla extract

¼ cup (50 mL) Limoncello (facing page)

¼ cup (50 mL) granulated sugar

5 egg yolks

Light and mousse-like, this sabayon is a delicious dessert on a hot summer night. Serve it with raspberries or almond cookies.

Slice the vanilla bean in half lengthwise then scrape out the seeds with the back of a knife.

Whisk together the vanilla seeds, Limoncello, sugar and egg yolks in a metal bowl over a pot of gently simmering water until thick and foamy, about 5 minutes. The mixture should triple in size. Adjust the heat so the mixture never becomes too hot (or the eggs may scramble) and the bowl should never touch the surface of the water.

Remove the bowl from the heat and continue whisking until cool. Spoon the sabayon into 4 serving dishes and freeze until firm, about 2 hours. Serve with mixed berries and sugar cookies, if desired.

SERVES 8

Menu

Jack Daniel's Sticky Ribs

Spicy Rum Punch Wings

Chipotle Black Bean Chili

Guinness Double Chocolate Chunk Ice Cream

Tailgate Blowout

PRE-GAME BEER BAR

Once the action starts it's "grab a cold one and pop the top," but before the game, set up a beer bar. Grab a selection of lagers, amber ales and stouts, and keep them cold in a big metal washtub filled with ice. Mixers like lime cordial, ginger ale, tomato juice—even sparkling wine (trust us!)—offer good choice for blending great beer cocktails.

Black and Tan—½ Guinness, ½ pale ale; slowly pour Guinness over the ale to form a clean layer

Black Velour—½ Guinness, ½ cider

Black Velvet—½ Guinness, ½ sparkling wine

Boilermaker—¾ pint of ale then drop a shot glass of whisky into pint (glass and all)

Lager and Lime—½ oz lime cordial, top with lager

Lager Tops — fill a pint glass almost full with lager then add a splash of 7-Up

Red Eye—¾ pale ale, ¼ tomato juice

Shandy—⅔ lager or pale ale, ⅓ ginger ale

Every good tailgate party has three important elements: cold beer, hot food and great seats to the game—or at least a big-screen plasma TV to watch it on. We must admit we're not exactly what you'd call a couple of jocks, but we do know something about fall-off-the-bone ribs and perfectly sauced wings. And beer might just go down as our favorite beverage. Whether you're hosting your bash from the back of an F150 or from the comfort of your La-Z-Boy we hope it's a "blowout" for you and your guests, and not the team you're rooting for.

Wine Pairing

Get real.

Setting the Mood

Dim lights and linen tablecloths are not gonna work for this type of bash. If you're in a parking lot you've got all the atmosphere you need. If you're at home, the TV will be the focus of attention, and you'll need to serve your guests in front of it. Set up a table with hot plates, bowls, cutlery, condiments and everything you'll need for the event. Get everything set up ahead of time so you won't be running back and forth to the kitchen and missing the game.

Forget the flowers and mood music, and instead hand out some face paint, giant foam fingers and air horns. That should rally the troops *and* please the neighbors.

Serving Suggestion

Make the ice cream the day before so it's good and firm when it comes time to serve. Likewise, the ribs and wings can be precooked, then heated and sauced right before serving. Start the chili in the morning and keep it cooking slowly all day. Have a bowl of shredded cheddar, chopped fresh cilantro, green onions and sour cream on the table and encourage your guests to garnish their own bowls.

SERVES 8

Jack Daniel's Sticky Ribs

Ribs

3 racks pork back ribs

1 Tbsp + 1 tsp (20 mL) extra virgin olive oil

1 Tbsp (15 mL) paprika

1 Tbsp (15 mL) ground cumin

1 Tbsp (15 mL) freshly ground black pepper

1 tsp (5 mL) ground cardamom

1 tsp (5 mL) salt

3 Tbsp (45 mL) Jack Daniel's

Sauce

1 cup (250 mL) chopped tomatoes

⅓ cup (75 mL) Jack Daniel's

⅓ cup (75 mL) fancy molasses

2 Tbsp (30 mL) balsamic vinegar

2 tsp (10 mL) chili powder

3 cloves garlic

1 tsp (5 mL) salt

Dash hot pepper sauce

The secret to fall-off-the-bone ribs is to cook them low and slow, and the secret to great flavorful ribs is to start with an aromatic spice rub and finish with an all-star barbecue sauce. Wouldn't ya know, the recipe to success follows?

Preheat grill to low or oven to 300°F (150°C).

Trim off any excess fat and remove the membrane from the underside of the ribs then rub them with the olive oil. Combine the paprika, cumin, pepper, cardamom and salt and rub this onto both sides of the ribs. Drizzle with the Jack Daniel's. Wrap the racks in 2 layers of aluminum foil and place on the grill, meat side up. Close the lid and cook for 1½ hours. Remove from the heat and allow to cool in the foil, about 1 hour.

Meanwhile, for the sauce, combine the tomatoes, Jack Daniel's, molasses, vinegar, chili powder, garlic, salt and hot pepper sauce in the blender or food processor and blend until smooth. Pour this mixture into a small saucepan and bring to a boil. Reduce the heat and simmer until the sauce is reduced by half. Remove from the heat and set aside.

Remove the foil from the ribs and cook on the grill over low heat with the lid open for 20–30 minutes, turning every 5 minutes or so. Brush with the Jack Daniel's sauce and cook for 5–10 minutes longer, turning once. Cut into 3-bone pieces and serve.

ALSO PICTURED: SPICY RUM PUNCH WINGS (PAGE 222)

SERVES 8

Spicy Rum Punch Wings

¼ cup (50 mL) brown sugar, packed
⅓ cup (75 mL) amber or spiced rum
⅓ cup (75 mL) pineapple juice
⅓ cup (75 mL) orange juice
¼ cup (50 mL) chili sauce
2 Tbsp (30 mL) cider vinegar
1 tsp (5 mL) hot pepper sauce
½ tsp (2 mL) crushed red pepper flakes
4 lb (1.8 kg) chicken wings
2 Tbsp (30 mL) extra virgin olive oil
1 Tbsp (15 mL) onion salt
2 tsp (10 mL) freshly ground black pepper

Perfect for fight-night or Friday Night Lights, *these sweet-and-spicy wings may cause a fight if you don't provide enough for your guests. If they won't fit in your oven in one batch, cook them on the grill over low heat for about 45 minutes, turning every 10 minutes until crisp.*

Heat the sugar and rum in a small saucepan, stirring to dissolve the sugar. Add the pineapple juice, orange juice, chili sauce and vinegar and bring to a boil. Reduce the heat and simmer until the rum mixture reduces by half. Stir in the hot sauce and pepper flakes and continue simmering until the mixture thickens, about 5 minutes. Set aside.

Preheat broiler.

Toss the chicken wings in the olive oil and sprinkle with the onion salt and black pepper. Arrange fat side up in a single layer on an oiled broiler pan (this may have to be done in 2 batches). Broil on the middle oven rack for 20–25 minutes, or until the wings begin to brown. Turn the wings and continue broiling for 10–15 minutes, or until crisp. (You may want to flip them again, depending on how well done you like them.)

Toss the wings in a large metal bowl with just enough sauce to coat them evenly.

SERVES 8

CHIPOTLE BLACK BEAN CHILI

2 Tbsp (30 mL) vegetable oil
1 lb (500 g) beef chuck, chopped into (½-inch/1 cm) cubes
1 Tbsp (15 mL) paprika
1 Tbsp (15 mL) ground cumin
1 onion, diced
1 green pepper, diced
3 garlic cloves, minced
1 jalapeño, seeded and diced
1 tsp (5 mL) salt
two 19 oz (540 mL) cans black beans
one 28 oz (796 mL) can diced tomatoes
2 cups (500 mL) sliced button mushrooms
1 cup (250 mL) fresh or frozen corn
2 canned chipotles in adobo, minced + 2 Tbsp (30 mL) adobo sauce
one 12 oz (341 mL) bottle amber ale or stout

Using chopped beef chuck in this chili adds a great meaty texture but ground beef or even turkey can be substituted. It could even be made vegetarian by using soy-based ground round or adding more beans (refer to the package for cooking times). Admittedly this saddens our carnivorous hearts, but you know we don't like to judge.

Heat the oil in a large, ovenproof stockpot over medium-high heat until smoking. Add the beef, paprika and cumin and cook until the meat is browned, 3–5 minutes. Remove the meat with a slotted spoon and set aside. Reduce heat to medium. Add the onion, green pepper, garlic, jalapeño and salt and cook for 8–10 minutes, or until the onion is soft and translucent. Pour in the black beans, tomatoes, mushrooms, corn, chipotles, adobo sauce and beer, stirring to combine. Add the reserved beef and bring to a simmer. Cover and cook on the stovetop for 2–3 hours, or until the flavors and texture of the chili are fully combined. Season to taste with salt and pepper.

NOTE: For a thicker chili, simmer with the lid off for 30 minutes to 1 hour. For extreme fire-ball chili, add the seeds of the jalapeño and all the chipotles you can handle.

PETER PIPER

Chipotle peppers are smoked jalapeños and sold either dry or in cans with adobo sauce, a mixture of puréed chilies, vinegar, tomatoes and spices. They can usually be found in the Mexican section of most major grocery stores.

SERVES 8

Guinness Double Chocolate Chunk Ice Cream

2 cups (500 mL) Guinness or coffee porter

2 cups (500 mL) heavy (35%) cream

1¾ cups (425 mL) whole milk

15 egg yolks

1 cup (250 mL) granulated sugar

1 cup (250 mL) finely chopped dark chocolate

1 cup (250 mL) finely chopped milk chocolate

As separate entities, beer and ice cream are not good companions, but when mixed into the same frozen dessert, they become the best of pals. The rich and malty flavor of the ice cream mixed with the creamy and bittersweet nature of the chocolate makes for a winning combo. If you don't have an ice cream maker you should run out and buy one immediately, if only for this recipe.

Fill your sink with a few inches of ice water.

Bring the Guinness, cream and milk to a boil in a large saucepan. Meanwhile, beat the egg yolks and sugar together in a large bowl until light and fluffy. Gradually pour the hot Guinness mixture into the egg mixture until completely combined and smooth, stirring to incorporate. Pour the mixture back into the saucepan and heat, stirring constantly until the custard thickens and coats the back of a spoon, about 5 minutes. Do not let the mixture boil or it will curdle.

Pour the custard back into the bowl and set it in the ice water. Stir the mixture periodically until it cools completely, about 30 minutes.

Pour the custard into an ice cream maker and freeze according to the manufacturer's instructions. (This may have to be done in 2 batches.) Stir in the chopped chocolate at the end. Store the ice cream in an airtight container and freeze until firm, about 4 hours.

A PROHIBITIONIST IS THE SORT OF MAN ONE COULDN'T CARE TO DRINK WITH, EVEN IF HE DRANK.

H. L. Mencken

A Quick and Dirty Guide to Wine and Beer

Wine

This guide is in no way exhaustive, but consider it a brief dossier of varietals, regions and food pairings.

WHITES

LIGHT-BODIED WHITES

PINOT BLANC

A fairly neutral-flavored grape means a wine with hints of pear, apple and minerals that's easy to drink. Best with mild cheese like brie.

PINOT GRIGIO/PINOT GRIS

Pinot Grigio hails from Italy and its light color indicates its delicate and fresh flavor. Best paired with salads, fish and oysters. Pinot Gris (same grape but grown outside Italy) features a fuller-bodied and usually sweeter wine that matches well with buttery seafood dishes, pâtés and mild cheeses.

RIESLING

Refreshing citrus flavors, light mineral notes and just a hint of spice define the best examples of wine made from this highly undervalued white. Dry versions still offer a touch of sweetness and match wonderfully with Asian dishes and seafood, while late-harvest varieties (left to mature and sweeten on the vine) are best served with lemon or almond desserts.

MEDIUM-BODIED WHITES

CHENIN BLANC

High-acid grape mostly grown in the Loire Valley of France and South Africa with a winemaking range from superdry sparkling to syrupy-sweet dessert wines. Good examples feature tart apple and pear aromas with notes of fresh herbs and honey. Drink with shrimp and other seafood dishes.

GEWÜRZTRAMINER

Difficult to say, especially after a glass or two (it's pronounced *ge-vertz-tra-meen-er*), but wonderful to drink, Gewürzt is one of the most exotic white grapes. Orange blossom, lychee, rose and cinnamon are just some of this wine's notes. Serve with mildly spicy dishes (such as light curries), creamy pastas or tangy salads.

SAUVIGNON BLANC/FUMÉ BLANC

Very pale in color with aromas of freshly cut grass, grapefruit and citrus, Sauvignon Blanc is crisp, clean and refreshing. It may also feature notes of passion fruit, elderflower and gooseberries and pairs well with baked or broiled fish, seafood pastas or mild cheese, such as chèvre.

SÉMILLON

Grown widely in Bordeaux for sweet Sauterne wines, and in Australia's Hunter Valley, this low-acid grape offers aromas of citrus and summer fruit softened by flavors of toasted bread, nuts and subtle spice. Pair Sauternes with desserts like crème brûlée and drier examples with buttery pasta dishes.

FULL-FLAVORED WHITES

CHARDONNAY

This golden-colored wine varies in flavor, depending on where the grapes are grown. Southern hemisphere Chards (think Australia, South Africa, Chile) tend to taste of peaches and pears or tropical fruit like bananas, pineapple and mango while northern hemisphere examples (France, USA, Canada) exhibit notes of sweet citrus, honey and roasted nuts. Aging in oak casks imparts spicy, vanilla aromas, making it one of the boldest whites which means it needs equally rich foods, such as roasted turkey and pork, creamy pastas or salmon.

VIOGNIER

Big, rich and elegant, this grape has it all. Floral notes accented by apricot and peach flavors and a naturally low acidity means it pairs wonderfully with spicy Asian dishes.

REDS

LIGHT-BODIED REDS

GAMAY NOIR

This grape put the Beaujolais region of France on the map. Gamay is very light in color and has low acidity and soft tannins, making it compatible with many dishes such as pâté, quiche, light pastas and crudités.

PINOT NOIR

The lightest of the reds, this has an easy-to-drink reputation. Berries, plums, minerals and light spice round out the flavors while fresh acidity and delicate tannins (the things that shock the side of your jaw) give Pinot Noir a light mouthfeel. Its earthy aroma pairs well with everything from roasted turkey and broiled salmon to mushroom soup.

MEDIUM-BODIED REDS

BARBERA

Low tannins, fresh acidity and pleasant berry characteristics make Barbera one of the easiest reds for quaffing. Serve alongside everything from barbecued ribs to mushroom risotto and lasagna.

CABERNET FRANC

Its high acid levels and relatively low tannins mean Cab Franc is often used in blends with Cabernet Sauvignon and Merlot to add structure. On its own it can feature prominent berry flavors with a mineral and herbaceous backbone. Serve with braised or roasted red meats.

MERLOT

This popular, easy-to-drink red has the flavor of ripe, full fruit and feels juicy and slightly sweet on the palate. Serve with veal, blackened chicken, fish or rich pasta dishes, such as lasagna.

NEBBIOLO

It's dry and tannic and has good acidity. These qualities mean wine made from this star of Italy's Piedmont region taste best after a good bit of aging. After a bit of time they soften to showcase aromas of black cherry, violets and tar. These need equally pungent cheeses, mushroom dishes or meaty stews.

SANGIOVESE

Earthy and fruit forward with aromas of cherry or plum *and* killer tannins, this grape (used widely in the making of Chianti wines) needs rich Italian dishes with a good fat content to help tame it. Creamy rosé pastas and sausage-based dishes should do the trick.

FULL-FLAVORED REDS

AMARONE

Not a grape but a technique for making some of Italy's most celebrated wines. Amarone-type wines are made in the Valpolicella region (see next page) and use the juice from partially dried grapes, namely Corvina, Rondinella and Molinara. This produces big wines with very ripe, raisiny flavors, low acidity and, alas, high prices.

BACO NOIR

Smoky and full-bodied, this hybrid varietal features a fruit-forward, inky wine with good aging potential. Serve with old cheddar, roast beef or spicy game dishes.

CABERNET SAUVIGNON

The king of all red grapes, Cab Sauv boasts a rich inky color and deep, tannic flavor full of black currant, cherry, wood and leather. Loads of acidity and high tannins mellow over the years if cellared. Best with pepper steak, brisket or wild meats, such as venison.

GRENACHE

A fruity, full-flavored grape with high alcohol and low tannins, Grenache is widely used to produce rosé wines. Notes of raspberry, plum and peppery spice dominate and match well with roasted game or grilled meats.

MALBEC

Argentina's big boy, Malbec is almost black in color and ripe with plum, berry and spicy flavors. Best matched with big, bold dishes like grilled meats and game.

SHIRAZ/SYRAH

Pepper, spice and bold hits of raspberry, currants and plums define Shiraz. Shiraz and Syrah are from the same grape, but Syrah is the name used in France where they produce lighter-tasting versions of this wine. Roasted lamb, stews or spicy sausage dishes all complement this wine.

TEMPRANILLO

Spain's noble grape translates to wines that are bright ruby in color, full of ripe berry and plum flavor and packed with savory aromas such as tobacco, leather and herbs. This *hombre* needs equally bold meals such as paella, roasted lamb or beef.

ZINFANDEL/PRIMITIVO

Notes of raspberry, blackberry, licorice and pepper define this heavy-handed grape grown mostly in California and the Puglia region of Italy. High sugar levels in the grape allow for high-alcohol wines full of sweet, ripe fruit. Primitivo-based wines tend to pack a little less punch then their California counterparts. Serve with grilled steak, bison and venison.

NOTE: White Zinfandel is a sweet rosé wine made from the red Zinfandel grape. The pressed juice spends only a limited amount of time in contact with the skins, imparting its pink hue.

REGIONS

Here is a highly abbreviated list of major wine regions throughout Europe, where geography provides insight on grape varietals used and style of winemaking.

ALSACE (FRANCE)

Situated on the border with Germany, this region is home to wonderful Riesling, Gewürztraminer and Pinot Gris wines—usually richer but drier than their German counterparts. Alsace is also home to much of the French beer industry as well, notably Kronenbourg.

BORDEAUX (FRANCE)

The country's largest wine-producing region is most famous for it pricy and delicious Cabernet Sauvignon blends although they also harvest huge amounts of Merlot, Cabernet Franc and Malbec. Whites focus mainly on Sémillon and Sauvignon Blanc used for dry table wines and famously sweet dessert wines from the subregion of Sauternes.

BURGUNDY (FRANCE)

Source of some of the most expensive wines in the world, Burgundy includes Chablis, Beaujolais and Côte-d'Or subregions, among others. To be a *true* Burgundy, red wine must only be made from Pinot Noir and/or Gamay grapes, while whites should be from either Chardonnay or Pinot Blanc, or a blend of the two.

CHAMPAGNE (FRANCE)

Not much explanation needed here—white table wines, usually made from a blend of white and red grapes (skins removed), then made fizzy and delicious and sold at luxury prices. Pinot Noir, Chardonnay and Pinot Meunier are the grapes of choice.

CHIANTI (ITALY)

Located in the Tuscany region, and home to one of the country's most recognizable wines, Chiantis are blends usually made up mostly of the Sangiovese grape.

DOURO (PORTUGAL)

Home to the country's premier, if nearly vertically aligned, vineyards, the Douro Valley is heavily planted with Tempranillo, Touriga Nacional and Tinta Nacional grapes, used to make both table wine and port (fortified wine).

PIEDMONT (ITALY)

Surrounded by the French, Swiss and Italian Alps, Piedmont is home to some of the best food and wine culture on the planet. Growing Barbera, Nebbiolo and Dolcetto grapes helps produce deliciously sexy wines.

RHÔNE VALLEY (FRANCE)

Syrah and Viognier grapes dominate in this South of France region, while Marsanne and Rousanne take up the slack. Highly recognizable wines from the region include Côtes du Rhône and Châteauneuf-du-Pape.

RIOJA (SPAIN)

Tempranillo reigns supreme in this north-central region of the country but gets some help from Grenache to produce some of the best wine that comes out of the country.

VALPOLICELLA (ITALY)

Situated in the province of Verona in northern Italy and home to light, fragrant table wines made from Corvina, Rondinella and Molinara grapes.

OTHER HELPFUL TIDBITS

SWEET SURRENDER

Wines are given a number based on how dry or sweet they are. For both red and white, the rating system starts at 0, which represents the lowest sugar content, and extends into the 20s (icewines are the sweetest). Wine should always be sweeter than the food it accompanies. For example, sweet chutneys or fruit sauces on roasted meat can handle a wine with a sugar content of 1 or 2. And those with a high rating, such as port, sherry or icewine, should be served with dessert.

ACID TEST

Wines with high acidity taste tart and feel lighter in your mouth than those with lower acidity. Unfortunately, there isn't a rating system for acidity, though the back label may mention it with descriptors such as "crisp," "tart" or "fresh." High-acid wines match best with high-acid foods like tomato- and lemon-based dishes (such as Chianti or Sauvignon Blanc), as well as rich or oily foods like cream sauces.

WARM UP AND COOL DOWN

Let white wine stand at room temperature for 20 minutes before serving. If it's too cold, all you taste is acidity. Red wine, on the other hand, is often poured too warm, creating a heavy feeling in your mouth. Place your bottle of red in a bucket filled with ice water for a couple minutes to cool it down a bit.

AIR IT OUT

Let red wine "breathe" before serving it to release its aromas and so you can taste its full profile. Simply popping the cork does little to help aerate it, as wine benefits from direct exposure to air. For best results, pour your wine into a decanter and let it sit for 5–10 minutes.

SNIFF THIS

The practice of sniffing the cork is all about show and little about substance. It's part of the ritual of "tasting" wine (cork sniffing followed by glass swirling then leg watching, bouquet smelling and finally tasting) but although decidedly pretentious it's not completely without merit. Placing one's nose to the wine-end of a fresh cork can indicate to the drinker if the wine is "off"—that is, turned to vinegar or displaying other marks of rebellion. However, the drinker won't know this for sure until he or she actually smells or tastes the wine, making the sniff just a tad redundant. And anyone who sends back a bottle of wine without tasting it first should be no friend of yours.

HALF DRUNK

While closing out your evening with half-drunk bottles of wine is considered sacrilege in many cultures (or at least it should), we recognize from time to time this can be unavoidable. Replace the cork, vacuum out the air or use a wine-preserving spray and place the partial bottle in the refrigerator where it will keep for up to three days. Alternatively, pour the remaining wine into clean ice cube trays and freeze. Store the frozen cubes in airtight freezer bags ready to use for sauces, marinades and other recipes.

GREAT PEOPLE TALK ABOUT IDEAS, AVERAGE PEOPLE TALK ABOUT THINGS, AND SMALL PEOPLE TALK ABOUT WINE.

Fran Lebowitz

A Guide to Wine Tastings

Depending on your personal preference and the type of evening you're organizing, you can opt for either a casual approach or a more structured tasting. Whichever approach you choose, it's always good to start the tasting with whites and light-tasting reds before heading in to full-bodied reds.

CASUAL TASTING

This is a relaxed and informal way to get your feet wet in the world of wine. Invite your friends to bring their favorite bottle of wine and taste them one by one. It's a good idea to make the person who brought the wine responsible for introducing it. This is a great way to create a fluid yet informal feel to the evening. Inform your guests of the plan in advance and encourage them to do some research on the wine they're bringing. The introduction to the wine should include some basic details about its region, the type of grapes that are used and any other notes of interest on its style or producer.

To help your guests track their favorites, label each wine with a card displaying the name of the person who brought the wine (this will also help the conversation) as well as the wine's basic details. Present your guests with a small notebook and pen when they arrive to record their favorite finds. To start out, open a few bottles and serve a taste of each wine to your guests, then introduce it, discuss it and move on to the next wine. Repeat this process several times over the evening as new bottles arrive and encourage your guests to slide up to the wine bar and have a glass of whatever tickles their taste buds.

FORMAL TASTING

Add structure to your event by comparing wines of the same style and region. This type of tasting is called a horizontal tasting and it's really easy to do. Start by selecting three bottles from one region; for example, the Côtes du Rhône region of France or the Marlborough region of Australia. You can assign your guests regions in advance and even pin up a map marking their names and wines.

You can also do a varietal tasting, where the focus is on a particular type of grape and the wines made from it. The idea of a varietal tasting is to explore how the *terroir* affects the flavor of a wine. *Terroir* is a French wine term with no direct translation into English, but it basically refers to the combined effects of the sun, soil, water, altitude and temperature on the grapes as they grow. The best way to create a varietal tasting is to select three wines that use the same grape from three different regions; for example, a Sauvignon Blanc from New Zealand, California and South Africa.

The final type of tasting is a vertical tasting. This is a great way to experience how wines develop with age. To do this you'll need to select three wines of the same type and from the same producer over three different vintages. This can be a bit tricky, so enlist the support of your favorite wine shop. They'll be able to direct you to what they have in stock. This type of tasting is best used to augment a horizontal or varietal tasting as it may be difficult (and possibly expensive) to build several vertical tastings.

WINE TASTING ESSENTIALS

The first thing that you need to know about tasting wine is that it's entirely subjective and all about personal opinion. There are no wrong answers and your plonk might be someone else's plum. Keep your comments critical but constructive. Try to express what you taste and not how you feel.

TASTING BEGINS WITH THE EYES

Hold the wine up to the light. Its color gives you clues to its flavor. With white wines, a clearer wine generally indicates a lighter flavor. More of an amber or straw color may mean more oak or sweetness. The same applies for red wines. More transparency usually means the wine is young and light-bodied. Red wines with a deep garnet or inky purple color tend to be more intense and full-bodied.

THE ALL-KNOWING NOSE

Now that your eyes have started to help you formulate an opinion, it's time to get your nose involved. It's important to understand that taste and flavor are different. The mouth tastes salty, sweet, sour and bitter, while the nose senses the aromas that make up flavor. Our brain wires these together to form a complete sensation. To maximize the experience with wine, swirl it gently in the glass and get your nose right into it (the glass not the wine). Take a few quick sniffs and think about what you smell. You smell wine, obviously. But does it smell like sweet strawberries? Spicy black pepper? Fresh like flowers or more like bread or nuts? How intense does it smell? Is it pungent enough to make your nose hair curl, or can you barely detect it?

DOWN THE HATCH

After you've teased your senses a little, it's time to taste. Take a sip, not a gulp, and make sure the wine is exposed to your whole mouth. Swish or chew if you need to. Figure out the wine's body. If it feels thick like cream then it has a heavy body. If it feels like skim milk, then it's light-bodied. Does it make the back of your mouth pucker? This is a result of the wine's tannic structure. Draw some air through the wine to help it open up in your mouth. Does that bring out any special flavors like citrus, berries or chocolate? Finally, swallow the wine and note how the flavor fades. This is called the finish. A long finish means the flavor stays around and a short finish means it disappears quickly. A clean finish means that there is no detectable aftertaste.

Repeat the above process again to reconfirm what your thoughts are then write them down.

CREATING A PARIS-INSPIRED THEME

The city of wine and romance is the perfect backdrop for an inspired wine tasting. This get-together is ideal any time of year and can be held inside, or under the night sky for added romance.

SETTING THE MOOD

The key to making this get-together work is to keep the focus on the wine bar. Make sure you have a table large enough to accommodate all the bottles as well as your glassware and lots of room to mingle and jostle around it. Also make sure you have plenty of water available. You can increase the chic quotient by serving both still and fizzy water. It's best to separate your food table from the wine bar to help keep people moving.

Introduce the French theme by creating a gallery backdrop to the wine bar. Print out mini versions of works by the great French painters like Gauguin, Manet and Cézanne. Place these in simple frames and hang them at eye-level behind the bar.

A good balance of lighting is important for this event. Your guests will need to see what's in their glasses, but at the same time the mood should be very romantic and relaxed. Scattered tea lights, or even white string lights on a tree create a great effect. Provide additional lighting by the wine bar so guests can make and record their wine observations without squinting.

SERVING SUGGESTION

The food pairings are designed to be light in flavor so they don't compete with the wine on the guests' palate. Refer to our Cheese, Please party (see page 177) for suggestions and keep the wine as the star of this party.

The slow romantic melodies of bistro jazz and bouncy notes of jazz quartets from the hot clubs of the 1920s and 1930s make a magical backdrop to this event.

> BEER, IT'S THE BEST DAMN DRINK IN THE WORLD.
>
> *Jack Nicholson*

ALE

Ale is a top-fermenting beer, brewed from malted barley. It's fermented at a warmer temperature than a lager causing the yeast to rise to the top during the process. Top-fermented beers tend to ferment quickly, giving them a sweet, full-bodied and slightly fruity taste. Most ales contain hops, which impart a bitter herbal note that acts to balance the sweetness and preserve the beer.

Ales represent a diverse range of beer, from pale to dark, bitter to sweet and hopsy to malty, and can be categorized by region, style, color or flavor. They tend to pack more of a punch than lagers, with pronounced elements that showcase fruit notes, spice, hops or malt. As in the world of wine, the color of the ale is generally a good indicator of its flavor. On the light end of the spectrum are Belgian white beers with notes of citrus rind and coriander seed. On the dark end are the rich malty-caramel flavors found in darks, stouts and porters.

Ales are traditional to Britain, Ireland, Belgium, Germany and the eastern provinces of Canada. They're also popular among the craft beer makers.

AMBER ALE

Wedged between the blonde and the stout lie the amber and red top fermented ales. The name refers primarily to the copper-colored tones that signify light sweetness, spice or nuts, hints of caramel and a balance between malt and hops. Ambers and reds tend to be easy-drinking and flavorful but not overpowering and are generally brewed to be a session beer—that is, a beer you can drink all night. Amber ales are great with fish and chips, breads, pizzas, meat pies and barbecue fare.

BOCK

A bock is bottom-fermenting beer and a subset of the lager family. Bock beer is typically the strongest of the lagers. It's higher in alcohol content than other lagers and richer in color and flavor. Popular in Europe, bock beer seems to be less popular in North America. Bock beers are traditionally special occasion beers served on holy high holidays such as Easter, Christmas and Lent. Bock beer pairs with grilled flatbreads, smoked or curried meats and salty cheeses.

LAGER

Lager is a bottom-fermenting beer made from malted barley. It's fermented at a cooler temperature than an ale, which causes the yeast to sink to the bottom during the fermenting process. Bottom-fermented beers are usually smooth and well rounded. While popular British beers are generally ales, the most popular North American beers are generally lagers.

Lagers originated in central Europe but are popular worldwide due to their approachable, light and refreshing characteristics. The modern definition of the term "lager" generally refers only to the method of fermentation as other characteristics may vary. Lagers pair well with Thai or Indian food as well as sushi, roast chicken and fish.

LAMBIC

Lambic beer is made from wheat and barley, but differs from a wheat beer in that it's spontaneously fermented. This process involves using natural airborne yeast and aged hops to ferment and preserve the beer. This natural fermentation process means that lambic beers are aged for up to 3 years. The most commonly available types of lambic are fruit infused: sour cherry, referred to as a kriek, framboise (raspberry) and pêche (peach). Fruit lambics frequently receive a second fermentation in the bottle, giving them added carbonation and a signature cork. Lambic beer pairs well with light and creamy blue cheeses, salads, cold-cut sandwiches, fruit pies and creamy desserts.

PILSNER

A pilsner is a bottom-fermenting beer and a subset of the lager family. Pilsner is typically light colored, crisp, clean and refreshing. A typical pilsner will feature a distinct hop aroma and slightly sweet to bitter flavor. Pilsners originated in central Europe but are popular worldwide and have strongly influenced North American mass-market products. Pilsners pair well with nuts and toasted snacks, barbecue dishes or sweet desserts.

STOUTS AND PORTERS

Stouts and porters are strong top-fermented ales that are rich, dark and full-bodied and can range from sweet to dry. They usually feature bitter and intense malt flavors and caramel aromas. There are several different types of stout including dry or Irish (such as Guinness) and imperial (a high-alcohol stout first shipped to the czars of Russia). Stouts and porters pair well with Irish stew, venison, pheasant or other hearty dishes.

TRAPPIST

Trappist beer is a top-fermented ale brewed under the control of monks in one of the world's seven beer-producing Trappist monasteries. These breweries follow various rules in accordance with the International Trappist Association to ensure quality and purity. Trappist beers vary in flavor and intensity but are generally full-bodied and well balanced with sweet malt and caramel qualities. Trappist beer is usually bottle conditioned, which means that the final qualities of the beer are determined in the bottle. This can include some refermentation which produces added carbonation. Trappist beer pairs well with grilled meats such as sausages, rich fowl such as goose or duck and light game.

WHEAT AND WHITE BEER

A wheat beer is generally a top-fermented ale brewed using wheat, but it may also contain malted barley. Wheat beers have a light, sweet flavor, pale color and creamy texture. Common wheat beer styles—including Belgian *witbier* (white beer)—appear cloudy and have a fruity note from the addition of fruit zests and coriander during the brewing process. Wheat beers originated from central Europe and are known by several names including *weizen*, *weissbier* or *weisse*, *Hefeweizen*, *witbier*, *witte*, *bière blanche* and Belgian white. Wheat beers are refreshing and pair well with light cheese, fish, chicken and creamy pasta dishes.

Glossary of Bar Terms

BITTERS — a very concentrated flavoring agent made from roots, barks, herbs and/or berries with about 45% alcohol. Typically sold wherever good spirits are available.

BLEND — to make a drink using a blender OR a type of spirit that has been blended as part of its production process.

BOSTON SHAKER — a two-part metal and glass shaker without a built-in strainer. Generally preferred by bar professionals.

CHASER — a drink consumed immediately after a strong spirit, generally to remove any harsh flavor or burning sensation.

COOLER — a drink made from a combination of liqor, flavoring, cracked ice, carbonated beverages and fruit rinds. Traditionally served in a collins glass.

CORDIAL — typically a nonalcoholic, sugar-based syrup, flavored using fruits, flowers, herbs, seeds, roots, plants or juices. Cordials are used as highly concentrated mixers.

DASH — a measurement equal to ⅓ tsp (1 mL).

DECANT — a technique generally used for serving wine that helps flavor develop by introducing air. Decanting involves pouring the wine from the original bottle into a serving vessel such as a carafe or decanter.

FIZZ — a drink made from liquor, citrus juices and sugar. It's shaken with ice and strained into a highball glass and topped with soda water or other carbonated beverage.

FLOAT — the technique of carefully pouring a small amount of alcohol on the surface of a drink so that it floats (see also *layering*).

FRAPPÉ — a drink using several liqueurs, combined and poured over shaved or crushed ice.

FROST — the process of dipping a glass in water, then freezing it to form ice on the outside surface.

GROG — a rum-based beverage with water, fruit juice and sugar, commonly served in large mugs.

HIGHBALL — any liquor served with ice, soda, plain water, ginger ale or other carbonated liquids.

LAYERING — a technique that involves carefully pouring various liquors over the back of a spoon into a narrow glass. The technique exploits the various densities of liquor to stack them on top of each other. Start from the heaviest (usually sweetest/lowest alcohol) first and end with a high-proof spirit.

MARTINI SHAKER — a container with a tight-fitting lid and built-in strainer to build, shake and decant drinks from.

MIX — to combine ingredients.

MUDDLE — to mash or crush ingredients with a spoon or muddler (a wooden rod with a flattened end).

NEAT — liquor served in a glass with no ice or other mixer.

ON THE ROCKS — liquor served in a glass with ice but no other mixers.

POUR — to transfer an amount of alcohol from one vessel to another.

PULL — a term typically reserved for draught products, referring to the action of pulling the draught handle to release a pint of beer.

PUNCH — a citrus drink that contains juices with two or more liquors or wines.

REAMER — a wooden or plastic handle used for squeezing juice from fruit.

RICKEY — made with lime, cracked ice, soda or sparkling wine and whisky, gin, rum or brandy. Served in a collins glass with a twist of lime.

SANGRIA — a wine- (or port-) based drink that typically contains fruit juice, whisky, gin, rum or brandy.

SLING — a coctail made with gin, cherry brandy, grenadine and club soda.

SMASH — a small julep, made from muddled sugar, ice cubes, whisky, gin, rum or brandy and soda. Garnished with sprigs of mint and fruit and served in a rocks glass.

SOUR — a cocktail made by combining liquor with lemon juice and a little sugar. Served in a collins glass.

STRAIGHT-UP — drink served in a glass with no ice.

STRAINER — utensil that fits over the mouth of a shaker to allow the liquid contents to be strained into a glass.

TODDY — drink made using sugar dissolved in a little hot water with liquor. Served hot or cold over ice, with nutmeg, clove, cinnamon or lemon peel. Often used to treat the sniffles.

TOP — to fill the remainder of the glass.

TWIST — small piece of fruit peel that is squeezed over or dropped in a drink.

WEDGE — triangular-shaped piece of garnish, usually skewered or cut and hung from the side of a glass.

WHEEL — slice of round fruit, typically citrus, usually hung from the side of the glass.

ZEST — tiny piece of a lemon or orange peel.

Glossary of Foodie Terms

AL DENTE — Italian term meaning "to the tooth," used to describe cooked pasta, rice or veggies that still offer a touch of resistance when bitten. Blah blah blah . . . slightly undercooked.

BAIN-MARIE — a double-boiler or other heat-resistant bowl set over a pot of gently simmering water. Used to melt chocolate and make custards, amongst other things.

BLANCH — to boil food (usually fruits or veggies) rapidly for a short period then plunge into ice water to stop the cooking. Used to remove skin from peaches and tomatoes and to set the color in veggies like broccoli and asparagus.

BRAISE — to cook tough cuts of meat in liquid for a long period of time. Helps render fat and tenderize meat.

CANDY THERMOMETER — a durable thermometer used to monitor the temperature of sugar mixtures when making candy. A digital-read meat thermometer may be substituted.

CARAMELIZE — to heat sugar until it liquefies and browns or to cook foods like onions until they release their natural sugars and brown.

CHIFFONADE — thin strips of leafy greens and herbs. Used to top salads and garnish plates.

CHOP — to coarsely cut food into ½-inch (1 cm) pieces.

CHOP FINELY — to coarsely cut food into ¼-inch (5 mm) pieces.

CREAM — to soften a fat like butter by beating it until smooth.

DEGLAZE — to pour liquid into pan where meat, seafood or veggies have been cooking. Liquid loosens all the delicious brown bits and begins the process for making gravy, sauce or jus.

DICE — to cut food into uniform pieces, about ¼ inch (5 mm). Cubes with dots on them, used for games and gambling.

DREDGE — to coat meat or fish in dry ingredients like flour or breadcrumbs.

DRIZZLE — to sprinkle drops of liquid over food in a casual, West-Coast way.

DUST — to sprinkle food with dry ingredients like cocoa powder, usually through a sieve.

FLAMBÉ — to set booze ablaze to burn off harsh alcohol flavor and impress your guests. Used for dishes like Crêpes Suzette and Cherries Jubilee.

FOLD — to gently incorporate light ingredients (beaten egg whites, whipped cream) into heavier ingredients (melted chocolate, cake batter) in order to maintain as much volume as possible. Use a rubber spatula to gently cut through center of mixture, lifting ingredients from the bottom of the bowl to the top then repeat while rotating the bowl.

GANACHE — a rich mixture of chocolate and heated heavy cream, used to make truffles, as a glaze or frosting for cakes and as a sauce.

INFUSE — to steep ingredients like herbs or spices in hot liquid to add flavor.

JULIENNE — to cut veggies into thin, matchstick-sized pieces.

JUS — a thin sauce made from the pan juices of meat and usually wine or stock.

MINCE — to chop into very fine pieces.

MOP — to brush barbecued meat with a thin sauce, adding flavor and moisture.

PINCH — amount of seasoning you can pick up between your thumb and forefinger.

POACH — to cook foods submerged or partially submerged in liquid.

PURÉE — to blend until the texture is smooth and consistent, usually with a blender or food processor.

REDUCE — to boil down liquid by evaporation to concentrate flavors and/or thicken.

RENDER — to make solid fat into a liquid by melting it slowly.

ROUX — a mixture of melted fat and flour, cooked in a pan and used to thicken sauces and add flavor. It's the basis for many French sauces like béchamel and Cajun cuisine, like gumbo.

SAUTÉ — to cook foods in a frying pan.

SCORE — to make shallow slashes into the flesh of meat or fish with a sharp knife.

SEAR — to brown meat quickly in a pan over high heat.

SHUCK — to remove the shells of oysters or other shellfish and to remove the husk from corn.

SIEVE — a metal strainer with very small holes used to sift flour, for example, or to smooth sauces, remove seeds, etc.

SIFT — to pass dry ingredients through a sieve to catch debris or smooth out lumps.

SIMMER — to heat a liquid gently so it barely reaches a bubbling stage.

TOSS — to combine ingredients with a lifting motion.

WHISK — to beat air into liquids such as egg whites or whipped cream, either by hand or with an electric mixer.

A List of Spirits

ABSINTHE (THE GREEN FAIRY)
Flavor notes: herbal, licorice
Main source: wormwood, herbs
Alcohol content: 70%
Substitution: anisette liqueur, Pernod

ALIZÉ (GOLD, RED, WILD, BLEU)
Flavor notes: passion fruit and other fruits
Main source: cognac, fruit juices
Alcohol content: 15%
Substitution: combine 2 parts cognac or brandy with 1 part orange liqueur

AMARETTO
Flavor notes: almond, maraschino cherry, marzipan
Main source: alcohol, caramelized sugar, apricot nuts, fruits
Alcohol content: 28%
Substitution: combine brandy or cognac with a couple of drops almond extract

AMARETTO CREAM LIQUEUR
Flavor notes: almond, maraschino cherry
Main source: amaretto, cream
Alcohol: 17%
Substitution: combine 2 parts amaretto with 1 part cream

AMARULA
Flavor notes: strawberry-like sweet fruit
Main source: marula fruit, cream
Alcohol: 17%
Substitution: none

ANISETTE/ANISEED LIQUEUR
Flavor notes: licorice
Main source: anise
Alcohol content: 25–40%
Substitution: Pernod, sambuca, ouzo, absinthe

APPLE LIQUEUR
Flavor notes: ripe apple
Main source: alcohol, apples
Alcohol content: 20%
Substitution: Calvados

APRICOT BRANDY
Flavor notes: apricot, caramel
Main source: brandy, apricots
Alcohol content: 24%
Substitution: combine 2 parts brandy with 1 part peach or orange liqueur

ARMAGNAC
Flavor notes: fruity, floral and woody
Main source: white wine
Alcohol content: 40%
Substitution: brandy, cognac

BAILEY'S IRISH CREAM (SEE IRISH CREAM LIQUEUR)

BENEDICTINE
Flavor notes: sweet herbal, citrus, medicinal, bitter
Main source: brandy
Alcohol content: 40%
Substitution: none

BENEDICTINE AND BRANDY (B&B)
Flavor notes: spicy, herbal, ginger, orange
Main source: brandy
Alcohol content: 39%
Substitution: combine Benedictine, brandy and orange liqueur in equal parts

BITTERS
Flavor notes: herbs, pepper
Main source: roots, herbs
Alcohol content: 40%
Substitution: none

BLUE CURACAO
Flavor notes: sweet candied orange, jammy
Main source: alcohol, orange rind, coloring
Alcohol content: 15–24%
Substitution: Cointreau, Grand Marnier, triple sec

BOURBON (SEE WHISKEY, AMERICAN)

BRANDY
Flavor notes: pronounced grape, caramel, wood
Main source: white wine
Alcohol content: 35–45%
Substitution: Armagnac, cognac

BUTTERSCOTCH LIQUEUR/SCHNAPPS
Flavor notes: butterscotch, vanilla, caramel
Main source: alcohol, butterscotch
Alcohol content: 15–17%
Substitution: honey or maple liqueur

CALVADOS
Flavor notes: apple, caramel, vanilla
Main source: brandy
Alcohol content: 40–43%
Substitution: combine 2 parts brandy or cognac with 1 part apple cider

CHAMBORD
Flavor notes: black raspberry
Main source: cognac, raspberry, herbs
Alcohol content: 23%
Substitution: crème de cassis

CHARTREUSE
Flavor notes: bitter herb, sandalwood, cloves
Main source: wine alcohol, herbs, botanicals
Alcohol content: 55%
Substitution: none

CHERRY BRANDY/WHISKY
Flavor notes: sweet cherry pie, spice
Main source: brandy or whisky, cherries
Alcohol content: 15–24%
Substitution: combine brandy or whisky with a couple of drops of cherry essence

CHOCOLATE CREAM LIQUEUR
Flavor notes: chocolate and/or fruit
Main source: distilled alcohol, chocolate, cream and/or fruit
Alcohol content: 12–17%
Substitution: combine 3 parts Irish cream with 1 part chocolate syrup

CIDER
Flavor notes: crisp apple, acidic
Main source: apples
Alcohol content: 5–7%
Substitution: none

CINNAMON SCHNAPPS (SEE GOLDSCHLÄGER)

COCONUT RUM (SEE RUM, COCONUT)

COFFEE CREAM LIQUEUR
Flavor notes: coffee, mocha, butterscotch
Main source: distilled alcohol, coffee, cream
Alcohol content: 15–17%
Substitution: combine 3 parts Irish cream with 1 part brewed coffee or espresso

COFFEE LIQUEUR
Flavor notes: coffee, vanilla
Main source: alcohol, coffee
Alcohol content: 20%
Substitution: Kahlúa, Tia Maria

COGNAC
Flavor notes: rich fruit, caramel, oak
Main source: white grapes
Alcohol content: 40%
Substitution: Armagnac, brandy

COINTREAU
Flavor notes: bittersweet, tangy orange
Main source: brandy, orange rind
Alcohol content: 40%
Substitution: triple sec, Grand Marnier

CRÈME DE BANANE
Flavor notes: sweet banana candy, spice
Main source: alcohol, bananas
Alcohol content: 15–23%
Substitution: combine brandy with a few drops of banana essence

CRÈME DE CACAO (WHITE AND DARK)
Flavor notes: sweet/dark cocoa, cream
Main source: alcohol, chocolate
Alcohol content: 15–24%
Substitution: chocolate cream liqueur

CRÈME DE CASSIS
Flavor notes: sweet black currant, jammy
Main source: alcohol, black currants
Alcohol content: 18–25%
Substitution: Chambord

CRÈME DE MENTHE (WHITE AND GREEN)
Flavor notes: sweet spearmint
Main source: alcohol, mint
Alcohol content: 15%
Substitution: peppermint schnapps

DRAMBUIE
Flavor notes: sweet herbs, smoky Scotch, honey
Main source: Scotch, honey
Alcohol content: 40%
Substitution: honey liqueur

FRAMBOISE (RASPBERRY LIQUEUR)
Flavor notes: sweet, candied raspberries
Main source: alcohol, raspberries
Alcohol content: 16%
Substitution: Chambord

FRANGELICO
Flavor notes: toasted hazelnut, cocoa, vanilla
Main source: grain alcohol, hazelnuts
Alcohol content: 24%
Substitution: walnut liqueur

GIN
Flavor notes: juniper berry, citrus, floral, herbal
Main source: wheat or rye
Alcohol content: 40%
Substitution: none

GOLDSCHLÄGER
Flavor notes: spicy cinnamon
Main source: alcohol, cinnamon
Alcohol content: 40%
Substitution: cinnamon schnapps

GRAND MARNIER
Flavor notes: sweet orange, brandy
Main source: cognac, oranges
Alcohol content: 42%
Substitution: Cointreau, triple sec

GRAPPA
Flavor notes: dry, spicy, pungent, unaged brandy
Main source: fermented grape seeds and skins (pomace)
Alcohol: 40%
Substitution: Pernod, absinthe

HONEY LIQUEUR
Flavor notes: honey, floral and herbal tones
Main source: alcohol, honey
Alcohol content: 40%
Substitution: Drambuie

HPNOTIQ
Flavor notes: grapefruit, peach, passion fruit, cognac
Main source: cognac, vodka, fruits
Alcohol content: 17%
Substitution: Alizé Bleu

IRISH CREAM LIQUEUR
Flavor notes: sweet nutty, slightly spicy
Main source: Irish whiskey
Alcohol: 17%
Substitution: none

IRISH MIST
Flavor notes: sweet florals, herbs, whiskey
Main source: whiskey, herbs
Alcohol content: 35%
Substitution: none

JÄGERMEISTER
Flavor notes: herbal, spice, citrus
Main source: alcohol, herbs
Alcohol content: 35%
Substitution: none

KAHLÚA (SEE COFFEE LIQUEUR)

KIRSCH
Flavor notes: cherries
Main source: cherries
Alcohol content: 37–45%
Substitution: cherry whiskey

LIMONCELLO
Flavor notes: sweet lemon
Main source: alcohol, lemons
Alcohol content: 30–35%
Substitution: combine 4 parts vodka with 1 part sugar and a few drops of lemon essence or see recipe on page 216

LYCHEE LIQUEUR
Flavor notes: sweet lychee nut, melon
Main source: alcohol, lychees
Alcohol content: 17–24%
Substitution: none

MADEIRA
Flavor notes: fruit, toffee, caramel
Main source: grapes, brandy
Alcohol content: 19–20%
Substitution: port or sherry

MALIBU COCONUT RUM (SEE RUM, COCONUT)

MAPLE LIQUEUR
Flavor notes: maple, coffee, butterscotch
Main source: alcohol, maple
Alcohol content: 26%
Substitution: butterscotch liqueur

MELON LIQUEUR
Flavor notes: sweet honeydew melon
Main source: alcohol, melon
Alcohol content: 15–24%
Substitution: none

ORANGE BRANDY
Flavor notes: sweet orange, nutmeg, slightly medicinal
Main source: brandy, orange rind
Alcohol content: 35%
Substitution: Yukon Jack

OUZO
Flavor notes: herbal, licorice, spicy
Main source: grapes, star anise, licorice, cloves, angelica root
Alcohol content: 40%
Substitution: anisette, Pernod

PEACH SCHNAPPS
Flavor notes: ripe candied peach
Main source: alcohol, peaches
Alcohol content: 15–24%
Substitution: apricot brandy

PEAR LIQUEUR

Flavor notes: pear, banana candy, slightly medicinal
Main source: alcohol, pears
Alcohol content: 30%
Substitution: Xanté Poire au Cognac

PEPPERMINT SCHNAPPS

Flavor notes: sweet peppermint candy
Main source: alcohol, peppermint
Alcohol content: 22–24%
Substitution: white crème de menthe

PERNOD

Flavor notes: sweet black licorice
Main source: alcohol, aniseed
Alcohol content: 40%
Substitution: sambuca, anisette

PIMM'S NO. 1 CUP

Flavor notes: slightly bitter citrus, herbal
Main source: gin, herbs
Alcohol content: 25%
Substitution: none

PORT

Flavor notes: sweet fruit, caramel, toffee
Main source: grapes, brandy
Alcohol content: 19–20%
Substitution: Madeira, sherry

RUM, AMBER, DARK

Flavor notes: molasses, vanilla, fruit
Main source: sugarcane
Alcohol content: 40–80%
Substitution: white rum

RUM, COCONUT

Flavor notes: sweet coconut
Main source: sugarcane, coconut
Alcohol content: 20–35%
Substitution: combine 2 oz rum and 2 drops of coconut extract

RUM, WHITE

Flavor notes: sweet, light, neutral
Main source: sugarcane
Alcohol content: 40%
Substitution: amber rum

RYE (SEE WHISKY, CANADIAN/RYE)

SAKE/RICE WINE

Flavor notes: subtle rice, fruit, grain, herbs
Main source: rice
Alcohol content: 13–17%
Substitution: none

SAMBUCA

Flavor note: black licorice, anise, sweet
Main source: witch elder bush, licorice, sugar, herbs, spices
Alcohol content: 38%
Substitutions: ouzo, anisette

SCOTCH (SEE WHISKY, SCOTCH)

SHERRY

Flavor notes: raisins, caramel, fig, almonds
Main source: grapes, brandy
Alcohol content: 19–20%
Substitution: port, Madeira

SLOE GIN

Flavor notes: mandarin, sloe berry
Main source: alcohol, sloe berries
Alcohol content: 15%
Substitution: none

SOUR LIQUEURS (APPLE, MELON, RASPBERRY, TANGERINE)

Flavor notes: sour, bitter fruit, candy
Main source: alcohol, fruit
Alcohol content: 15%
Substitution: none

SOUTHERN COMFORT

Flavor notes: sweet peach/apricot, whiskey
Main source: whiskey, fruit
Alcohol content: 35%
Substitution: combine 5 parts whiskey with 1 part peach juice

STRAWBERRY LIQUEUR

Flavor notes: strawberry jam
Main source: alcohol, strawberries
Alcohol content: 20%
Substitution: Chambord, raspberry liqueur

TEQUILA

Flavor notes: herbal, pepper, citrus, vanilla, caramel
Main source: blue agave
Alcohol content: 40–50%
Substitution: none

TEQUILA CREAM LIQUEUR

Flavor notes: strawberry, vanilla, tequila
Main source: tequila, strawberries, cream
Alcohol content: 15%
Substitution: none

TIA MARIA (SEE COFFEE LIQUEUR)

TOFFEE CREAM LIQUEUR

Flavor notes: toffee, butterscotch
Main source: distilled alcohol, toffee
Alcohol content: 17%
Substitution: combine 5 parts Irish cream with 1 part butterscotch syrup

TRIPLE SEC

Flavor notes: sweet, tangy orange
Main source: alcohol, orange rind
Alcohol content: 22–35%
Substitution: Cointreau, Grand Marnier

VANILLA LIQUEUR/SCHNAPPS

Flavor notes: sweet vanilla, marshmallow
Main source: alcohol, flavorings
Alcohol content: 24%
Substitution: none.

VERMOUTH (DRY/WHITE)

Flavor notes: herbal, citrus, bitter
Main source: wine and brandy, herbs
Alcohol content: 18%
Substitution: white wine

VERMOUTH (SWEET/RED)

Flavor notes: bittersweet, citrus, spice
Main source: wine and brandy, herbs
Alcohol content: 16–17%
Substitution: red wine

VODKA

Flavor notes: light herbal
Main source: grain, corn, potatoes
Alcohol content: 40–50%
Substitution: grain alcohol

WALNUT LIQUEUR

Flavor notes: toasted walnut
Main source: grain alcohol, walnuts
Alcohol content: 24%
Substitution: Frangelico

WHISKEY, AMERICAN/BOURBON

Flavor notes: smoke, caramel, floral, spice
Main source: corn, other grain(s)
Alcohol content: 40–75%
Substitution: rye, Scotch, whisky

WHISKEY, IRISH

Flavor notes: smoke, fruit, butter, oak
Main source: barley, wheat, corn
Alcohol content: 40%
Substitution: bourbon, rye, Scotch

WHISKY, CANADIAN/RYE

Flavor notes: grain, vanilla, toffee
Main source: rye
Alcohol content: 40%
Substitution: bourbon, Scotch, whiskey

WHISKY, SCOTCH—BLENDED AND SINGLE MALT

Flavor notes: caramel, honey, herbs, floral, spice, smoke, peat
Main source: barley, wheat, corn
Alcohol content: 40–75%
Substitution: bourbon, rye, Irish whiskey

Index

CHEERS!

There are so many people we'd like to raise a glass to, and others on which we'd like to plant a big sloppy kiss right where it counts. A huge thank you to both of our families for all their love and support. And for teaching us so much about booze and the joys of entertaining—we wouldn't be the drinkers we are today without you.

A huge, heartfelt thanks to Yaman, Jamie, Gord, Dennis and McKizzo—friendship like yours is once-in-a-lifetime.

To our friends at Whitecap—Robert, Nick, Lesley, Michelle, Five and Taryn—for helping us create something we are incredibly proud of. And to Geoffrey, Jeff and Michael, your photographic talents are unmatched and are more appreciated than you know. And to Horia and Dekla Kitchens for providing the perfect backdrop upon which to shoot our shiny mugs.

To Aum and Graeme in Scotland, a big thanks for getting us live on the web from half a world away!

David Adjey, you're an inspiration and a friend. We're honored to have your words greet the readers of this book. Thanks for taking a chance on us, and for enjoying the bottle as much (or more) than we do.

And finally, our sincerest thanks to the passionate brewmasters, distillers and winemakers all over the world. Your dedication to the art of booze-making continues to inspire us.